How Do You Score
on This Communication Quiz?

Take my advice (you'll find some in chapters 2 and 21). Relatively speaking, learning the answers to good communication is the smartest thing you can do to succeed in business.

Are You Communicating?

"After 28 years with AT&T, how come you never learned to communicate?"

Are You Communicating?

You Can't Manage Without It

Donald Walton

McGraw-Hill Publishing Company

New York   St. Louis   San Francisco   Auckland   Bogotá
Caracas   Hamburg   Lisbon   London   Madrid   Mexico
Milan   Montreal   New Delhi   Oklahoma City
Paris   San Juan   São Paulo   Singapore
Sydney   Tokyo   Toronto

Library of Congress Cataloging-in-Pubication Data

Walton, Donald (Donald W.)
  Are you communicating? : you can't manage without it / Donald Walton.
    p.   cm.
  Includes index.
  ISBN 0-07-068052-3
  1. Communication.   I. Title.
P90.W24   1989
001.54—dc19   88-35658
                                                                           CIP

    4567890   DOC/DOC   943210

ISBN 0-07-068052-3

*The editors of this book were Martha Jewett and Edward N.
Huggins, the designer was Naomi Auerbach, and the production
supervisor was Dianne L. Walber. This book was set in Baskerville.
It was composed by the McGraw-Hill Publishing Company
Professional & Reference Division composition unit.*

Illustrated by Dennis Atkinson.

Printed and bound by R. R. Donnelley & Sons Company.

A sixty-minute audio program to accompany this book
is now available. Ask for it at your local bookstore
or phone toll-free 1-800-2-MCGRAW.

*For more information about other McGraw-Hill materials,
call 1-800-2-MCGRAW in the United States. In other
countries, call your nearest McGraw-Hill office.*

Contents

Part 3. Writing

Part 4. Priceless Ingredients of Communication

Preface

The Skill That Can Make or Break Your Career

Countless times throughout my business career I've noticed a paradox. Perhaps you've noticed it too. A person who has everything (or almost everything) needed for success—intelligence, education, ambition, stamina, integrity, outstanding technical skills—is passed by consistently at promotion time or, if given responsibility over a larger staff, fails to perform as well as expected.

What's missing? It's not the ability to handle the technical aspects of a job, and not the willingness to work hard, but *the ability to handle people*. It's knowing how to listen, talk, write, and establish rapport with others—how to guide and motivate them to perform desired actions. It's *communication,* the skill essential for people who must constantly interact with others. It's not the only ability you need in business, of course, but you can't manage without it!

As David P. Reynolds, the chairman of Reynolds Aluminum, expressed it to me, "The ability to communicate and listen effectively is probably the most important skill at a manager's command, because all other management skills depend on it."

Alvin Toffler, author of *The Third Wave*, has estimated that 80 percent of a manager's day is spent in 150 to 300 information transactions. This doesn't leave time for much else. The paradox is that although you may spend three-fourths or more of your business day in meetings and in listening, talking, and writing to people, supervisors typically receive less training for these activities than for any others. Often no training at all.

Ideas from Leading Executives

How widespread is the feeling that poor communication is causing endless management problems? To find out, I wrote to the heads of dozens of leading firms. The answers poured in. They came from the top executives of American Express, AT&T, Coca-Cola, Goodyear, W. R. Grace, H&R Block, ITT, Mobil, Prudential, State Farm, United Airlines, Wal-Mart, Whirlpool, and others.

Not only did these executives write me long letters, but many agreed to personal interviews so that I could explore their views in detail. They all agreed, often vehemently, that communication must improve. And they spelled out for me many practical ideas that have worked in their companies.

This book presents their ideas and some of my own.

I've been a professional communicator most of my life, starting as a writer and then as a creative director in major national advertising agencies. I've written books (including a best-seller), developed people skills as the vice president of a large advertising department, and honed these skills in corporate marketing and new-product development that required dealing with people in many countries. As part of a fast-growing, innovative marketing company, I've seen communication come directly from the top: "That sounds good. Do it!" And for 10 years in the General Motors building in Detroit, I've seen just the opposite in a giant corporate client, whose decisions filtered down slowly from the gods on the plush-and-mahogany fourteenth floor. Finally, as a professional speaker at conventions and seminars, I understand how to use words, voice, and personality to warm people up and win them over.

In short, I know what does and doesn't work in communication. *I've been there.*

"So," I reasoned, "let's combine other executives' ideas with mine and tell people what I wish I'd known when I was younger—how to progress faster in business through better communicating."

You won't take my word for everything, of course. But perhaps you'll accept a tip or two from those who've climbed to the pinnacles of the biggest corporations in this country. And I bet you'll listen to advice from such famous communicators as Art Linkletter, Andy Rooney, and Barbara Walters.

A Distillation of the Key Elements

Instead of writing a comprehensive text on the multitudinous facets of communication, I've sifted out for you the important, practical things that experienced business managers and I have discovered to be the *keys* to successful communication—what worked for us and what can work for you.

I've aimed to create a book that would have helped me, both in my career and personal life. Sure, I managed to get by, even achieving more than most people. But I bumped my nose often while learning too many things the hard way.

Perhaps you can avoid some of the scars and disappointments and can do more climbing with less stumbling as you move through life. If some of the hundreds of *proven ideas* in these pages can show you useful shortcuts to effective communication and enable you to become a winner, I'll be happy.

And so will you.

Donald Walton

1
Where Do You Stand in the Information Age?

We can lick gravity, but sometimes the paperwork is overwhelming.
WERNHER VON BRAUN

This is not a textbook concerned with grammar or vocabulary. It's not a handbook full of standardized sales and collection letters, memos, etc., to be copied. It doesn't try to teach you what you should have learned in high school or college English classes.

What you'll find here is what you were never taught in any classroom. It focuses on the people skills that are crucial to success in today's information age—on communication and the practical things that really make it work. They are among the most important things in your life.

To succeed in business today, and in your social and family life too, you need all the skill you can master in every type of communication. This involves language, of course, both spoken and written. It also includes nonverbal expression, such as smiles, gestures, and body language, which can be equally important in communicating your ideas and feelings to people.

Listening is another critical facet of communication. It can do more to help you win friends and score points than any amount of slick talk. Establishing rapport with others is also a crucial skill. Unless you can establish it, you'll find that no matter what you say, people won't pay attention to you and will simply ignore your suggestions.

You and Abe Lincoln

Abraham Lincoln was criticized (usually by the opponents he beat) as lacking a sophisticated style of speaking and writing. "A crude backwoods orator," they scoffed. But could he communicate! That's because he listened to people, understood them, and used simple, clear words to touch them deep inside. No one did it better.

You should be so lucky as to possess some part of the charm that enabled Honest Abe to reach people and motivate them. And you can. Like anything else, the ability to communicate clearly and persuasively is a skill that can be learned.

It's not just in government that this ability is admired. In the politics of today's corporations (and don't be so naive as to believe that business life is not political), those who become leaders are the ones who can best *transmit* their views, ideas, and enthusiasms to others. That's what being a leader is.

The Qualities of Leadership

Look around you. At the start of a career, ability in a professional specialty tends to be the overwhelming factor in success. The young engineer, accountant, chemist, editor, banker, or whatever, wins respect and a rising income by personally using the techniques peculiar to his or her craft. But as these individual accomplishments are rewarded with an assistant or two, the emphasis begins to shift. The need for communication, always present in any group human activity, multiplies with each addition to the staff. By the time the upwardly mobile manager wins promotion to department head, everything becomes heavily dependent on communicating.

As you approach that situation, you still need superior knowledge of your industry and your specialty within it so that you can aim your helpers in the right directions and then evaluate and polish their work as necessary. But now your chief activities become sharing your knowledge with subordinates, making clear to them what needs to be done, keeping them convinced and enthused about each job, hammering heads when occasion demands (without crushing spirits), pushing your people beyond what they think they can do, and building pride in themselves and the group.

All these essentials of management are mostly communication.

You Can't Manage Without It

The higher you go, the wider spreads the network of communication that will make or break you. It extends not only to more people below, but to new levels above. And it extends all around, to endless other departments and interests interacting with yours. You'll be communicating constantly with a multitude of individuals helping you and demanding help, questioning, calling for reports and meetings, showering you with memos and suggestions, evaluating, criticizing, and always competing for attention, budgets, and plaudits.

At the end of some days you may wish that all the people wired into your communications network would tune out and go away. But they won't. And you shouldn't want them to, because the problems they present are your greatest opportunities for demonstrating your worth. Lick the challenges and you become the Golden Knight, beloved by the troops you lead and treasured by the great leaders at the top. It's your route to the top.

Here's what the head of one of the world's largest companies has to say about that:

> A key element in determining a manager's potential for advancement is skill in communication...the ability to present ideas and information concisely and effectively, orally and in writing.
> RAWLEIGH WARNER, JR., CHAIRMAN
> Mobil Corporation

This attitude is shared by the heads of many other major corporations. Of all the senior executives I've been able to observe closely, I can't recall a single one who wasn't a good communicator and who didn't seem partial to others with similar qualities.

How Managers Rate Their Own Skills

When Dr. Harold T. Smith of Brigham Young University wanted to rate the various skills required for efficient management, he decided to go to a group of professional managers for the answers. The Academy of Certified Administrative Managers (CAMs) agreed to cooperate with him in this research.

listening so important here in skills

First, Dr. Smith made a list of all the managerial activities he could think of. The academy helped him whittle down his all-inclusive list to activities it regarded as most critical to good management. All members of the academy were then asked to rate these key competencies according to importance in their jobs. In decreasing order, here are the 12 they chose as the most essential to them:[1]

*1. Listen actively.

*2. Give clear, effective instructions.

3. Accept your share of responsibility for problems.

4. Identify real problems.

5. Manage time and set priorities.

*6. Give recognition for excellent performance.

*7. Communicate decisions to employees.

*8. Be effective in oral communication.

9. Shift priorities if necessary.

*10. Explain work.

*11. Obtain and provide feedback in two-way communication sessions.

*12. Write effectively.

Note that the two top vote getters in the CAM poll are language skills. In fact, as indicated by the asterisks, *8 of the 12* are essentially forms of communication.

Does the Story Fit?

Humorist Art Buchwald told the story of the little girl who visited her father's office. On her return home, a friend asked, "What does your daddy do all day?"

"He sends pieces of paper to other people," she replied, "and they send pieces of paper to him."

That line got a laugh from those working in offices because there's so much truth in it. Would it sound even more like your place of work if the child had added, "And when my daddy puts down the pieces of paper, he hurries to a meeting room where he talks to people for hours and hours"?

That story was told years ago; today it would apply equally to mothers and fathers since present-day offices are staffed about evenly with both sexes. If it presents an all-too-true (and not so funny) picture of your

---

[1]Based on data published in *Management World*, January 1978.

typical day, you're a bona fide member of the modern business world. Efficiency experts who've done many studies of office operations come up with a profile of the modern manager's workday that looks something like the pie chart in this illustration.

The activities in this pie chart, concentrated almost exclusively on communicating with people, would not have been typical of managers a generation ago. But they certainly are a part of the Third Wave and the overwhelming mass of information transfers that Alvin Toffler describes as revolutionizing the office of today. Similarly, when John Naisbitt writes of the 10 directions transforming our lives, the number one megatrend he lists is the dramatic shift from an industrial society to an information society where the game is *"people interacting with people."*

How Do You Spend Your Day?

How much a part of that game are you? Maybe it's time to ask yourself, "Exactly how *do* I spend my day?"

The easiest way to find out is to clock your activities throughout a day or two. Put a memo pad on the center of your desk, where you can't forget it, and keep a time record of everything you do. This needn't be fancy or onerous; if you just record 15-minute intervals, that'll be close enough. At the end of each day, break down your activities into the five categories shown in the accompanying chart. (You can pencil in the results directly on this chart.)

Listening*	Talking*	Reading	Writing	Other
Total hours	Total hours	Total hours	Total hours	Total hours

*Divide the time you spent in *conversation* by 2, putting half under listening and half under talking. Divide the time you spent in *meetings* between listening and talking; if there were five people in a meeting, you might have spent four-fifths listening and one-fifth talking.

Once that analysis is completed, it may alter your perspective on the relative importance of various managerial skills. If you discover that big chunks of your day are spent in listening, talking, reading, and writing (maybe far more time than you devote to other activities you've always considered paramount), you may need to do some reassessing. Common sense dictates that whatever you do most often deserves major attention to make sure you're doing it as well as possible.

Any skills in which you don't feel particularly strong will need to be sharpened. *Average won't do.* If you're not the type to settle for a mediocre career and lifestyle, you need to be damned good at whatever is going to play a major role in your future. And you can be.

A Common Complaint

In general, many intelligent career people, skilled in most of their daily activities, fall far short of what they could be when it comes to communication. Both *The Wall Street Journal* and *Business Week* have reported that one of the commonest complaints they hear from top executives about their newer managers is "Many recently graduated MBAs don't know how to write understandably." Richard West, dean of the prestigious Amos Tuck school, echoed this with "The vast majority of MBA students need to improve their skills in oral and written communication." And remember, this is supposedly the cream of the crop these experts are talking about.

What Employers Don't Like

All too many businesspeople who start out as weak communicators don't improve much; therefore, they fail to reach their full potential as they try to climb the ladder. Companies don't like this, for trying to correct the problem uses up a great deal of time, energy, and money. In fact, the American Society for Training and Development estimates that U.S. employers spend $40 billion annually for employee education, much of it directed toward helping managers in *"writing clearly, reading better, being able to speak before audiences, and working harmoniously in groups."*

The Carnegie Foundation for the Advancement of Teaching believes that the expense for trying to improve these people skills is far higher. Charles L. Brown, when he was chairman of AT&T, informed me that the Bell System spent more than $1 billion a year on education and training—more than it devoted to its famed research and development.

Why People Get Fired

Inadequate people skills can cause as much trouble for a manager as any other factor—maybe more. Personnel managers agree almost unanimously that terminations result not from a lack of technical ability or industriousness, but most often from difficulties in relating to and dealing with people.

A Harvard University study of people fired showed that for every dismissal based on a failure to do work properly, there were two for personality factors. Poor communication is generally an integral part of this.

Computers Are Not the Solution

In general, the advent of the computer has not solved communications problems as some hoped it would. The top executive at the Bell System made this observation:

> Even in the age of the computer, we must have some reasonable degree of competence in the English language. It is still the principal language in which business is conducted in this country.
>
> The issues we in business confront do not come in the form of true-false or multiple-choice quizzes. "None of the above" is the most likely answer to the questions we confront, and usually that answer requires original—and precise—articulation.
>
> CHARLES L. BROWN, CHAIRMAN
> *AT&T*

The new electronic machines can spew out more words and data at an amazing rate, but this may merely exacerbate the difficulties. As John Naisbitt has so aptly pointed out, we can be "drowning in information but starved for knowledge." Companies that have invested millions in new electronic office systems, hoping to find the magic solution, discover instead that employees may latch onto the new marvels as a means of amplifying the avalanche of words and data to build ever greater mountains of garbage. Always, it gets back to *people* who must know how to put the right *language* into the machines.

Meeting the New Challenges

When I asked Robert Anderson for his views on the latest developments in management, this was his reply:

> Careful listening and clear writing are important ingredients of effective communications, but these days managers face a new and important communications challenge—assuring maximum productivity through proper use of office information systems.
>
> The tools now readily available range from briefcase-size communications terminals to large systems for word processing, electronic mail, and information retrieval. These marvelous devices are worthless investments, however, if they are improperly or inadequately utilized.
>
> The most successful managers will be those who not only embrace the new technology, but also learn to obtain every advantage it can provide in creating and delivering carefully crafted messages.
>
> ROBERT ANDERSON, CHAIRMAN & CEO
> *Rockwell International Corporation*

The very fact that the number one executive skill is so often the weak spot of otherwise efficient managers presents *you* with an opportunity. The generally poor performance of others gives you that much more chance to shine by comparison. For every loser, there's a winner. You simply have to make up your mind which you want to be.

You Have What It Takes

Probably more than you realize, you're well-equipped to learn the people skills required to make your way upward in the business world. (You'll find some interesting facts about your inherent language ability in the next chapter.) What you need to do is sharpen your God-given abilities to communicate. Because all humans have them, more or less, they're often taken for granted and allowed to atrophy. Don't you make that mistake. Strengthen your inherent skills; build on them. If you do, you can move ahead of your peers—maybe even ahead of those who've had a head start in technical training or educational background.

To succeed in your career, you don't have to be a genius or to graduate cum laude from a prestigious school. If you happen to be so lucky as to enjoy that sort of fast start, congratulations. But wherever you stand on the ladder now, the amount of climbing you're apt to do depends heavily on whether you apply yourself and how willing you are to learn. You can take the word of one of America's most respected business leaders for that:

> *Despite all the educational and analytical infrastructure built up around the alleged science of management, it still reduces itself simply to homework, common sense, and good communication.*
> DONN B. TATUM, CHAIRMAN
> *Walt Disney Productions*

2
Your Special Gifts

Language is the light of the mind.
JOHN STUART MILL

This is primarily a book about language. All kinds of language—not just spoken or written, but also nonverbal communication, such as smiles, gestures, and body language. It's about all the tools you use every day to transmit your ideas, feelings, and desires to people, hopefully in such a way that they'll understand you and respond as you want them to.

It includes hundreds of specific ideas on how to use language more skillfully. But before you plunge into the explicit ways of handling it, you ought to know more about this basic tool of communication. (Experts always understand their tools.) Two questions need to be answered:

1. Exactly what is language?
2. Can you have confidence in your own language abilities? In other words, do you have what it takes to succeed in communicating?

To gain a better understanding of what language is and how it works, you need to take a brief look back into history. Don't worry—history can be interesting, particularly when it's about things that make you what you are today. And about your family. You're going to like that, because I assure you, you come from a wonderful, talented family.

The Legacy from Your Ancestors

It started so far back in your family tree that your folks' home address was probably a cave. But this legacy, the skill of language, is the most valuable gift you've received from your ancestors.

We don't think much about language. After all, everyone except deaf-mutes can talk, and this ability seems to develop more or less automatically.

Even a little child can express herself in words. Dr. Mario Pei, author of more than two dozen books on languages, cites research which shows that a four-year-old child is likely to have a vocabulary of about 5000 words. By eight, she'll know 5 times that many. By adulthood, her vocabulary can be 35,000 to 70,000 words. (I've used feminine pronouns because girls are generally ahead of boys in language skills. Feminists may interpret this as they wish.)

Your Vocabulary and Your Intelligence

If you're significantly above-average in intelligence, your vocabulary may possibly exceed 100,000 words. This is because intelligence and vocabulary tend to parallel each other.

The ability to communicate with words, rather than through growls or chirps, is universal. *No people on earth, no matter how primitive, lack a language.* Before many small tribes were exterminated by the benefits of civilization, more than 5000 languages were spoken throughout the world. About half of them survive today, according to Dr. Gordon C. Baldwin, an anthropologist at the University of Arizona.

Don't jump to the conclusion that what we consider primitive cultures have merely rudimentary languages; some of them are much more complex than ours in certain respects.

Be Glad You're Not a Bantu

The Bantu language of Africa separates nouns into 17 classes by means of prefixes. Some aboriginal Australian languages have five future tenses. In the languages of people who live close to nature, a noun may have dozens of different forms; for instance, the Inuit in northern Canada have a wide variety of words for snow, indicating whether it's expected, falling, swirling, driven, light, granular, large-flaked, wind-blown, on the ground, piled high, packed into ice, slushy, melting, old, new, etc. Solomon Islanders use 20 different genders.[1]

---

[1]You'll find thousands of strange and fascinating facts about languages in Charles Berlitz's *Native Tongues*, Putnam, New York, 1982.

So we can't say our language is superior, judged on the basis of grammatical complexity. Be glad you speak English; it rates far down the list in that regard.

You're Different from All Others

In contrast to human language and its universality, not one animal has anything remotely resembling this ability.

Don't animals communicate? Of course they do, in a variety of ways. The European honeybee, in its tail-waggling dance, can tell its hive mates how far to fly to reach a rich source of food and in exactly what direction in relation to the sun. There's evidence that some birds teach their chicks the distinctive calls of their species by chirping to them while they're still unhatched. A female moth communicates to her mate over a distance of several miles by odor. Certain deep-ocean fish and fireflies use light to send signals. Mammals employ facial and body gestures, growls, howls, etc.

But such messages tell little except to warn of danger, invite procreation, or lead to food. Limited to the emotion of the present, they tell nothing of the past or future and have none of the rich texture of human speech or its vast scope of meanings.

Why Animals Can't Talk

Experiments by scientists to find out if any animals have any true language potentials have shown minimal results, despite what you read from time to time in the popular press.

For example, linguists Keith and Helen Hayes attempted to teach a chimpanzee, one of the smartest of all animals and a good mimic, to speak English (1951). After six years of concentrated daily expert tutoring, the chimp, named Vicki, could speak four words with some clarity: "momma, poppa, cup," and "up." Compare these with the more than 10,000 words we'd expect from a typical six-year-old child or from an adult we'd consider stupid.

How About Sign Language?

Part of Vicki's problem was that a chimp lacks the flexible vocal apparatus that you and I were blessed with.

To avoid this factor, another pair of linguists decided to teach a chimp American Indian sign language—a medium of communication they figured correctly would be much more natural to the primate. After nine years (1966 to 1975), Alan and Beatrice Gordon succeeded in teaching their pupil, Washoe, to make 160 signs, mostly to indicate food, other objects, or simple commands such as "give me."

In contrast, the "savages" who populated precolonial America could make pictures with their fingers and hands to express thousands of words taken from 20 to 30 tribal languages, and they could do it as fast as speech, just as deaf-mutes do today. In fact, they were so adept at sign language that they often used it within their own tribes in place of talking.

So what does this all mean? It means:

You and I are different from all other species on earth. Unique not just in some minor details, but by a quantum leap.

It's a difference not just in vocal apparatus; songbirds and parrots certainly have considerable agility in making sounds. The advantage you have over all other creatures is intellectual, not mechanical.

The magic of a language is not merely the production of about 50 sounds.[2] It's your ability to combine these sounds into the thousands of building blocks we call words and to structure the words into phrases and sentences that provide an infinite combination of messages.

It's *your brain* that enables you to speak, and to *think*, in an entirely different way—to think in ideas, to speak of the past, to dream of the future, to be human.

The uniqueness of man—the superiority of man in the world of animals—lies not in his ability to perceive ideas, but to perceive that he perceives, and to transfer his perceptions to other men's minds through words. ALBERT EINSTEIN

---

[2]Our vocal chords can produce hundreds of different sounds, but most major languages select about 50 of these. The 50 or so selected give each language its peculiar tone.

Your Incredible Brain

Your brain makes one of today's most advanced computers look like an antique adding machine. Sir John Eccles, the Australian Nobel-prize-winning scientist, calls it *the most complex device in the entire universe.*

For example, it contains about 10 of the 12 billion basic nerve cells (neurons) of your nervous system. Your 3 pounds of gray matter can store 100 trillion bits of information. That makes your brain a supercomputer. But this analogy doesn't begin to do justice to the wonders of your thinking apparatus; it merely indicates big capacity.

Far more amazing to me is the connecting system between the brain cells. They're interconnected in a three-dimensional network of incredible complexity. Unlike other cells in your body, each brain cell has numerous projections branching from it. Some of these threadlike projections are receptors (dendrites), which carry nerve impulses into the cell body, and one long sending antenna (the axon) carries messages from the cell to others. Although microscopically thin, the axon of one tiny brain cell may be several feet long. Multiply this length by 10 billion (the number of cells in your brain) and you have enough nerve thread in your axons alone to stretch 3 times as far as the moon.

Beyond Comparison

In trying to understand the incomprehensible, we liken our brain to devices that represent the pinnacle of human technology. A generation ago it was common to compare it with a telephone network; today we often say it's like a computer. Such comparisons are no more illuminating than likening a jetliner to a wagon because they both have wheels and carry things.

Comparisons between the brain and our modern electrical marvels miss the mark in several ways:

- *Capacity.* There are more connections in one human brain than in all the telephone networks in the world. Similarly, the brain outstrips the capacity of any computer.

- *Live versus dead.* We build computers out of standardized parts that always act in a standardized way. No two of your brain cells are precisely alike, and their reactions vary under different physical and chemical conditions in the body.

- *Wet versus dry.* The neural network floats in a solution of chemicals. These chemicals facilitate some messages and inhibit others. Your brain is a chemical device just as much as it's an electrical device.

How You Think

When one brain cell sends out a message to others (as many as 40,000 others may be affected), the impulse starts out as an electrical signal. The cell "fires." But the impulse must jump the gap to the connectors of other cells. It does this by chemical action that is affected not only by the condition of the other cells but also by the adrenaline, sex hormones, peptides, and other substances in the fluid in which the brain floats.

In other words, one cell doesn't simply send the message along to be accepted routinely by others. Of the hundreds or thousands of cells that receive a given electrochemical signal, each one decides whether to respond to it or not; some do, some don't.

Unlike the dumb mechanical computer, each of your brain cells makes a decision. And on the basis of these multiple decisions, your brain takes a vote of whether the signal seems to be a good, important one that should be acted upon or whether the majority of brain cells involved have determined that it should be ignored. *Unlike the computer, it thinks.*

You're Smarter than Any Computer

If you tend to be intimidated by computers, you needn't be. Even those of us with ordinary intellects are way ahead of the most advanced models...ahead in many respects. For example, every day you perform the miracle of hearing or seeing something, analyzing its meaning, formulating a reply, encoding it into the symbols we call language, and then activating the hundred or so muscles of your vocal chords to speak your reply. And you do it all within seconds!

While we stand in awe of electronic devices, it's a pity we know so little and wonder so seldom about the marvel in our own heads. It would take many books thicker than this one to begin to explain all the wonders of the human brain, but the box on the next page lists a few facts you may find titillating:

If this is a book about language and communication, why have I taken several pages to write about the brain? Just to make you feel good, knowing that you're so smart?

Partly. It's important for you to start your program of self-improvement with self-confidence, assurance that for the job of communicating you're equipped with a fantastic, incredible, unique-in-the-universe tool.

Thinking and language (communication) are inescapably intertwined. They're two sides of the same coin. The more clearly you think, the more clearly you'll be able to communicate. And as you learn to communicate better, you'll discover that you think better.

I hope you'll remember that, because the link between your language and your thinking is one of the most significant things about you.

**Some Amazing Facts
About Your Amazing Brain**

- If your brain cells were people, there'd be enough of them to populate 25 planets like ours.
- More than a million nerve fibers are required just to connect your eyes to your brain.
- Your brain operates on a type of electricity (and chemical action too). It uses about the same amount of current, during full consciousness, as a 20-watt light bulb. If the current ever goes completely off, so do you.
- A large elephant has a brain about 4 times as big as yours, and a giant whale's may be 6 times as big, but neither animal has nearly as many interconnections between brain cells. Ergo, their thinking capacity is not nearly as great.
- About 100,000 years ago there appeared a new kind of early human beings (Neanderthals) with a brain far superior to that of their predecessors. In fact, they had a brain very similar to ours in kind and size, were probably as smart as we are, and developed language.
- We have not just one brain in our cranium, but three. Innermost is the ancient "reptilian" brain, similar to that of turtles and lizards. Encircling it is the old "mammalian" brain of a type we share with all lower mammals. These two older brains deal with our emotions, instincts, etc. Wrapped around them is the neocortex, the seat of our conscious processes—thinking and language.

Your Words, Your Brain, and Civilization

Washoe, the educated chimp, could break you in two with one hand, but you have a power far beyond hers. While she knows the sign for "banana" and can indicate "give me," that's the limit of her horizons. The world is your banana.

What Washoe and Vicki couldn't do after years of patient coaching, even the little children of humankind have been doing for maybe a thousand centuries. Which came first? Did God first bless your ancestors, the Neanderthals, with a superior brain that enabled them to develop the complexities of conversation, or did God grant the unique gift of language that caused the human brain to expand and evolve into something special? Nobody knows.

One thing's for sure, though: The two are inextricably linked together. If you learn to speak better (and write better), you'll also learn to think more clearly. That's because...

Words Are the Medium You Think In

Since apes and other animals have no words, is that why they can't think as you do? Consider this: Don't you often talk to yourself? Of course you do; admit it. We all do because it helps us formulate our thoughts.

Dr. Rudolf Flesch, a renowned authority on language (author of *Why Johnny Can't Read* and many other books[3]), says that he worked in his field for almost 20 years before he fully realized the connection. Gradually the truth dawned on him. *Thinking is silent speech, and speech is simply thinking out loud.* The written word carries this one step further. *Writing is a way of speaking on paper.*

Put them all together, and you have the elements of civilization. When one member of the tribe could talk to others, the elders could pass on their wisdom to the next generation. Knowledge didn't have to be rediscovered constantly; it could grow and grow. Writing greatly expanded the process.

> The palest ink lasts longer than the most retentive memory.   CHINESE PROVERB

So important was the discovery of written language to early societies that it was considered to be of divine origin. Ancient Egyptians called their hieroglyphics "the speech of the gods." The Mayans believed that their chief god, Itzamnu, had three attributes: He was Lord of the Heavens, Creator of Mankind, Inventor of Writing. Lesser gods took care of lesser things.

Writing was a product of its times. It developed as urban societies replaced the simpler farming or hunting societies. This created a need for permanent records between merchants, artisans, taxpayers and collec-

---

[3]His books include *The Art of Plain Talk* (1946), *The Art of Readable Writing* (1949), and *The Art of Clear Thinking* (1951), all published by Harper & Row, New York.

tors, debtors and creditors. Because this happened in various places between roughly 3000 to 1000 B.C., writing was invented, independently, in several different societies.

How Writing Started

The ancient Sumerians in southern Mesopotamia (the Tigris-Euphrates valley, now in Iraq and Syria) are thought to be the first inventors of writing at some time between 3500 and 3000 B.C. Not much later the Egyptians, nearly a thousand miles away, developed their own different system of pictographs and symbols. About 500 years after that, the Elamites (in an area now included in Iran) created a script that scholars have not yet deciphered. Other distant places where writing appeared in the two millenia before Christ were the Indus Valley (Pakistan), Crete, and China.

The Sumerians were also the inventors of a great advancement over the earliest pictographic writing. They simplified their symbols into wedge-shaped marks (cuneiform writing) that could be rapidly impressed with a stylus into a clay tablet, which was then baked for permanency.

The Greatest Invention

The crowning achievement in the history of writing—and one of the greatest achievements in all our history—was yet to come. It was the invention of the alphabet.

As with most great discoveries, its simplicity was its beauty. Instead of requiring hundreds of symbols to depict words, it substituted a very few symbols (22 to 30) that could be put together to form any word. This made writing immeasurably easier and faster.

Exactly when and where the alphabet was invented are a matter of debate. There's evidence that it happened somewhere along the eastern edge of the Mediterranean, probably where the ancient Canaanites lived, and perhaps as early as 1700 B.C. We'll never be able to honor the genius who made the discovery, but we can give thanks to the seafaring Phoenicians (from the coastal areas of Canaan) for carrying the alphabet to many other lands. By about 1100 B.C. the Phoenician alphabet was spreading widely. Modified over the centuries, it has come to you, a greater gift than the wheel.

The alphabet started the information explosion that affects your life so dramatically. When it was followed by the invention of paper to replace expensive parchment and then by the invention of movable type, books became available to everyone.

They tell you about things that happened before you were born: the Civil War or what Plato said. About places you'll never see, like a galaxy a billion light years away or what's inside a sodium atom. About adventure and romance: plots with horrifying intrigues and steaming passions that gallop your pulse deliciously.

One of Life's Greatest Blessings

So you see, if it hadn't been for the gabbiness of those cave men and women, the ingenuity of Sumerian scribes, the inventiveness of Gutenberg, and the accomplishments of an additional host of your ancestors, you'd be missing one of life's greatest blessings.

Sure, we grumble at times about the deluge of words, spoken and written, that bombard us in our modern world, especially in the world of business. But as we say when moved to complain about old age, "Think of the alternative." Without it, we couldn't accomplish anything.

> *I hadn't yet learned what I know now—that the ability to communicate is everyone.*
> LEE IACOCCA, CHAIRMAN & CEO
> *Chrysler Corporation*
> (from his autobiography,
> *Iacocca)*

There's magic in language. You may never have thought much about this wonderful gift. But with it, you have what it takes to deal with your fellow humans so they'll understand you, like you, and cooperate with you.

Proceed with confidence to learn the fine points of using this important tool with exceptional skill...so you can be exceptionally successful in your work and in your life.

PART 1
Listening

3

Your First Step toward Success

Women like silent men. They think they are listening.

MARCEL ACKARD

Television star Barbara Walters claims that it doesn't matter what you say at a cocktail party, because no one is listening to you anyway. She says she knew a woman who was so tired of having people at parties ask her, "How are you?" and then pay no attention whatever to her answers that she decided to answer outrageously. In response to their stereotyped "how are you's," she responded gaily, "I'm dying!" All through the party she kept this up, and the only replies she got were stock comments, such as "That's good" or "You certainly look great."[1]

I've been at cocktail parties like that, where the tongues were all in high gear and the ears were mostly turned off. Maybe you have too. But I've also been at business meetings where the situation wasn't much different.

The Truth about a Universal Complaint

It's prevalent everywhere. Marriage counselors and divorce lawyers will tell you that day after day they hear their clients complain, "He (or she)

---

[1]From Barbara Walters, *How to Talk with Practically Anyone about Practically Anything*, Doubleday, New York, 1970.

doesn't listen to me!" How many times have you said that about your spouse or your children? How many times do you think it's been said of you?

Presidents of many a corporation have expressed the same gripe, as have several Presidents of the United States, when they thought they'd made their wishes known but found that the bureaucracy hadn't gotten the message at all. Companies, or even entire industries, don't pay attention when customers murmur about products and services—until finally the public yells, "You're not listening to us. Good-bye!"

What the Psychiatrist Does

More and more people are going to psychiatrists, where they may pay $100 an hour or more. For what? For one thing, the doctor *listens*, carefully and sympathetically. If you learn to listen to people—really listen in the right way—your rewards can be as great or greater.

Robert Beck, head of Prudential Insurance, considers the failure to listen and understand to be one of the greatest weaknesses in business. Here's what he wrote to me about it:

The Best Chance of Success

Starting my Prudential career as an agent, I understood quickly that although people may listen, they don't always hear. I had to make sure, therefore, that my presentations were clear, concise, and to the point. In addition, I taught myself to listen to and understand others, another crucial point in making sales.

Clear communication is an important component of any career foundation. I have seen bright, ambitious people fail simply because they were unable to understand the importance of this. The person who has the ability to make his or her point simply and effectively, while clearly understanding what is being said by others, will have the best chance of success in a society and business environment as complex and multi-dimensional as ours.

ROBERT A. BECK, CHAIRMAN & CEO
The Prudential Insurance Company of America

Just the fact that you spend such a big part of each day listening makes it important. If you made a survey of your daily activities (as described on pages 5–6), didn't you learn that listening is at or near the top of the list of where your time goes?

Besides the enormous amount of listening you do, the transient nature of this activity makes it imperative that you pay close attention. If you fail to understand a written message, you can always go back to it later. It's a permanent record. But what you hear is fleeting; either you get the message and remember it, or it's gone forever.

A Game You've Played

Garbling verbal messages is easy to do. Have you ever played the party game where one person hurriedly whispers a sentence to the next person in line, who then passes it on down to the next? By the time the original message has been relayed through several sets of ears, it no longer even vaguely resembles the original thought.

A similar scrambling of messages occurs all the time in organizations large and small. It's costly.

The High Cost of Scrambled Messages

In a social group, if you pass on to someone incorrectly what another told you, you can lose a friend. In selling, if you pass on information you haven't heard or interpreted correctly, you can lose a customer. In a business office, the garbling of a few words results time after time in letters having to be retyped, in schedules going wrong, and in faulty procedures being instituted.

Some of the errors resulting from poor listening habits may seem inconsequential. If a secretary misses something in dictation, a memo or letter may have to be retyped. No big deal; it happens every day. But that's the point: Multiply that few dollars in extra cost by the many spoiled letters and memos per week throughout the company. In a year it adds up to big money. So do the little delays in schedules, the little mistakes in purchasing and shipments, the little misunderstanding that someone said, "Go," when she really said, "No."

"No, no! I didn't say that I *insist* on that line of action. I said we must *resist* that kind of action."

How big a disaster can result from not listening? The biggest!

Remember Pearl Harbor?

No one paid attention to a diplomatic message just a few days before the Japanese attacked the Hawaiian Islands. No one listened to the radio operator on that fateful morning when he reported squadrons of planes approaching from the northwest. Such an occurrence was ruled out as impossible—only it wasn't.

In recent years a similar scenario was repeated in Lebanon. Intelligence reports warned of rumors that our Marine headquarters would be blown up, and it was, with the gates wide open. A few months later another warning came that our embassy would be bombed, and again, *no one listened.*

You aren't likely to encounter such life-threatening situations, but you still must guard against business Pearl Harbors—the kind that can undermine trust built up over many years, destroy careers, lose good friends.

We Hear What We Wish to Hear

An apochryphal story relates that a zoologist was walking with a friend down a busy street past a construction site where a jackhammer was ripping up the concrete. Amid the ear-shattering cacophony, she stopped her friend and said, "Listen—there's a cricket hiding back of those boards." Amazed, her friend asked, "How can you possibly hear a little bug chirping when we have all these cars and machines roaring around us?" The answer was, "It's easy. I don't like car horns or jackhammers, but a cricket is music to my ears." Then she dropped a coin onto the sidewalk. As it bounced, a dozen heads turned toward the sound. "See," the zoologist indicated, "we hear whatever interests us."

If your eardrums are in reasonably good working order, you can hear what's said to you. But that's not the same as listening. Just because the sound enters doesn't mean that the message is assimilated…and re-membered. The sad truth is: *People fail to understand about half of what they hear. And they quickly forget half of that.*

This conclusion has been confirmed many times in studies that started more than 35 years ago and has been confirmed by researchers at several universities (the University of Minnesota, Michigan State, Ohio State, and Florida State). In the researchers' tests, a variety of people listen to a brief talk and are asked to recall details of what they just heard. On average, their recall is only 50 percent. When quizzed again a few hours later, their recall drops still lower. By the next day, their retention of information is usually down to only one-third or one-fourth of what they were told. After those early lapses the drop-off continues, but at a slower rate.

These dismal results, based on testing thousands of people, including business and professional persons as well as students, were obtained even though the subjects were trying to concentrate because they knew they were going to be quizzed on what they heard. Isn't it likely that the scores might be as low or lower if you and your colleagues were to be quizzed on what you could remember after sitting through a long meeting?

How Good (or Bad) a Listener Are You?

Nobody is perfect. It's easy to "turn off" at times when you should be keeping your mind open to what someone is telling you. Whatever the cause, you'll miss whatever knowledge, instructions, or mental stimulation you might have gained.

The accompanying chart lists some of the common reasons for a turned-off attitude. Check off on the chart the reasons for not listening that apply to you. Skip those which you feel never, or almost never, apply in your case. Indicate the frequency with which you indulge in the others. Then total the check marks at the bottom of each column.

Common Reasons for Not Listening

What you say to yourself	How often you say it		
	Now and then	Fairly often	Very often
I want to talk first.			
I'm thinking about what I'm going to say.			
I'm not interested in the subject.			
That's too hard to understand.			
I don't like you.			
I don't like the way you talk.			
I'm too upset, or worried, about other things.			
I don't want to believe what I know you're about to tell me.			
I'd rather give my attention to people or activities around me.			
I'd rather daydream or doodle.			
Total check marks			

If you placed no check marks next to most of the items on this list, and maybe just two or three in the first column, you can adjust your halo. You tend to be unusually open-minded about listening (although you still may not analyze and remember what you take in as well as you should).

If most of your check marks are in the "Now and then" column, that's not too bad. We all slip at times. But if there are any check marks at all in the last two columns, particularly the "Very often" column, you have a problem. Several checks there indicate that you're closing the door to any reception at all.

Now that you're aware of any problem habits that may exist, think about them. Try to stop yourself when you realize that you're "tuning out" for one of these reasons. If you do that, you'll make an important first step. You'll at least give yourself a chance to listen—and to gain some benefits from one of the most important of all human activities.

You're Too Smart!

It may be assumed that poor listening habits are restricted to those with low intelligence. But that's not true, not at all.

Those with high IQs may not pay attention; therefore, they'll miss much that whizzes through their ears. In fact, the faster your thought processes, the more tempted you are to let your attention wander.

The crux of the problem is that if you have a keen intelligence, you can comprehend words 3 or 4 times as fast as the average person talks.

Human speech varies widely in speed. Women tend to talk faster than men—at a rate of about 175 words per minute, versus 150 for men. In the south, the tempo gets slower. Tempo varies by countries too. French and Japanese machine-gun out half again as many syllables as English or Americans; in the South Seas the pace may be only one-fourth as fast as ours.

Somewhere around 160 words per minute is probably about average for rapid conversation. That's rattling right along, not allowing for frequent pauses or for peppering the conversation with such slow-down words as "you know, ummm, well," etc., as we tend to do.

But with your high intelligence, you can assimilate the meaning of speech at least 3 times that rapidly—maybe even faster. You can understand at the rate of about 500 words per minute. So what happens?

You Get Bored

You begin to wish that Joe, who has been talking for such an interminably long time, would hurry up and finish his long harangue. Gradually, you turn your mind off to what he's saying, and you completely miss the one crucial bit of information Joe tosses to you.

The two-thirds of your mind that's been idling while waiting for Joe's slow tongue finds other things to think about. You're so smart that you subconsciously figure you can listen to him and at the same time let your thoughts wander back to that marvelous (lucky) golf shot made Sunday. Or ahead to what you're going to do tonight. Or off to the side to that extremely attractive new employee walking down the hall.

What Are You Going to Say?

Even more likely, since you're a conscientious and ambitious person, you direct two-thirds or more of your terrific brainpower to something that can do you some good. Instead of concentrating on Joe, you think about what you're going to say as soon as he shuts up. That's the most important part of the conversation, isn't it?

As a *Harvard Business Review* article expressed it, *"We listen past ourselves."* You may recall that you tend to do that when you can't wait to get on stage yourself. That's when you listen only for that pause in the conversation that allows you to break in with your own message.

> No man would listen to you talk if he didn't know it was his turn next.
> ED HOWE

What it all boils down to is that if you have bad listening habits, you outsmart yourself.

How to Improve Your Wicked Ways

Many experts have formulated many different suggestions on how to listen better. They all have some merit and mostly tend in similar directions. This variety of helpful ideas can be boiled down into a few simple rules.

Half the battle is to open your mind as well as your ears—to get past the many distractions and bad habits that prevent you from really hearing what's said and paying attention to it. Until you do that, you're nowhere. So the first step is...

Remove the Barriers to the Message

Approach with a Positive Attitude

The check chart "Common Reasons for Not Listening" listed many negative attitudes: "I'm not interested," "That's too hard," "I don't want to believe it." Instead of saying any of those things when you're about to hear someone talk, either in a small group or a large one, say to yourself, "I'm going to like this; I'm going to get something worthwhile out of it."

It's as easy to say one as the other. The negative approach makes listening, or pretending to listen, a painful ordeal. The positive attitude makes it a pleasure.

Keep Your Emotions from Sidetracking Your Reasoning

Maybe you don't like the speaker. Maybe that person's looks, mannerisms, or background don't appeal to you. Maybe you don't like the voice or style of delivery. Maybe the speaker's grammar is not perfect, or he or she uses words that seem contrived or that grate on you.

Ask yourself, "Is that what's important to me?" Is that why you came to the meeting, or the church, or the seminar—to analyze somebody's clothing, personality, or rhetorical skill? Or did you come to learn something?

Actually, if you let your attention get sidetracked for emotional reasons relating to the speaker or the subject, you're really only looking for an excuse to sulk rather than listen. So don't indulge in emotional excuses. Concentrate on what's important.

Tell yourself, "Miss Jones isn't as polished a speaker as I expected, but that's her problem. She's an expert in her field, and I want to find out all I can about it."

Similarly, it doesn't pay to let your personal emotional problems or worries interfere when you should be listening. Dwelling on them is also just an excuse for letting your mind wander and wasting time. Put them aside. Focus instead on what's being said; maybe it'll include some happy thoughts that'll cheer you up.

Maintain Concentration

Keep alert for signs that you're allowing your attention to wander. You'll recognize them: daydreaming, looking out the window instead of at the speakers, doodling on a notepad during a meeting.

In one-to-one or small conversational groups, it's also imperative to concentrate on the speaker's words. Sometimes you may lose this concentration because you're overly concerned with making a good impression, particularly if you've just been introduced to someone. By trying too hard to make a favorable impression, you concentrate on what the speaker may think of you, rather than on what he or she may be saying, and instead you create a bad impression.

Find Something to Get Interested In

Instead of saying to yourself, "I'm not going to like this" or "I know what this fellow is going to say," make up your mind at the outset that there's bound to be some nugget of valuable information or some thought stimulator somewhere in what you're about to hear.

Decide that you're on a treasure hunt, searching for those valuable nuggets hidden in the words that will be forthcoming. Make it a game, a challenge. That's more fun than enduring boredom, and it's much more rewarding.

You'll find it easier to concentrate on the speaker and on the message. Even if the speaker is dull and verbose, decide that you can beat him at his game and find something to treasure in spite of his shortcomings.

Don't Get in a Hurry-Hurry Mood

It has many causes. You may be busy and impatient, you may think you know what the speaker's about to say, or you may be overly anxious to please. But hurrying too much can cause you to miss the message and get into trouble.

Example: When the speaker gets halfway through a sentence, you're so sure you know what the end of it will be that you cut in and finish the sentence yourself. Your interpretation is likely to be wrong and the speaker is bound to be irritated—maybe so irritated he won't bother to correct you, or maybe too polite to do so.

Example: When your boss says, "We won't revise the proposal until the new cost figures arrive," the first five words are what you're pleased to hear. You tune out the last part of the sentence. At the end of the week, she demands, "Why haven't you revised the proposal yet? The new cost figures came in on Thursday."

Put Yourself in the Speaker's Shoes

The old American Indian adage says, "You can't understand another person until you've walked a mile in his moccasins." Similarly, you can't understand what anyone is saying until you've put yourself in his or her shoes. Art Linkletter made this point when he wrote me about an incident that occurred on one of his shows.

As he indicates in the following letter, you shouldn't judge others too hastily:

A Child Can Teach You

Number one on my list of requirements for a good communicator is being a good listener. By this I mean a totally focused, receptive attitude which communicates to the speaker that I consider him or her to be the most important person in the world during the time we are speaking.

I learned this with children, who are easily distracted and sensitive to attitudes. I've even been accused of hypnotizing them to get them to tell me the secrets of their family life, and in a sense you might say I have, because my eyes never leave theirs and I do not appear shocked or critical no matter how outrageous their remarks may be.

I recall an incident that taught me not to judge hastily, but to try to understand the other person's point of view:

On my show I once had a child tell me he wanted to be an airline pilot. I asked him what he'd do if all the engines stopped out over the Pacific Ocean. He said, "First I would tell everyone on the plane to fasten their seatbelts, and then I'd find my parachute and jump out."

While the audience rocked with laughter, I kept my attention on the young man to see if he was being a smart alec. The tears that sprang into his eyes alerted me to his chagrin more than anything he could have said, so I asked him why he'd do such a thing. His answer revealed the sound logic of a child: "I'm going for gas...I'm coming back!"

ART LINKLETTER

Active Listening Gives Meaning to the Message

OK, so you'll at least hear what's being said if you follow the preceding suggestions and open up your mind as well as your ears. As previously indicated, that's half the battle. But stopping at the halfway mark doesn't accomplish much for you.

You need to *do* something with what you hear. To get meaning and real benefits from the message requires active listening. Rand Araskog, former head of ITT, had this to say about what active listening involves:

The Manager Who Listens

As a manager, you make or break your support people by your attitude....Sometimes it's as simple as taking the time to listen. But listening is more than hearing. It's an *active* process that involves thought and an expenditure of energy.

You must analyze what's being said; separate the relevant from the irrelevant; test your understanding of what you hear; consider the implications; and anticipate—but don't prejudge—where a particular line of thought is leading.

A manager who learns to listen, and encourages his subordinates to listen and question, enriches the jobs of his subordinates by giving them a sense of participation which helps both them and himself.

RAND V. ARASKOG, CHAIRMAN & CEO
ITT

You know by now that you have oodles of surplus brainpower that's just idling along because the human tongue is so much slower than the marvelous gray matter between your ears. If you allow your brain to idle too long, it'll go off on a tangent and take you into unproductive daydreaming, doodling, and extraneous thoughts. You can't allow that, because, as Mr. Araskog correctly points out, there's important work to be done.

Bounce the Message Around

So the second step to good listening is to listen *actively*—to bounce the message around.

As the bits of information are fed into your mind, don't just let them lie there and pile up. Bounce them around; look at them from various angles.

Sift and Sort

Talk rambles, repeats, backtracks. It often contradicts itself and can confuse you. It may be loaded with unimportant details that hide just a nugget or two of worthwhile information. So you have to sift and sort— bounce the raw input around until you can identify the gold from the mass of gravel.

For example, here's what you want to search for:

- *IDEAS—not details.* You can't remember everything, especially in a meeting of any length, and you don't want to. A mass of details will only confuse you and blur your memory if you try to retain it all. So as you listen, keep your mind active in sorting out the one or two real ideas from the mass of niggling little details.

- *Underlying FEELINGS that may belie the words.* Active listening may involve the eyes as well as the ears, strange as that may seem. If you watch the speaker's face closely, you may sense that he or she doesn't really mean what's being said. Tone of voice may also indicate certain feelings that will alter your perception of the message.

- *The CENTRAL point of the message.* As talkers ramble along, they may digress into many byways and make many peripheral statements. You need to focus on the core of the message.

You Be the Judge

Remember, everything you hear isn't necessarily true. Just because "they say it" doesn't mean you have to believe it.

Some of what you hear will be true, some false, some valuable and worthy of your consideration, and some inconsequential nonsense. It's up to you to differentiate and to decide what the message means to you.

To do this, you might keep in mind the name of the old TV game show, *Truth or Consequences.* You be the game-show host or hostess and keep asking these questions:

- *Is it TRUE?* Does it sound right to me? Is it contrary to or in line with facts I've previously heard? Is the speaker someone with a reputation for veracity, accuracy, trustworthiness? Is there any reason why the speaker would want to mislead me?

- *Is it GOOD advice or opinion?* Regardless of factual accuracy, is the speaker interpreting the facts in a doubtful way? Are the opinions and advice I'm getting sensible and reliable? Or do they sound silly or dangerous?

- *What are the CONSEQUENCES to me?* If I believe what the speaker is telling me and act on his advice, what can the result be? What are the probabilities that it will be good or bad? For him, or for me?

Don't Hesitate to Question

Some listeners are too shy—overly passive. Afraid to contradict others, they hesitate to interject questions even though they may not understand some point fully or may not agree with it.

Don't hesitate to question when you're listening. That's the only way you can be sure of getting everything straight. It's far better than merely nodding your head or keeping quiet throughout a conversation. Far from resenting your questions, the speaker is likely to welcome them, because your questions show that you're genuinely interested in what's being said and understand it.

In fact, questions are one of the most important elements in communication. They not only help you listen. They also help you direct a conversation, get feedback on what you say, and establish rapport with others. The numerous benefits of asking questions are discussed in Chapter 21.

Ways to Improve Your Memory

Plan Some Use for the Message

Try to relate what you hear to yourself—to some useful purpose it will serve. Information is not much good if you can't put it to use, either soon or later. So, one of the problems you can pose to your idling-along brain is, "What can I do with this?"

Often there's no immediate opportunity for action, but you can still think where a new thought or bit of data might come in handy someday. If you do this, you'll "put a label" on it, so it'll be easier to retrieve from your mental computer when you need it.

Repeat the Main Points to Yourself

It helps to repeat any ideas or information you need to remember. Once you've sifted out a key idea or an instruction that applies to you, repeat it a couple of times silently, before it slips away. Once you've mentally heard yourself saying it, it becomes your thought—a part of you—that you're not likely to forget.

Take Notes, but Don't Get Carried Away

As you already know, writing something down helps you remember it. During meetings, seminars, etc., it's generally advisable to take a few notes.

But observe that I said *a few*. Whenever I see someone scribbling constantly during a meeting, I wonder if that person is really listening or merely indulging in a form of mindless doodling. Is it possible, while immersed in encyclopedic note-taking, to think about what's being said? Taking endless notes, how can you still be analyzing for veracity, sorting out key ideas, and planning some use for them? It's far better to be concentrating on these activities.

As your mind bounces the message around and squeezes out the essence, this essence is the part you want to write down—as concisely as possible. In my experience, if you can come away from a half-hour meeting or presentation with half a dozen pertinent points jotted down in a sentence or two each, it was an unusually productive get-together. The important thing then is to *do* something about those few points; you know you're kidding yourself if you think you'll take action on a book full of notes. They're headed for the circular file.

Listening Is Your First Skill

Listening probably ranks first in the amount of time you devote to it. If you're a typical business executive, you may spend half or more of your day in meetings alone. They're principally listening activities, unless you're one of the characters you'll read about in Chapter 8 who monopolize meetings.

Did you know that listening is also the first type of communication you ever experienced? You started listening *before* you were born. No kidding!

Obviously, you couldn't use your eyes before birth, and babies don't do much talking before they're a year old. But doctors who concentrate on infant studies have reason to believe you were listening to mama when still in her womb—not just listening to her heartbeat, but actually hearing her voice.

Medical researchers have found that, unlike the eyes, a baby's ears function even *before* birth. The newborn arrives with a whole set of auditory reactions. By the time they're born, babies prefer female voices. (Perhaps this explains a tendency I've noticed for tiny babies to be frightened if a man speaks to them. Or maybe I just scare kids.) By the time they're a few weeks old, babies can recognize the sound of their mother's voice.

And there's a third reason why listening ranks first among the various means of communication. It's the beginning of wisdom—what the wise person does before speaking, and the secret of success of the person everyone likes. As one of those smart old Greeks advised:

> Nature has given us one tongue, but
> two ears, that we may hear from others
> twice as much as we speak.   EPICTETUS

4

Listen with Your Eyes

You can observe a lot just by watching.
Yogi Berra

You can't believe everything you hear. Sometimes you'll pick up visual signals that are contradictory. Keep in mind the words of the song that goes, "Your lips are saying 'no, no,' but there's 'yes, yes' in your eyes." In business matters, the opposite is more likely to be true: You may be getting lip agreement to your requests, but if you read the visual signs carefully, you'll know you'd better not bank on it.

Such signals are often referred to as *body language*. Actually, the parts of the body you're apt to read mostly are the face and especially the eyes. They can be tricky to analyze correctly because everyone tries at times to hide feelings by showing a poker face to the world. Posture and body movements aren't always easy to read. Yet it behooves you to be more observant, as Yogi Berra advises, to be sure you're not led astray by words alone.

You Have a Head Start

The task of listening with your eyes is not a formidable one, though you might think so if you pick up a book that attempts to attach a meaning to every nuance of body or facial movement. After all, you've been reading nonverbal cues since infancy. What you need to do now is go back to some basics you already know. Pay more attention to them. Be more observant.

Some Signals Are Obvious

Imagine you come near a stray dog. He growls at you and bares his teeth. His tail goes up and he advances toward you. Understand what he means? Of course you do, very clearly.

Similar messages are transmitted between humans, but they're usually more subtle, so you may sometimes miss them. People also growl (tone of voice) or make friendly sounds. They bare their teeth figuratively (facial expressions) or smile. They make threatening movements (gestures) or ones expressing friendliness, boredom, nervousness, eagerness, assent, or dissent.

Long before you could talk or understand many words, you were deciphering such messages. In fact, specialists on infant development would tell you that an infant can read nonverbal messages better than you can. They mean everything to the baby, while you've become educated and oriented toward words, so you may have lost the sensitivity toward unspoken language. That's the key word: sensitivity.

How to Resurrect Sensitivity

How can you again get as smart as you were in your childhood, when you watched every expression flickering across your parents' faces and knew precisely whether they really meant what they said or whether it was safe to ignore their words? You need to do the same as you did then: Watch carefully for the little movements of face and body, and add them all up for assessment.

To accomplish this, you don't require any intricate study of body language any more than a child does. Gestures or posture can't be catalogued in any precise way. The fact that people shift their legs or slouch in a chair is no infallible guide to anything. They may merely be tired or have hemorrhoids. Human behavior is complex and subtle, and it varies from person to person and time to time.

Go to the Movies or Watch TV

One good way to practice sensitivity to silent language is to go to a foreign movie. There you'll automatically look intently for nonverbal clues to supplement the sparse subtitles. In Tokyo, I once went to a classical Noh play where the actors all wear masks, so I couldn't even pick up any clues from facial expressions, but gestures alone told me fairly clearly what the demons, warriors, and maidens were up to.

Probably the best way to practice nonverbal listening is right at home. Watch your TV set with the sound turned down. On a dramatic program, if the actors are skilled and if you do a careful job of observing, you'll discover many indicators of how the story is progressing. Try this. It's challenging fun, and it'll make you much more aware of the silent signals of those around you.

Facial Expressions Are Fleeting

As you'll learn when you watch a foreign film or a drama on TV sans sound, you must stay alert to catch changing facial expressions. Actually, the actors you see there are playing broadly—exaggerating and holding their movements to telegraph them to their audience. In real life, you get less time to read the signals.

Facial expressions have been timed in slow-motion films. They show that an expression can flit across a person's face and disappear in a fifth of a second, so if you let your attention lag, you'll miss it.

That's a hazard. But like most problems, it has a positive side. Because emotions flash to the surface of people's faces so quickly and instinctively, they're difficult to hide. These almost instantaneous reactions, therefore, are often more reliable clues to real feelings than what people say to you. They may pause, reflect, and then speak a lie to you, but if you're sharp enough to note the quick emotional flash that escaped to the face, you know what the deep-down thought is.

Watch the Eyes

Spoken language is easy to control. So are some body movements; people can fake a smile and lean forward as if interested when they're not. Some may even be pretty good at maintaining a frozen face that yields few clues. But it's practically impossible to control one's eyes.

Even the Chinese, noted for inscrutability of facial expression, can't control the pupils of their eyes. The wily old merchants of China knew this. One of their trade secrets was to focus on the eyes of an important customer as they suddenly uncovered a beautiful piece of jade or other precious bauble. That might elicit not a word or a facial quiver, but if the customer was really pleased at the sight, *the pupils of his eyes would inevitably, involuntarily open wide*. Then the merchant knew that although the haggling might be long, this was the piece of merchandise the customer really wanted, and that it could be sold for a top price.

What the Camera Discovers

Some of today's market researchers have utilized the same physiological phenomenon. They focus a camera straight into the eyes of a person they're testing to determine his or her interest in various things. For example, the person tested may be shown different pictures to be used in advertising ... or different television commercials ... or different packages ... or colors of a product, such as a lipstick. The camera will show the pupils widening (as much as 45 percent) when the viewer experiences pleasure. That's what the researcher wants to know—what's most pleasing to typical prospective purchasers.

A Lesson from X-Rated Pictures

As far back as 1960, Ekhard H. Hess conducted a number of studies which showed that pupil sizes increase when people look at other people they like. Not surprisingly, men's pupils dilated when they were shown pictures of nude women.

Dr. Hess tried photos of political figures next. I don't know if the dilation was as extreme, but the pupils opened when the subjects looked at politicians they admired, and contracted when they viewed public figures they disliked. So if you notice a substantial shrinking of the pupils when you shake hands with someone, don't let any warmth of handclasp fool you.

Gestures Are a Cultural Code

Gestures are a form of sign language. Some are peculiar to a given country or part of the world. A few strange (to us) regional gestures are listed in the box on the next page.

There are many others. Waving is a serious insult in Greece. So is beckoning with the finger in the Middle East. Tapping the head means "I'm thinking" in Brazil, but it means "crazy" in other places; it can mean either to us. Tapping the nose means "Keep it secret" in England and is a warning sign in Italy. Most countries have a much wider variety of gestural "words" than do the British and Americans.

Universal Gestures

Despite the peculiar differences, a lot of gestures are universal. For example, if you travel where you can't speak more than a few words of the native language, you find yourself communicating reasonably well by the use of basic human gestures. You spread your hands to say, "I don't know." You hunch your shoulders to indicate "I'm not sure," and at the same time you may raise your eyebrows. You face your palm toward the listener to mean "No!" You nod (hopefully in the right directions for that culture) to indicate "yes" and "no." You point for things you want. You may clap to show approval. The number of gestures you use may exceed the number of words you can command.

Strange Symbolic Gestures

In parts of southern India, here's a gesture of respect that we might resent.

- Thumb and first finger forming a circle means "OK" in the United States but is obscene South of the Border, means "worthless" in Southern France, and means "money" in Japan.

- Winston Churchill's famous V-for-Victory sign is closely akin to the insulting gesture in many cultures that means "You have horns; your wife is cuckolding you."

- The English hiss actors to show extreme disapproval. In Japan, hissing expresses social deference.

- There are many ways to indicate "yes" or "no." Our up-and-down or side-to-side nods of the head mean the opposite in parts of Greece, Turkey, and India. In Sicily you tilt your head back slightly and thrust out your chin for "no." An Abyssinian tilts her head back and raises her eyebrows for "yes." She jerks her head toward her right shoulder to show disapproval.

- In many places, spitting is a gross sign of contempt, inviting violence. But if a Masai warrior spits in your presence, you needn't run; he's trying to show friendship and respect.

- In our culture, we stand up (or used to) to show respect for women and elders. Fiji Islanders sit down before a superior. This is akin to the ancient oriental tradition of groveling before a ruler, since anyone who dared raise his head higher than the King's risked losing it.

- One of the most interesting signs of respect is found in the Friendly Islands, aptly named. There the natives take their clothes off to show esteem for others.

- Conversing with your hands in your pockets is impolite in France, Belgium, Finland, Sweden, and Indonesia. In Fiji it's bad manners to raise your arms, but crossing them over your chest is very good.

You constantly transmit nonverbal signals. You cannot *not* communicate, even if you try.

Although we Americans and the British don't "talk with our hands" nearly so much as other peoples do, we use those basic gestures unconsciously as we converse. Sometimes you'll see people let a gesture slip out that contradicts what they're saying. At other times, gestures may help the verbal message in one of three ways:

- *Accent.* You say, "Yes," and nod your head at the same time to project a strong affirmative.

- *Repetition.* You admonish a child not to do something. If the warning is ignored, without saying anything more, you may waggle your finger as a repeated caution.

- *Substitution.* Without speaking, you may use a gesture alone to transmit a message.

Loosen Up!

In our culture, we probably don't use gestures enough; they complement what we say, adding to the strength of our messages. It wouldn't be appropriate for you to throw your hands around whenever you talk (that's not the norm here as it is in some other countries), but you don't need to stand like a statue either. *An occasional gesture shows enthusiasm!* And everyone likes to see enthusiasm, especially in a dynamic young executive who has the potential to go places.

Gestures should also be used more frequently than they are during presentations or public speaking. (You'll read more about this in Chapter 7.) Too many speakers allow themselves to freeze in rigid postures, or they grip the podium in front of them with white-knuckled intensity. Some body movement and gestures are needed to unlock that rigidity and to bring the audience closer to you.

In social conversation, only about one-third of the social meaning is transmitted by words. The other two-thirds is conveyed in nonverbal clues.

The Message of Distance

When you're talking about friends or acquaintances, you ask, "How *close* are you to him or her?" Distance tells a great deal about relationships—in social situations or in business. You'd like to be "like that" (make the gesture of two fingers aligned touching each other) with the president of your company, certainly not "on the outs" with that important individual. It's no accident that you use such words to convey warmth or coolness of relationships. Actual physical distance indicates

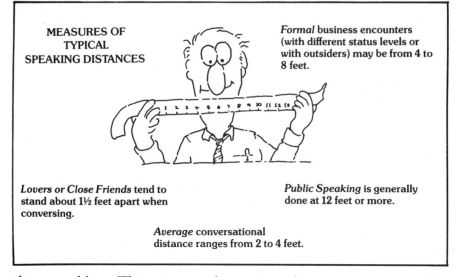

MEASURES OF TYPICAL SPEAKING DISTANCES

Formal business encounters (with different status levels or with outsiders) may be from 4 to 8 feet.

Lovers or Close Friends tend to stand about 1½ feet apart when conversing.

Public Speaking is generally done at 12 feet or more.

Average conversational distance ranges from 2 to 4 feet.

the same things. The accompanying cartoon shows some common distance clues.

In future, whenever you're in meetings where people are free to move around (as opposed to sitting around a table), keep an eye on the distances. They may tell you more than the conversation does about what's really going on.

Status Behavior

Status behavior varies from country to country. The distance maintained between people is more rigid in Japan than it is in the United States. But in Latin countries and in the Middle East, conversation gets almost nose to nose.

Perhaps you've heard the story about the Englishman and the Italian talking. Wanting to be friendly, the Italian moved a step closer to the Englishman. He, in turn, feeling embarrassed at having his companion so uncomfortably near—almost brushing his chest—moved back a step. This two-step was repeated again and again, the Italian advancing and the Englishman retreating, until the two of them had danced the length of the room.

In one of his books, Theodore H. White describes people's innate reluctance to encroach on the space of someone who holds or may soon hold great status. The following excerpt describes what happened when John F. Kennedy met with some of his supporters:[1]

[1]Reprinted with permission of Atheneum Publishers, an imprint of Macmillan Publishing Company, from *The Making of the President, 1960*, by Theodore H. White. © 1961 by Atheneum House, Inc.

[Kennedy] descended the steps of the split-level cottage to a corner where his brother Bobby and brother-in-law Sargent Shriver were chatting, waiting for him. The others in the room surged forward on impulse to join him. Then they halted. A distance of perhaps 30 feet separated them from him, but it was impassable. They stood apart, these older men of long-established power, and watched him. He turned after a few minutes, saw them watching him, and whispered to his brother-in-law. Shriver now crossed the separating space to invite them over. First Averell Harriman; then Dick Daley; then Mike DiSalle, then, one by one, let them all congratulate him. Yet no one could pass the little open distance between him and them uninvited, because there was this thin separation about him, and the knowledge they were not as his patrons but as his clients. They could come by invitation only, for this might be a President of the United States.

In corporate structures, there are codes of distance that indicate status. As you well know, you don't crowd the CEO or anyone substantially above you in the pecking order.

However, a person at a higher level has the option of narrowing the distance. If your boss moves close to you—especially in a group situation—you can interpret this as a nonverbal signal to you and the others that you're being singled out in a favorable way. That's called a "good" gesture. Conversely, if the head honcho gets into the habit of staying an extraordinary distance away, it's time to polish your résumé.

How You Can Label Yourself

Position around the conference table is an indicator too. If you're in the corporate world, you're familiar with the unspoken rule that the seat at the head is reserved for the head person. And you also know that in formal corporate cultures the chairs immediately adjoining usually go to those next on the organization chart—except for the brownnoser who often slips in at the right hand of the power. That's hazardous.

The tendency of nonpushy people to relegate themselves to the outfield at meetings is also dangerous. If you do that, you label yourself as the least important member of the group. But even if you are unimportant, organizationally, you can sometimes arrive early and seat yourself midway to the throne. It's a simple, nonpresumptive gesture that says you deserve to be higher up and will eventually get there.

Touching Is the Ultimate

Touching is the ultimate reduction of distance. When it occurs, it's the ultimate expression of closeness or confidence. You don't see much of it in business, which is basically a formal relationship. When it does occur, it's often deliberately intended by the initiator as a gesture to be understood by the receiver as a special one.

If a word of praise is accompanied by a touch on the shoulder, that's the gold star on the ribbon. But in dealing with your subordinates, remember that the special value of the gesture is derived from its rarity. If you go around patting everyone all the time, this will become not a singular accolade, but what's expected of you routinely.

Voice Cues Alter Your Message

Voice cues (technically known as *paralanguage*) are not body language or something you see. But they are nonverbal, and they certainly change the meaning that's derived from your words.

Just as gestures do, these clues slip out unconsciously at times and indicate to the alert listener that caution is required in interpreting what's being said. It may be a change in the rate of speech, a loudness or gruffness, a tightness, a hesitation. No need to spell them out; you're familiar enough with the many variations of the human voice and what they indicate. You hear them all the time when you listen to others, and you automatically read them as clues to the true sincerity, enthusiasm, etc., of the speaker.

How Do You Sound?

Most people have little idea how they themselves sound when they talk. Do you? Have you ever taped yourself and carefully analyzed the paralanguage you transmit to others? If not, get a recorder and speak into it the conversation you hope to have soon with your boss, or tape part of the important presentation you must make.

Listen not to the words, but to the enthusiasm and sincerity you hope to convey. Listen for little hesitations that betray uncertainty, for tightness of throat (more uncertainty), for hurried delivery, and for drops in tone when your voice should be firm and strong. Then do it over and over until you get a tape that says, "This is the way I want people to read me."

A Case History:
Lt. Col. Oliver North

On July 13, 1987, the cover of *U.S. News & World Report* was a grim black-and-white drawing of Ollie North, who had to date said little to congressional probers except that he took the Fifth Amendment. The following week, North appeared again on the magazine's cover, this time in full color. The caption describing his testimony at the House-

Senate Iran-contra hearings read, "How Ollie Stormed the Hill." For yet a third week, images of Ollie and others involved in the probe were shown on the magazine's cover with the bold headline "Television's Blinding Power." By that time, the Marine colonel who seemed destined to become the silent scapegoat of a muddy mess had transformed himself into the hero of millions who wanted him to run for President and who were avidly buying T-shirts and bumper stickers extolling his virtues.

It's not the intention here to express any opinion as to whether Lt. Col. North is really Sir Galahad or a misguided bum. But in the context of communication, the question is, "How could any such fantastic transformation take place? What did he do?"

Sometimes It's Not the Words that Count. The opening paragraph of the article in the July 27 issue of *U.S. News & World Report* gave a clue to his success: "Lt. Col. Oliver North had already stolen the show, not so much with *what* he said, but with *how* he said it—and with how it played on television." The italics are theirs. The caption under the main picture in the article was: "A formidable capacity to convince 55 million viewers it's not the words that count."

Do you recognize in those statements—and in North's performance (if you watched some of it)—a relationship to what you've just been reading about facial movements, eyes, body language, and voice cues? Let me help you recall some of what viewers saw and heard.

What they heard Col. North describe was a chronology that included a long series of lies, dealings with shady characters and terrorist nations, scrambled Swiss bank accounts, and the shredding of documents. It was a litany far worse than even his interrogators ever expected. As some of them stated, it was mind-boggling. Without being moralistic or judgmental as to whether these shenanigans were justified (that will be determined in court), would you agree that if North's words had been presented coldly on paper, they'd have elicited little sympathy?

What America Saw. An impersonal written documentation is not what America saw. What appeared to the TV audience was a sincere, likable man sitting ramrod straight in his Marine uniform bedecked with row upon row of richly deserved medals (body language). He leaned forward, eager to tell his story. He looked the audience straight in the eye (eye movement). His voice had a hoarseness that bespoke his sincerity and patriotic passion (voice cues). It broke with emotion at appropriate spots. He was a clean, lovable Clint Eastwood with sad basset-hound eyes. And Laurence Olivier could not have surpassed his performance in that difficult theater with the cameras focused on his face hour after hour.

Just as you do every day, Ollie North used paralanguage. He did it superbly well, while millions *listened with their eyes* and were persuaded to believe him.

Electing a President

The power of body language was demonstrated clearly during the 1988 presidential election—a media event, from start to final balloting, that shocked many people with its emphasis on form over content. In commenting on the predominant use of visuals and short sound bites by the candidates, Kevin Delaney, a consultant to politicians, explained: "Impressions are what voters are guided by. Our surveys show that *only 10 percent of impressions are based on the candidates' words. Forty percent is voice, 50 percent is general appearance and body language.*"[2]

Newsweek magazine, in a special postelection issue of November 21, 1988, spoke at length about the major role that image expert Roger Ailes played in coaching George Bush for his television appearances. Ailes, who had been a consultant to both Nixon and Reagan, faced a difficult challenge with the vice president; he had to slow his speaking down to deepen his voice, and also get his body language into better sync with his words. As the magazine said, "Ailes trained him in the tricks of nonverbal communication—how to show calm with a smile and strength with a stab of the hand; ... how to steady his darting gaze and lean into the camera in a debate or an interview, as if invading the enemy's space."[3]

Whatever you may find yourself campaigning for, remember that it's not just *what* you say, but *how* you present it.

[2]From an article by Dick Polman in the *Kansas City Times*, September 27, 1988, with permission from Knight-Ridder Newspapers.

[3]Excerpted with permission from Newsweek Inc.

5
Companies That Listen

The number one managerial productivity problem in America is, quite simply, managers who are out of touch with their people and out of touch with their customers.
TOM PETERS AND NANCY AUSTIN
(from A Passion for Excellence)

Companies are like people—some listen, some don't. Those which are good listeners tend to become popular everywhere: with their employees, customers, investors, and the general public. And often they get to know some things, useful knowledge, not widely shared by their less open-eared competitors.

You're familiar with companies that have these characteristics, and with many more that do not. If you think about them, you'll recognize that the differences stem from the attitudes in the executive suite.

In the companies that don't listen, there's what I call a BMW complex. I'm not referring to a motor car, but to the tendency of the top executive and his or her chief aides to hide *b*ehind *m*ahogany *w*alls. Safely ensconced where no one can reach them, they live in a cozy private world free from all thoughts of unruly employees or unhappy customers. Their doors are closed to such distractions while they concentrate instead on management by statistics, systems, legalities. They focus on cutting costs rather than on ways to build better products. If this leads to customer complaints, they refuse to talk about them except through their lawyers.

That's the closed-door, closed-ears attitude. Fortunately, there's an increasing number of prominent, successful American companies in which the atmosphere is refreshingly different. I'd like to point out several outstanding examples of *companies that listen* and discuss some of the things they do to earn a warm regard and enviable record of accomplishment.

H&R Block

If Henry and Richard Bloch hadn't listened to their customers, they'd have washed their hands of tax preparation 30 years ago. They hated it!

The two brothers had a nice little bookkeeping business that went along smoothly most of the year, until tax time. Then they had to help their clients prepare returns, and they were also innundated with neighboring businesspeople and friends of clients who wanted tax help too. Each succeeding spring became more of a nightmare, with the Blochs working killing hours on IRS forms for paltry income. "We were making about $400 apiece each spring on tax returns and working seven days a week to do it," Henry Bloch recounted to me.

Finally Henry and Richard told their customers they'd had enough. Everyone except their regular year-round bookkeeping clients was advised, "Please take your tax business somewhere else. We're through with it."

That set up a howl among the once-a-year customers. They told the Blochs, "You can't do that to us; we need you." The message the brothers heard was that they could probably get a big volume of business—maybe a very profitable amount—if they went after it and added some springtime help to handle it.

One Last Try

Reluctantly, they decided it might be worth one more try. The next year they advertised their tax-preparation services and trained a few part-time people to assist with the basic chores. The response from that first public solicitation faced them with a new decision: Should they forget the bookkeeping business and go full tilt into the tax business? They did. Today H&R Block, Inc. (they changed the "h" at the end of their names to a "k" because that's how most people spelled it) prepares about *10 percent of all U.S. returns—more than 12 million of them.* It also prepares millions more in 16 other countries.

Would This Scare You?

Henry W. Bloch, the president and CEO, admitted to me that the initial plunge into new fields was a scary proposition. That's understandable. How would you like to go into a business where (1) you're not offering anything new or unique (CPAs and bookkeeping companies have always provided tax help); (2) you make a sale in most cases only once a year; (3) you expect to lose money three-quarters of the year and make it up, plus a profit, in just one quarter; (4) about 20 percent of your customers move away to a new location (maybe to another town) every year; and (5) 25 percent of your office force is brand new each year?

Mr. Bloch credits communication with being a key factor in overcoming the strange problems of such a peculiar business and in building it into the large, profitable corporation it has become. Here are some of the precepts his company follows.

The Block Formula for Success

"We Listen to Our People in the Field."   About half of all H&R Block offices are franchises, often run by people who have other businesses throughout the year. Mr. Bloch said, "When we started out, we tended to tell them exactly what to do...give them rigid rules to follow. That didn't work out. Now we suggest, but we recognize that different people in different situations are going to do better if they're allowed flexibility. When they tell us what needs to be done in their location, they're usually right."

"We Turned Our Viewpoint Upside Down."   He explained that this policy of "listening to the field" created a new organizational concept at H&R Block—a different way of looking at things. Instead of viewing the operation as a pyramid with headquarters at the top (in the heavens) and command filtering down to the field offices, as is done in most companies, they have exactly the opposite concept.

He told me, "We view our operation as an *upside-down pyramid*. The district offices are at the top, because that's where it's at. Below come the regional offices, then our three divisional offices, and finally our corporate headquarters. We're there at the bottom to help. That's how we want everyone to view our operation."

An interesting concept. Certainly unlike that in most corporations. Perhaps it's one of the reasons why H&R Block manages a sprawling international operation with a small headquarters staff and only two levels of management between headquarters and the district field offices.

"Customers Tell Us What They Want—We Listen."   "What we emphasize in our advertising," Mr. Bloch said, "is what customers tell us. You may have noticed some ads which quote actual customers who are pleased because we helped them get tax refunds—larger refunds than they believe they could have gotten by themselves. Our surveys show that three out of four customers who receive refunds share that belief. "Another thing we've heard our customers say repeatedly is that they dread going to an IRS office alone if they're called in for an audit. So we tell them that if there's ever an audit, we'll go with them, free of charge."

"Our Tax Preparers Listen for a 'Thank You' from the Customer."   It's common for a supplier of services to say "thanks" to its customers, but I'd never heard of one that expects to get a "thank you" *from* customers. Evidently that occurs often during the trauma of tax time when it feels so good to have all those receipts and scraps of data neatly assembled onto an IRS form and sent off by an expert.

In fact, Mr. Bloch informed me, "We figure something must be wrong if it doesn't happen. The customer may not be as pleased as he should be about something ... and may not come back to us next year. We depend on repeat business. So we train our preparers to *listen for the 'thank you.'* Whenever they don't hear one, they're supposed to ask if the customer is completely satisfied with everything. We don't want any unsatisfied customers."

H&R Block is no longer entirely a tax-preparation company. It's moving into other areas—personnel training, computer information services, and seminars—to spread its revenues beyond the hectic tax-paying season. It plans to use the same management attitudes and principles in these fields. They've worked well so far. In 30 years, profits at H&R Block have increased every year but one.

Whirlpool

Whirlpool is a big company (probably the largest appliance manufacturer in the world) located in a small town. As such, it operates on a combination of worldly up-to-the-minute sophistication and a low-key country casual manner. The latter is exemplified by a story they like to tell about the time Jack Sparks, who was then president and chairman, tried to shut people out of his offices for a few hours.

This happened on the day a TV crew arrived to film an interview with Sparks. The director wanted to start shooting just inside the double doors to the hallway leading to the boardroom and the CEO's office.

"No problem," Mr. Sparks agreed. "We'll just close the doors so no one will come barging in to spoil your filming." His communications staff working with the camera crew thought maybe they ought to put up a sign explaining why this area was temporarily off-limits, but Sparks saw no need for that. After all, if the chairman shut the doors, wouldn't everyone know this meant "keep out" because he didn't want to see anyone?

At almost any company I can think of, that would be a logical assumption, but not at Whirlpool. People kept blundering into the hallway, to the exasperation of the photographers, until someone was stationed outside to deter them. *They couldn't believe Jack would close them out.* Must be a mistake. He wouldn't do that. He was always available if someone needed to see him.

No one, not even the head man, could alter the open-door policy at Whirlpool.

Starting a Cool Line

When I first knew Sparks, he was marketing vice president and deeply involved in the advertising our agency created for Whirlpool. At that time, Whirlpool initiated a consumer program that has set a precedent for many others since then.

Based on the concept that it was truly prepared to *listen* to any and all consumer troubles, Whirlpool offered toll-free telephone calls over an 800 "Cool Line." This received a warm response from appliance owners.

In its first year of operation, the Cool Line handled 10,000 calls from consumers with questions about sales, service, or the use of their appliances. In recent years, about 30,000 queries come in annually. They're answered by knowledgeable consultants from the service, research, sales, manufacturing, or engineering departments—mostly long-time employees or retirees with extensive knowledge of the company's full line of appliances.

Some of the calls can be handled quickly and easily. (A frequent solution to an appliance that won't work: simply check to see if the electrical plug has been pulled accidently from the outlet.) Other calls require lengthy, detailed answers. For example, a growing number of do-it-yourselfers get patient step-by-step advice on how to install or repair an appliance.

Someone Always Available to Listen.   Whirlpool owners can be sure there's always someone knowledgeable prepared to listen to them—24 hours a day, 365 days a year. To many consumers, that means a lot.

Besides doing much to build goodwill and confidence in products and service (Whirlpool consistently rates at or near the top in these respects in independent surveys), the Cool Line has an additional important benefit. It's relied on as a major management tool that supplies reliable information throughout the company.

Supervisors and Managers Get an Earful. Not just the consultants who answer the telephones listen to the calls that pour in over the Cool Line. The phone lines also go to every department of the company: to loudspeakers in the offices of managers and supervisors. And these management people are expected to switch on the speakers regularly to hear what's being said out in the real world.

> **From bottom to top, Whirlpool management listens *directly* to the ultimate boss, the consumer.**

They hear first-hand what people like or don't like about product design, convenience, quality, durability, service, and sales. In making decisions, management doesn't have to say, "I think the consumer wants." They can say, "I know."

The Payoff

For numbers-oriented people, is there any way of quantifying whether or not all this effort to be a company that listens really pays off? Consider a few facts, and draw your own conclusions:[1]

- Since the mid-1970s, the Whirlpool brand has about doubled its share of the market.
- While sales increased, service incidence went down.
- In these perilous times when many firms bewail their inability to match overseas productivity, that's no problem at Whirlpool. Its output per employee is about twice the U.S. average.
- Whirlpool produces more appliances than any other manufacturer—more than $4 billion worth.
- Despite intense competition, it's still growing strongly, at an average rate exceeding 12 percent annually.

Wal-Mart

If you're a Northerner or from either of the coasts, you may not be familiar with Wal-Mart or the Walton family of Arkansas. (No relatives of mine, unfortunately.) Even though it's predicted that Wal-Mart will be the nation's largest retailer before too long, you may never have seen one of its discount stores, because they're concentrated in the middle of the Sunbelt in small communities. Very small, mostly.

The first one opened in 1962 in Rogers City. If you can't place that, it's in the northwest corner of Arkansas and has a population of about

---

[1]Data from author's personal interviews and from Whirlpool's 1987 annual report.

18,000. That store's still there, but it's been joined by *more than 1200 others*. Company headquarters is now in nearby Bentonville, about half as large as Rogers.

Despite it's expansion, you could still regard Wal-Mart as a small-town family company. Sam Walton, though past 70, is still very much in charge as chairman and CEO. There are three other Waltons on the board of directors. Nearly all the executives and the 80 district managers scattered throughout the territories are home-grown talent recruited from the Ozarks and thereabouts. The family still owns 39 percent of the stock. That's nice for them because the total value of the company at the time this book went to press was a bit over $18 billion.

Unwelcome Publicity from Malcolm Forbes

It wasn't until Malcolm Forbes put those statistics into his calculator a few years ago that the company and the family began to attract national attention—attention that hasn't pleased them. Malcolm announced in his magazine that Sam Walton, according to his figuring, must be the richest man in America. That caused many financiers and corporate moguls to exclaim, "Sam who?"

It also prompted editors throughout the nation to order their reporters aboard an Ozarks Airlines flight to find out what's happening out there, wherever it is. They learned that Mr. Sam, though a friendly courteous gentleman, does not cotton to journalists who insist on asking impertinent questions about his bank accounts (the Waltons own the local bank) and his net worth. While hounding the elusive businessman for interviews, they uncovered many quaint facts about the corporate world in Bentonville.

Examples: There are no chauffered limousines; the chairman drives himself to work in a beat-up old car or pickup truck and parks wherever he can find a spot in the company lot. He used to bring his favorite hunting dog to the office occasionally. His alternative to the infamous three-martini business lunch is sharing a couple of hamburgers and some fries at McDonalds or the Ramada Inn coffee shop—Dutch treat, since no one at Wal-Mart ever accepts free meals from suppliers.

The Advantages of Focusing

These exotic trivia may have some news value, but they don't explain how Mr. Sam propelled Wal-Mart forward at a 40 percent compound growth rate during the 1970s and early 1980s. This growth (which has now slowed down to 25 percent, or only a few billion dollars a year) hasn't come from plunging into debt to buy up other chains or different businesses; that has no appeal to Walton.

Rather, he believes in *focusing*—a word he uses frequently—on the business you know and on the few key essentials that make it successful. No need to change your methods or thinking because you've gotten big. You just do the same kind of things in more locations. What are these things?

Going Where the Action Is

One reason it's difficult to catch Mr. Walton in his office is that four days a week he travels to various Wal-Mart locations so he can personally listen in on what's happening there. *When the company was smaller, he called at every store every year!* That's no longer possible, but he still tries to hit 50 percent of them annually, and he also tries to attend as many new store openings as he can. That's difficult too. During the week I visited him, Wal-Mart opened 11 new outlets.

"What does he do there?" I wondered, expecting that the chairman's visits would be largely ceremonial, involving a speech or pep talk to the local troops. Not so, I was told. Mr. Walton goes not to make speeches, but to *learn*.

Talking and Listening to Customers. He wanders throughout the store to observe customers and their reactions. And at some time during his visit, he'll station himself alongside a checkout clerk. If you should ever happen to be in a Wal-Mart when Mr. Sam is there, you might be surprised to find a distinguished-looking, gray-haired man in a conservative suit packing your purchases into a bag for you as he chats amiably and asks probing questions about what you bought and why, how often you come to Wal-Mart, or how the service, merchandise, and people compare with those at competitive stores nearby.

As you'd suspect, if the chairman sets this kind of travel pace, others throughout the organization follow suit. The corporate headquarters, a nondescript building next to the warehouse just off highway U.S. 71, is the emptiest main-office building I've ever seen. That's because most of the executive staff is out in the field most of the time.

Talking and Listening to Associates. On every store visit, Mr. Walton makes it a point to talk individually to every associate there, from the manager to the newest stock boy. Not only are such contacts the ultimate in employee relations, but Walton believes that the person who does the work knows the most about it.

If a checkout clerk or stock clerk has any suggestion that will improve service or save money, Mr. Sam wants to hear it. Such suggestions, passed on to him or other executives, save Wal-Mart millions of dollars a year. And that's important in a business where every penny counts, as it should in any business.

Unusual Interaction

Besides visits to stores, which far surpass the volume of contacts of this sort I've ever heard about in any large retail chain, there are other unusual programs to ensure open, stimulating communication.

Grass-Roots Meetings.   At the store level, it's company policy that the manager must have a get-together and free-for-all discussion with all his or her people once a year. This is held away from the store, often at the manager's home. Topics for discussion include anything about the store or the company that anyone wishes to talk about.

Open-Door Communication.   This name is applied to a unique policy of guaranteeing resolution of any employee problem. It means that if a clerk, for example, has a serious disagreement with his or her manager and doesn't reach a satisfactory solution, that clerk can take the problem to the district manager. And if the district manager can't work it out, the clerk can go still another step higher, or two steps, or up to the president or chairman if necessary.

At a typical place of employment, any such attempt to go over the boss's head would be the quickest way to land out on the street. At Wal-Mart it must not only be tolerated, but the immediate supervisor, when advised of such an action, must *congratulate* the complainer on his or her persistence in seeking a solution.

Walton wants his store teams to work in harmony, as friends. There's a legend in the company that once when constant bickering persisted at one store, Mr. Sam put an end to it dramatically by firing everyone at that location and installing a completely new staff. Everyone understands the dictum: "Backbiting and bickering will not be tolerated; you must get along."

A Back-to-Basics Week for All Executives.   Once a year, every executive must spend one week at a Wal-Mart store. Not observing. Not giving high-level advice. But *working*—unpacking merchandise, marking it, inspecting it, stocking shelves, checking inventory and the physical condition of the store, waiting on customers, listening to complaints—all the unglamorous things that home-office brass may tend to put out of mind.

It can be a humbling experience for high-salaried managers, some of whom have $1 million or more in Wal-Mart stock. And it's intended to be. But it assures *focusing on what the business is all about.*

The People Business Isn't High-Tech

Mr. Walton told me that his company is in "the people business" and that this means "*giving the best possible service to the people who want to buy*"—the six million who come to Wal-Mart stores in a typical week. And he does it, he says, *"with a hard-working staff of good intelligent people who deserve to be treated with respect and dignity. They are important partners in the business."*

Nothing mysterious or high-tech about that, is there? Just common sense and fair play. It sure works for Wal-Mart.

Marion Laboratories

If you're a baseball fan, you may have seen Ewing M. Kauffman when the TV cameras invaded a locker-room champagne celebration at the end of the 1985 season. He's co-owner of the Kansas City Royals, the cinderella team that came from way behind in both the pennant race and the World Series that year to clobber the competition.

Ewing Marion Kauffman is also the founder and chairman of the board of Marion Laboratories—another cinderella outfit that regularly shocks bigger competitors in the pharmaceutical field. From the very beginning, it has been an unusual company.

If Mr. Kauffman has a favorite song, it should be the Loretta Lynn classic, "Take This Job and Shove It." He was a salesperson for a small firm in Illinois, doing exceedingly well; too well, in fact. He sold so many pills that his earnings began to exceed those of the president of the firm. Not considering that proper, the president decided to slash Kauffman's territory and commission schedule. The proposal was not well received.

How to Become an Entrepreneur

Rather than meekly accept a reduced income, Kauffman told his boss what he could do with his job. This proved to be a fortuitous move for Kauffman but not for his former employer; that company is no longer in business.

Kauffman proceeded to empty his bank account of the $4000 it contained so that he could set up his own pharmaceutical business in the basement of his home. He called on doctors and pharmacists during the day; he filled orders at night, because he was the only employee of the new little company. But after the first few rough years, Marion Laboratories expanded, expanded, and expanded.

You Could Have Made a Million

If you or I had been astute enough to invest just $8000 in Marion stock 20 years ago, we'd be millionaires today. Of course, Mr. Kauffman did better than that. He and his family and trusts own about $1 billion of the stock.

Marion has become one of the big 10 in the pharmaceutical industry, and one of the most profitable. Its profits per employee are consistently *double* the industry average. At this writing, the company's profits have grown by more than 50 percent in each of the past six years. And the people at Marion have many incentives to keep that growth on track.

A Constant Flood of Information

An Annual Update for Everyone.   Where does communication and listening come into the picture? Throughout the operation. I saw some of it at firsthand when I was invited to a two-hour meeting of the entire work force. And I mean entire.

Four times a year, everyone at Marion from the janitor on up is given a complete update on what's happening—sales, new products being developed, projected earnings, everything. And it's a rapt audience that listens intently.

Stock Options for Everyone.   There's a reason for this intense interest by all categories of associates (never called employees). It would be equally appropriate to refer to the more than 2000 of them as *stockholders* because *everyone* at Marion owns stock in the company. Some own quite a bundle of it.

Mr. Kauffman recounted to me that he decided from the beginning to offer stock options to everyone, "not just the big shots, if we have any of those here, but to everyone on the payroll. That way they all take pride in the company because it's *their* company. They're interested in their fellow workers, too, and want to know about everything that goes on here. And we tell them everything."

He related an incident about a newly hired associate who'd attended her first quarterly meeting and went home all fired up about the company and full of facts about its operation and future. She relayed this abundance of information to her husband, an attorney. Evidently he was amazed at what she, a nonexecutive employee, had learned. He told her, "I'm a partner in my law firm, and nobody tells me as much about what's going on as you know about what's happening at Marion." Few CEOs communicate like Mr. Kauffman.

A Suggestion Program That Works.   Like many companies, Marion Laboratories has a suggestion program. As you might expect, though, it's not a token program paying piddling amounts and garnering sparse ideas that top management doesn't listen to. I was told that some of the suggestions could save millions over the years, and that a top award a few years ago for an especially fine suggestion was a trip anywhere in the world for the winner and her family, plus a chunk of stock then worth about $90,000. That's considered a stimulating incentive at

Marion. It encourages others to think hard about other worthwhile ideas.

Mr. Kauffman, usually referred to as Mr. K, has been criticized for spoiling people with overgenerous compensation plans. He maintains, "Those who produce should share in the results." Maybe he's remembering the picayune president years ago who preferred to lose his best salesperson rather than pay high commissions for high performance.

Accent on the Positive

Mediocrity versus Pride. Mr. Kauffman told me, "Those who work here know we take good care of them if they produce. They 'own' their jobs if they do well at them. They can count on steady work, excellent compensation. And by the time they reach retirement, their pensions and stock options are likely to provide a bigger income than they made before. But they also understand that *we don't tolerate mediocrity*. We communicate that very clearly."

Throughout this communication to employees, the importance of *pride* is emphasized—pride in yourself and your company. At the quarterly meeting I attended, Mr. K told everyone, "I'm so proud of you— all of you." And he urged all the associates to be proud of themselves.

Don't Complain Sideways or Downward. Mr. Kauffman pointed out that one of the dictums at Marion is: "Don't ever complain about anything either sideways or downward. In other words, don't complain to associates on your level or to those who work for you, because it destroys morale. If you have any complaint, take it up to your boss, or up to the top if necessary." That's part of his belief that pride in yourself and in your company is of prime importance.

No Standardized Sales Presentations

Communication with physicians is one of the main keys to Marion's success. An unusual aspect of it is that standardized, rehearsed sales presentations are verboten. They're replaced by "consultative selling." This means that instead of launching into a canned presentation, the sales representatives first *ask questions* to learn what most concerns the physicians and what particular needs they have in treatment. The Marion sales rep then points his or her consultative discussion in that direction.

This type of selling requires intense training and a high-caliber person capable of in-depth discussion with doctors, but Marion has little difficulty finding the right talent. It ran an ad to hire 45 new salespeople and received 15,000 applications. When you have an elite company, the news gets around.

But as Mr. K advised me, "You don't build a favorable culture in your firm overnight or just by talking about it. You do it through your *actions* over a period of years."

Gromer Supermarket

A company doesn't have to be one of the Fortune 500 to do an outstanding job of listening and otherwise communicating. In fact, the smaller it is, the more important those skills may be to its survival and prosperity.

Gromer Supermarket, Inc. is one store, though a supersize one. It's located about 50 miles northwest of the Chicago Loop in the small town of Elgin, Illinois, population a bit short of 65,000. Yet it was analyzed by *Inc* magazine as one of the best-managed companies in America.

Ridiculous? Don't jump to conclusions. The most educational experience I can imagine for those tycoons who are being cut up by competition, plagued by unfair export practices, and fighting unsuccessfully to retain fickle customers would be for them to get out from behind the mahogany walls and go shop at Gromer. If that didn't open their eyes, nothing could.

Although there are only 65,000 potential customers in its immediate trading area (counting all the men, women, children, and infants), Gromer pulls an average of 34,000 shoppers past its cash registers each week. Obviously, most of the adults in Elgin must come in the doors of Gromer Supermarket every week, with some of them making two or three visits in that period.

How to Pamper Customers

What's the big attraction at Gromer? There are many, but they all stem from the fact that Dick Gromer doesn't just serve his customers—he pampers them. He listens when his customers tell him what they want in the way of products, services, and conveniences, and then he gives them all of that and more.

Perhaps you think of a supermarket as consisting of aisles stacked with groceries, a meat counter, a fruit-and-vegetable department, some frozen-food bins, maybe a small deli section. That's not Gromer Supermarket. When you walk in the door, you're greeted by the appetizing sights and delicious smells of a taco bar, a gyro bar, bubbling cauldrons of soup, steaming baked potatos, chickens turning and browning on a spit, a salad bar, an ice-cream counter. It's worth a visit just to smell the aroma from the bakery in the back, where you can get your rolls hot

from the oven. Or to drool past the deli counters heaped with an incredible array of sausages, salamis, hams, pastramis, shaved turkey and
chicken, corned beef, pepper loaf, head cheese, Capicola, Cotto, jellied
luncheon meats, etc., etc., plus aromatic wheels of cheeses from all
around the world. Or to ponder in front of more than a hundred bar-
rels of nuts, dried fruits, bulk candies, coffees, and cereals. Shopping
here is not a chore. It's a delight, because all the goodies a shopper
could ask for seem to be here in profusion.

Courtesies and Conveniences. The pampering of customers doesn't
stop with proffering a cornucopia of delicious groceries and ready-to-
eat foods. There are many courtesies and conveniences. For instance,
you can get a cup of coffee...free, of course. Also, without leaving the
store, you can pay your utility bills, get new license plates, buy a lottery
ticket, have photo film developed, replenish your money supply from
the bank teller machine, or buy stamps or mail a package at the contract
post office. All this at the four-window Service Center that enables Dick
Gromer's customers to save time and travel by getting many little chores
done when they make one stop at his store. (The Service Center also
builds traffic for neighboring merchants in the 22-store shopping center owned by Gromer.)

What's more, these conveniences are available here at times when
they might not be elsewhere in town. The supermarket is open 24 hours
a day. That's one of the accommodations his customers told Gromer
they'd appreciate; so they get it even though traffic is merely a trickle in
the wee hours.

The Paradox of Loss Leaders. "Those sound like loss leaders," you
may be thinking. "How can a store afford all that, along with a vast inventory? My grocer would never listen if I suggested he provide half
that variety or any of those conveniences."

You have a good point. Gromer admitted to me that he's lucky to
break even on some of the conveniences offered and that he loses
money on others. For instance, it's a total loss (from an accounting
standpoint) if a gal from the supermarket staff jump-starts your car on
a frigid day. But how could you ever get angry with friends like that, or
take your business elsewhere, or quibble about a nickle or two above
some special price advertised down the street?

The payoff is in the high traffic generated by the many incentives to
visit this particular store. When you come in for a 25-cent ice-cream
cone (a real bargain these days) or to buy a stamp or to pick up a hot-
from-the-oven cinnamon coffee cake, you'll find a few other items to
purchase. There's no way you can pass by all those delights without
yielding to temptation.

How About Some Shish Kebab in Your Business?   Many of the conveniences that customers enjoy at Gromer are high-profit producers. The customers are happy to pay extra for things that save them work, save them time.

For example, they pay extra to have vegetables cut up for them and made into a salad they can pick up. They expect to pay more for cold cuts and cheeses arranged on a party tray by the catering department— a profitable operation.

They like the convenient shish kebabs that consist of vegetables, mushrooms, and squares of steak on a skewer, all ready for the grill. The meat department manager likes them too; instead of grinding his steak ends into low-cost hamburger, he can utilize them with relatively inexpensive onions, peppers, etc., and sell the lot along with a stick for nearly $5 a pound.

The Number One Priority

Dick Gromer told me that the most important thing he does is to get out into the store every day to talk to customers and listen to them. "It's my number one priority," he said. "With an operation that covers more than an acre and nearly 250 employees, we have a lot of office work here. But I have good people who handle most of that—inventory, purchasing, accounting, and so forth. They can do it better than I can, so I delegate much of the management activity.

"But I'll never get away from the customer contact. I have to find time for that, part of every day."

He listens not only to the people who patronize the store but also to those who work in it. "I meet with all the department managers every Monday night," he explained to me. "And every Friday noon we have lunch together. That gives us a chance to discuss any aspect of the business. And we also sample the groceries. Anything new we try. And we eat different food every time, so we know ourselves if it's up to quality. We invite customers to those meetings too."

When complimented on his success, Gromer said to me, *"We're always trying to do better. The only way I know how to do that is to learn from the customers, try to sharpen up management all the time, and keep striving for higher volume."*

That's a good formula for "making it" in any business or location.

Reynolds Aluminum

An international firm that mines and refines metals may seem a million miles apart from the operation at bustling little customer-oriented Gromer Supermarket.

In many ways it is. Reynolds is the second-largest metals company in

America. It is "heavy industry," operating mines in several states, the Caribbean, and South America and operating giant smelters and more than 40 processing plants. It produces about 20 percent of all our aluminum. It has been called "a semifeudal state, largely owned and operated by the aristocratic Reynolds family of rural, fox-hunting Virginia."[2]

Yet the scions of wealth who moved their headquarters out of the bustle of Manhattan back to the gracious life of beautiful Richmond don't fit the stereotypes you might expect. When it comes to marketing, they're hustlers with their eyes and ears attuned to the wants of consumers. Unlike Alcoa, their bigger competitor that sells almost all its aluminum by the ton to other industries, Reynolds has elected to sell much of its metal by the ounce on the shelves of supermarkets. A decade ago, *Forbes* magazine commented, *"The Reynolds boys changed aluminum from an exotic industrial raw material into a fabricated end product."*

The Top-Rated Skills

David P. Reynolds, who became chairman and CEO more than a decade ago, is responsible for much of that change—and also for the strong company emphasis on communication and listening that was essential to it. He rates these skills at the very top in importance because, as he says, "All other management skills depend on this ability."

Listening is of special concern to him. He pointed out to me that his company has courses on how to speak and write effectively and also tries to teach its managers to listen. Then he added, *"I think one of the saddest comments I hear about a manager is that he or she doesn't listen."*

Innovations in Marketing

Kitchen Products. When you consider some of the many innovations that Reynolds Aluminum has marketed aggressively, you realize how carefully it must have listened to consumer desires, especially for kitchen products. In 1947 it introduced Reynolds Wrap and quickly took over leadership in the foil-wrap field. A variety of cookware and kitchen utensils followed. In recent years, disposable aluminum cake pans and the package in which you microwave your popcorn are likely to be Reynolds products. The company introduced flexible aluminum food pouches (now used by the military and campers) for preserving rations without the weight of the traditional "tin" can.

---

[2]From Milton Moskowitz, *Everybody's Business: An Almanac,* Harper & Row, New York, 1980, p. 566.

Billions of Cans.   Any beverages you drink generally come in aluminum cans, and Reynolds is a leader in this field. When the public became concerned with the litter of beer and soft-drink cans over our landscapes, Reynolds listened and initiated the most extensive recycling program. It has paid more than $100 million to encourage the collection of aluminum, and it now recycles more than half as many cans as it makes.

Building Products.   Another major market area that Reynolds has explored is building products—aluminum doors, siding, garden and farm sheds, etc. Of course, it also produces metal for airplane and auto parts, and it has long been trying to convince automakers to save vehicle weight with aluminum engine blocks. Reynolds has never been able to communicate the benefits of aluminum engines as well as it hoped to, but you can bet the people from Richmond will keep trying.

Training Is Popular

As David Reynolds stated to me, *"Nothing is more crucial in management than sound, effective communication. That's not to say that good communication will ensure success in business. But poor communication or none at all will vastly increase the risks."*

Since Mr. Reynolds had mentioned that courses in communication were available throughout his company, I checked to determine what they were. I learned that seminars in listening are designed for a full day's session. They employ taped materials developed by Xerox and are designed principally for managers and sales personnel. Courses in effective writing are held two or three times each year. They're two-day sessions conducted by a professor from the University of Richmond. The university also helps provide an extensive course in public speaking that involves 54 hours spread over a five-week period. It's regarded as particularly useful for salespeople, but it's open to any manager.

At Reynolds, no one is forced to take any of these courses in listening, writing, or speaking, but they're popular companywide. This is not surprising, for bright managers there are aware that their prospects, like those of the firm, depend on these skills.

As David Reynolds said, "I don't know of any good manager who doesn't respect the need for effective ongoing communication that goes two ways, up and down the ladder of management responsibility." And who doesn't respect the views of the chairman of the board?

In companies that listen, the chairperson invariably has such views and makes them known to all around.

There's a wide diversity in the companies described in this chapter—appliances, tax services, retailing, groceries, mining and metals, pharmaceuticals. But they're all alike in one important respect. They're all companies that listen.

Individual people who listen have a much better chance for success too. For one thing, it helps them be better conversationalists. You'll read about this in the next chapter.

PART 2
Speaking

6
Conversation, the Ping-Pong Game

If only everyone talked the way we do in
my household. I mean ... if only everyone
... like ... talked ... you know ... the
way we do ... right? It would be so much
... like ... easier ... you know ...
understand ... right?

ROBERT NORDELL

Everyone can talk. You've probably been doing it since you were about a year old. But some people learn to talk more interestingly and effectively than others. And "having a way with words" is an attribute that's admired and expected in those who become leaders—in business, government, schools, social groups, clubs.

Conversation—the kind of talking you do every day—is an interchange with a single person or a small group of two or three people. Your conversation varies widely in style and tone. It has to. Your purposes differ, so you talk in different ways to different people at different times. Basically, your conversation falls into three general categories: social, emotional, and intellectual.

You use all three types of verbal conversation at various times. Sometimes they get blended together. Let's consider them one by one.

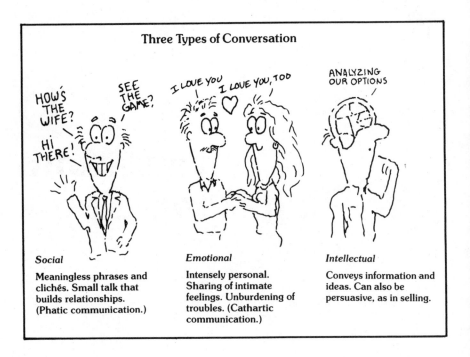

Social Conversation Is Verbal Touching

This is not limited to strictly social settings. Almost every human interaction has some social overtones and conventions, and that includes business.

This sort of verbal touching is used to get acquainted with people, to size them up, to cement friendships. It's technical name is *phatic* conversation, which means a sharing of feelings. Next time someone accuses you of yakking over the phone or spending a long time at the coffee machine, tell them you're engaged in phatic conversation and that it's an important element of communication.

There are cliché phrases you use often merely to acknowledge someone's presence or as a preamble to an informational transaction. You pass someone on the street or in a hallway and you say, "How are you?" You don't expect an informative answer; you have merely acknowledged that you know a person (maybe slightly) and that you recognized him. The usual answer is "Fine," regardless of how that person feels. The same noninformational exchange may take place when you enter a store. If you're browsing around, the proprietor may ask how you are or comment on the weather, as a way of introducing herself into your space. Then she may ask if she can help you, and you go on to exchange information.

Social Conversation Is an
Important Lubricant in Business

Among business colleagues there's often a polite interchange of small talk, however brief, as a preamble to the business at hand. It's a way of saying, "We're friends, aren't we? Let's relax and cooperate with each other."

Contrary to what efficiency experts might say about this sort of chitchat, it's an important lubricant in the machinery of any organization. It's our way of sounding people out, getting comfortable with them. Without it, there'd be difficulty in starting romantic courtships, no need for cocktail parties, less closeness and esprit de corps within organizations.

Where Does Emotional Talk Fit in Business?   Emotional communication is limited mostly to family and close friends. In business, you may aim to avoid emotional interchanges and personal confidences that may interfere with the job. But that's not always possible, or even desirable.

At times, you need to listen sympathetically to the fears and troubles of subordinates. The boss who shows no human side gets no trust. And whether you like it or not, emotional outbursts do occur when pressures build up in the business, and you must deal with them.

The Blowfish in the Office.   There are executives (as you may know from past encounters) who deliberately use emotional outbursts as a surprise tactic to throw their rivals off balance and get their way. These characters are like the blowfish who puff themselves up to frighten you. The way to handle them is to ignore the emotional blowup totally, and calmly resume the factual level of the conversation.

When Emotions Are Good.   Of course, there are good emotional elements in business conversations. Enthusiasm is one of them; you'll read more about it in the next chapter. Sympathy for the problems of others is another emotion that lubricates any conversation, whether it be in an office or at home. And anytime you can interject the warmth of an emotional approach that will touch on the basic feelings and beliefs of the people you're talking to, you stand a much better chance of getting through to them.

That's basic sales ability. And aren't you selling something—whether it be a product, proposal, or yourself—much of the time?

The Key to Successful Selling.   Successful salespeople are invariably skilled at building friendly relationships through social talk that recognizes the emotional interests of others. And they appeal to the emotions, however subtly, as they convey information and suggestions.

They don't sell the most expensive car model because it's a good investment, though that may be claimed. The deal is clinched by getting the prospect to slide behind the wheel and then by hinting how great it'll feel to roll this beauty past the envious gazes of neighbors and friends.

Intellectual Conversation Is Aimed at Information and Ideas

In the world of business, you have to do more than kill time or cement friendships. Besides social and emotional conversations, you also need intellectual ones that deal with facts and ideas.

That's a different ball game. In that case, your communication must be aimed toward a specific goal you have in mind. It can't be loose, as in social chitchat. *It's more like a Ping-Pong game.* As you bounce ideas back and forth, the conversation will veer in various directions—but to come out the winner, you must shoot it back onto the table and keep it going in the way you desire.

This doesn't mean monopolizing the conversation. As in Ping-Pong, the flow must go two ways. Mr. Robinson of American Express makes this point. Those who run off at the mouth, leaving others no chance to get a word in edgewise, are not conversationalists. They are bores.

Two-Way Communication

We are talking *at* each other instead of to each other. That is not communication; it is monologue.

Effective communication runs in both directions. We must improve the ways in which we listen to our publics, and then respond to what we hear.

There must be a change in the attitude toward the function, power, and role of communication. They are too important to be left entirely to professional communicators. It's an all-hands job.

Talking, listening, and reacting to our customers, shareholders, and employees and the public must become a part of the manager's responsibility. And managers at every level must become as skilled in the communications arena as in other business disciplines.

JAMES D. ROBINSON III, CHAIRMAN & CEO
American Express Company

If you keep the Ping-Pong analogy in mind, it will remind you that good conversation must involve give-and-take. The give-and-take occurs on two levels: *verbal* and *nonverbal*. These two channels, or wavelengths, of communication are affected by two other elements. They are interfered with by *static*, either within ourselves or in our surroundings. And they are reinforced by *feedback*. The accompanying diagram illustrates these four elements of a conversation.

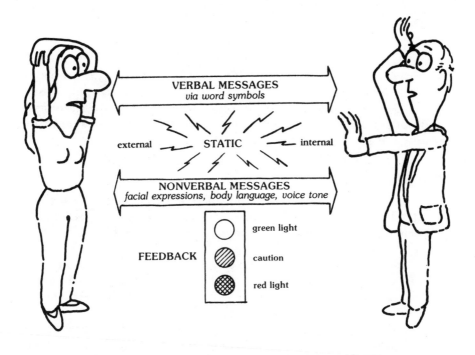

Before considering how to make the most of the words that will carry your thoughts, let's think about the static that can hamper them. What preparations may be needed?

Getting Ready for the Game

No special preparations are necessary for the kind of casual or brief conversations you engage in every day. But suppose you have a lot riding on a particular contact:

- You plan to hit the boss for a raise.
- You need to get an important person lined up on your side so you can start a new project.
- There's an awkward situation you must explain that may not look good for you.
- You'd like to escalate a new friendship quickly into a warm and loving relationship.

These things require the right setting, whether it be a quiet office or a cozy spot with wine and roses.

The Right and Wrong Time and Place

You can't always pick the time and place for a conversation, but the wrong setting does contribute to the static around your talk. Obviously, you want to avoid interruptions. The morning your boss is preparing for a big meeting or packing to catch a plane is no time to initiate a sensitive discussion. A hallway or an office where people are running in and out is no place to get started on a complicated explanation or the planting of an idea that requires careful thought.

Don't Be Impatient

Sometimes we let ourselves get stampeded into a situation we know isn't good. This can cause a worthwhile proposition to be trampled on, and we may never get a chance to present it again, once it's labeled as a reject.

What's the alternative? What do you do when you're caught in a hazardous setting, but someone asks, "Tell me about that new plan I hear you have" or "I'd like to hear what happened to delay the Colorado project"?

Stall. But don't appear to be stalling; tell why it will be advantageous to the questioner to get an explanation at a later time. You might say, "I'm anxious to tell you about my new plan, but ..." or "There are several things that happened in Colorado, and I'd like to set up a meeting with you to go over them."

Here are some reasons you can give for stalling:

1. You have a quantity of information at another place; you want to give the questioner a complete picture.

2. There are many statistics involved; you want to give the precise figures or costs.

3. More information is coming in; it will complete the picture, or may change it.

4. You'd like to have a colleague involved in the discussion because she or he can contribute some other data or viewpoint.

5. You must leave in a few minutes (for a meeting?) and you'd like to have ample time for a thorough discussion of the situation in question.

The Butterflies Inside Us

The static that interferes with our communication is often not the obvious distraction, such as noise, interruptions, or lack of privacy. It's internal, emotional—affecting either one or both of the conversationalists. Everyone gets these distracting butterflies in the stomach at times, because all human communication has an emotional as well as an informational content.

Listen to Barbara Walters. No one is a more skilled conversationalist than TV star Barbara Walters; she has a rare ability to make people feel at ease and to draw them out when she talks to them. Some years ago, Miss Walters wrote a delightful book on the secrets of conversation. Here's an excerpt from it:[1]

How to Keep Your Cool

I've learned that the skills I use every day in my job as a professional television interviewer are portable, and have been a boon to me in hundreds of everyday situations. The same techniques that result in fifteen minutes of smooth informative chat with the Queen of England are just as helpful when I meet a new neighbor, or the austere aunt of a friend, or someone trapped with me in the eye of a cocktail party.

Inner confidence is the key to making genuine contact with another person. Nervous people are too involved in their own alarm bells and flashing signals. To offset panic, try to envision the worst thing that can happen and consider how it can be handled. A television performer friend of mine gets her composure together before a show by saying over and over, *"They can't kill me."* My own talisman is Abigail McCarthy's serene observation, "I am the way I am; I look the way I look: I am my age."

There's a gimmick I use for emergencies when I need to recover my well-being in a hurry. I follow the suggestion that photographers give their subjects when they're posing and looking glum. They're told, "Think of the happiest moment you've ever had," or, "Think of the person you love most in the world." When you do this, the tension goes out of your posture and your face, and softness floods in. You look and feel refreshed. It's really a form of method acting. You recreate the best version of yourself by remembering when you felt your best.

BARBARA WALTERS

---

[1]Reprinted with permission from *How to Talk with Practically Anyone about Practically Anything*, Doubleday, New York, 1970. © 1970 by Barbara Walters.

Help the Other Person Relax

Showing interest in the other person is the way to start a friendly, productive conversation. It begins with a warm greeting, a warm smile, a warm handshake (or hug, if your relationship makes this appropriate).

Tell the person you meet that you're glad to see her, and mean it.

As you talk, *maintain eye contact.* You know this is essential to good listening. It also helps put the other person at ease because it shows you're interested in her, not just in yourself. Don't let your eyes wander to anyone else or anything else in the room. Get absorbed in her and in what she's saying.

In her *Book of Modern Manners*, Charlotte Ford advises that this is not only the polite thing to do, but that it promotes better conversation. She observes that when you become self-absorbed, it kills spontaneity and inhibits conversation.

Once you get yourself relaxed and your partner relaxed too, you've eliminated much of the static that can inhibit an important conversation. Then you're ready to start the game.

Rules of the Game

A few pages back, conversation was compared to a Ping-Pong game. At times it can be more like football—the back-lot, no-holds-barred variety.

It can contain good-natured banter, and sometimes remarks not so good-natured. Maybe you've heard the anecdote about the jealous author who asked another, "Who *wrote* your new book for you?" The quick retort that paid back the questioner: "Who *read* it to you?"

In the locker room or at a poker game, insults are apt to be part of male banter, with no offense intended or taken. This is a characteristic of male social play that tends to confuse women. In female groups, there is greater sensitivity, so a friendly insult is a rarity.

There are business offices where discussions can become loud and rough on occasion. I've been in many a raucous creative session in advertising agencies, which tend to be populated by free-wheeling types, where a dozen views were being shouted at the same time. That's enthusiasm gone wild. It often included someone returning from a wet lunch who tried to compensate for weak ideas with a loud voice. Order was usually restored when the senior person present quieted the melee, or when the rest of the pack turned on the chief offender.

If you find yourself in that sort of milieu, defend yourself as best you can.

But that's not the norm in American business, where conformity to rules seems to receive increasing emphasis as the size of the organization grows. In most workplaces, and certainly in social situations, it behooves you to "talk unto others as you would have them talk unto you."

Here are five points of etiquette that apply.

Don't Hog the Floor

If you make a habit of monopolizing the conversation, people will soon get out of the habit of listening to you. This applies even if you're the boss and they're forced to sit still while you go on and on; they'll simply turn off their minds to much you say. A prime example of this turnoff to monologues is what happens in many classrooms when teachers "lecture" instead of inspiring participation.

> *Remember—birds are entangled by their feet and men by their tongues.*
> FOUND IN A FORTUNE COOKIE

Don't Change the Subject

You've witnessed this. A group will be in the midst of a conversation about one thing—let's say it's on how to keep crabgrass out of a lawn (Is that possible?)—when someone breaks in with a comment straight out of left field. Example: "A funny thing happened to my car yesterday." You never do learn the solution to the crabgrass problem, and you resent the lout who has so rudely interrupted what the rest of you were discussing before you've had a chance to finish. Remember, conversation is a Ping-Pong game and you have to go along with the discourse of others before you can take your own swings on subjects of special interest to you.

Don't Step on the Sentences of Others

This sort of interruption is not caused by disinterest, as changing the subject is, but it still can be considered rudeness. It's generally the result of overeagerness to show the other person you agree with or are greatly interested in what he's trying to say.

Let's suppose the crabgrass expert states, "I put the control chemical on my grass in May because that early application ..." In your eagerness to agree, you cut in with "That's the only time to do it. Won't accomplish a thing in the fall." Unfortunately, that isn't what he meant at all. He corrects the thought: "No, I start in May because the early application gives me time to spread the chemical on again in September. I find that ..." Again you jump to conclusions and step on his sentence by saying, "The more you put on, the better it is." Again the speaker, thoroughly irritated by now, corrects it: "No, I'm careful not to overdo it; that kills the grass. I apply a half dose in the spring and a half dose in the fall. I find that spreading out the application is better than a lot at once."

Suggestion: Be interested and eager, but avoid the temptation to jump to conclusions that may not be correct. Even if they are, people like the courtesy of being allowed to finish their sentences themselves.

Do Hold Your Temper

Unless you want to terminate a conversation totally, and perhaps a relationship for all time as well, you'd better keep your temper under control. Losing it doesn't gain much; it puts you at a disadvantage as far as coming out ahead in a verbal disagreement.

When you argue a point, you want to do it with skill, not with a rising voice and increasing invective. That only hardens your opponent's conviction that she's right and you're a stubborn dunce. Butting heads may accomplish something for rams in mating season, but there are better ways for us to come out ahead. Present your reasoning logically and quietly. Also, here are a couple of tricks you can use.

Silence.   This can be a simple way to deflate a ridiculous, inflammatory statement. It's not an agreement, particularly if you accompany it with a quizzical raised eyebrow, or even a slight smile if you wish to goad the speaker into further nonsense that will expose his ignorance completely. Let's imagine that some "Archie Bunker" character shouts out, "Women are too emotional. That's why so few of them get to top levels in business."

Any woman's instinct would be to react angrily to this, which is what the speaker wants and which would partially prove his premise. But you know that any of the many available answers will have no effect anyway, so why not let him hang himself?

If your silence or a quiet "Really?" draws no further statement, the initial declaration will hang in the air exposed as an uncorroborated inanity. If the speaker takes the bait and goes further, he'll simply dig himself in deeper, especially if you can keep him going through two or three more similar statements until he runs down in front of his audience. Of course, if there is no audience—just you two—don't bother. Walk away and make it a onesome.

Questions.   These are an excellent means of turning an argument around. A question puts the burden of proof on the other person, and proving almost anything can be difficult. Use such phrases as "Why is that? What do you mean by that? What's that based on? How do you explain that?"

The question approach accomplishes two things. First, it dissipates some of the heat if the discussion was tending to get noisy; the other person has been given a chance to say everything he wishes and gradually to cool down. Second, it commits the other person to expose his entire store of facts right at the start, leaving you in a flexible position to wind up the debate. No need to butt heads with him point by point. You can select whatever you wish from what you've heard—possibly a few weak points—and make them the center of the discussion, now that it's your turn.

> When angry, count to ten before you speak. If very angry, count to a hundred. THOMAS JEFFERSON

Don't Forget—There's Always a Tomorrow

When a discussion gets heated or you've had to offer sharp criticism, try to pour a little oil on the waters at the end of it. Allow the other person to save face. Without backing down on your own (possibly hard-won) position, you might say, "I respect your views, Martha, but I believe the decision we've reached will be best for all of us in the long run." Or, "I appreciate the problems you faced, George, but when you get them all cleaned up, we can all breathe easier."

You may have put the other person on the defensive during your talking, but you don't want him or her to go away feeling resentful. Once the battle's over, it's time to start thinking about the peace treaty. Tomorrow and tomorrow, you'll have to communicate again with the same people, hopefully on a cooperative basis.

> Once a word goes out of your mouth, you can never swallow it again. RUSSIAN PROVERB

If you observe the rules of the game—the five points of etiquette just enumerated—you'll be regarded as a civilized conversationalist. One with whom people like to talk. That's a good starting point. But you must also be clear in what you say.

Being Clearly Understood

Did you say what I think you said, or did I think I heard what I thought you were going to say?

A friend of mine told me about his talking to a subordinate who had been doing a poor job—so poor that he was close to getting fired if he didn't correct some of the things he'd been warned about. It was one of those unpleasant chores we all approach reluctantly. My friend tried to ease into it gradually by saying one hopeful thing before getting down to the nitty gritty.

He said, "Marty, you've made considerable improvement in your punctuality. I see you haven't been late even once this past month. But there are still several areas where you must shape up, and time's running out." Then he went on to detail several serious failings that were still to be corrected. At the end of his stern lecture, he asked, "Now what do you have to say to this? Do you have any questions?"

Marty had only one question. He smiled hopefully and asked, "Am I going to get a raise the first of the year? You said I've improved a lot in getting to work on time, and I haven't had a raise in a long while."

Marty heard clearly what he wanted to hear: "considerable improvement." All the unpleasant parts of the message went right past him as he concentrated on the good part. Personnel people tell me that Marty's case is by no means unique; employees frequently shut out or moderate what they don't wish to hear. So do we all.

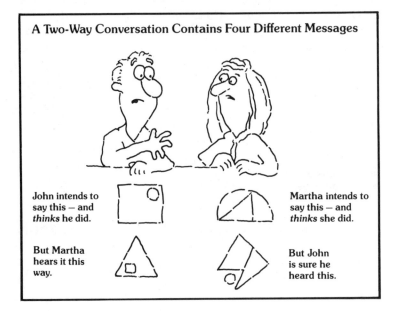

A Two-Way Conversation Contains Four Different Messages

John intends to say this — and *thinks* he did.

Martha intends to say this — and *thinks* she did.

But Martha hears it this way.

But John is sure he heard this.

How Messages Become Twisted

A single conversation is likely to end up as many different conversations. One version is what you and I each believe we said. (This may vary from what we actually did say.) Then each of us twists the messages we hear and interprets them to suit ourselves. So a conversation between two people quickly splits up into four different trains of thought, as shown in the cartoon on the preceding page.

When more than two people are involved, the conversational patterns get more complex. With three people, there can be nine different interpretations of what was said; with four people, it escalates to 16 different versions.

Factors That Cause Misunderstandings

- *High hopes.* The biggest culprit is, "I think I heard what I expected (or hoped) you were going to say." If I'm hoping strongly for a certain message, I'm going to tilt my interpreting mechanism in that direction.

- *Muddled message.* You may not express your thoughts clearly. Your language may be vague or incorrect, or I may not understand the language you use. If there's much "static" nearby, I may not hear all you say over the noise and distraction.

- *Blank...blank.* When talk is batted back and forth rapidly in short, interrupted bursts of speech, you may leave out part of what you intended to say, assuming that I'll fill in the blanks. That I'll do—only I'll fill them in *my way*, which may not be at all what you had in mind.

What's the solution to this confusion? There is no absolute solution; conversation is seldom a precise art. But you can strive for clarity in your words and manner of speech. And you can ask for feedback to check what I'm receiving against what you think you're sending. Give feedback, too, to make sure the circuits are working in the other direction.

Feedback Is the Insurance Policy

The way to make sure you're being understood is to get feedback from the other person.

This may come automatically in the form of nonverbal signals—smiles or nods that indicate your partner agrees with what you're saying. But beware the trap. Sometimes this nodding or smiling can be simply a cover-up; the other person may have her mind on other matters while she nods and smiles politely to hide her boredom until you leave.

Even if the other person seems to be listening and seems to be on the same wavelength with you, always double-check by asking for verbal feedback on important conversations. This doesn't mean just asking, "Do you understand?" or "Do you agree?" Such queries get simply a yes or no answer. I may tell you, "Yes," when I really don't understand but don't want you to think I'm stupid. If I'm an employee of yours receiving instructions, I'll tend to be affirmative about everything you ask, even if I'm not quite sure of your meaning.

The Right Way to Ask for Feedback

The trick is to get the other person to interpret what you've said into his own language. Then you'll really know if he got the message clearly and completely. Here are some phrases that call for a response in the listener's words:

- "What should we do about this?"
- "How will you handle this?"
- "We ought to decide on priorities. What should come first? Second? Third?"
- "I hope I've been clear. How do you see the situation?"
- "That's my view. How would you describe it?"
- "To be sure we're on the same wavelength, why don't you run this by me in your words?"

You need to *give* feedback as well. On complex or especially important matters, you want to be sure that what you think the other party said is what he or she really meant. So paraphrase it. You may say, "Let me see if I've got this straight. What you want me to do is...."

Words can be tricky. Words can be wonderful. It all depends on how you use them and how well you understand them.

7
Without the Yeast, the Beer Won't Bubble

Nothing is interesting if you're not interested. HELEN MacINNES

There is one priceless ingredient in every conversation. It makes all the difference, whether you're chatting socially, sharing intimate feelings, or trying to get a stranger to warm up and give you information.

This ingredient is *enthusiasm.* Without it, conversation goes flat. Your speech may be fluent and clever, but it will lack the effervescence that lifts an ordinary exchange of words into something memorable.

When You're Enthusiastic, You're Warm

Your enthusiasm makes the casual acquaintance you run into on the street glad that you met, and thinking good thoughts about you. You make your lover feel happy because you show that your words come from the heart—not just "trippingly from the tongue." Business associates like to talk to you and include you in their groups because it's a pleasure, not a struggle, to discuss their plans and ideas with you.

Enthusiasm can cover a multitude of faults. Even if you don't yet

83

know as much as you should, this may be forgiven if you show you're enthusiastic about learning. Even if a presentation may not be as smooth and professional as you'd wish, it can still be persuasive if you show your heart's in it.

So don't try to be Mister or Miss Cool. Warm up, bubble up. Let your true wonderful self show, and people will mean it when they say, "Nice talking to you."

Nobody Likes a Phony

But here's a caution: Your enthusiasm must be real. Nobody likes a phony. So you can't just put on an act. You need to open yourself up to becoming truly warmed up to the forthcoming discussion and to the person with whom you'll be having it.

Turn Your Sights in the Right Direction

You know that one of the biggest handicaps you face in listening is getting overly concerned with yourself—with how you look, with the impression you're making. This same me-centered attitude also keeps you from saying the most productive and interesting things.

The people you're talking to don't care beans about hearing how great you are, what smart thing your kid did in school last week, or what *you* want out of the new project you'll be working on.

You're looking down the barrel of the gun if that's the way much of your talking is oriented. Turn yourself around and get behind the sights, where you can focus on your true target.

How to Turn Yourself Around

This requires that you keep your eye on the others in the conversation and on the broad scope of their interests.

If the target is to persuade, it's obvious that you'll have a better chance of doing so if you present your ideas in terms of the other person's best interests. If the object of the conversation is to provide information, be sure to include all the facts the other person needs. Ask yourself if you've given her all the data that's important from her viewpoint, not just from yours.

Expect the same kind of treatment in return. Remember, conversation is a Ping-Pong game; it's not all one way, carried on exclusively either for you or for others. A 50-50 deal is the ideal, so if you're not getting all the information you want, don't hesitate to insist politely on receiving all the facts you need.

To Be Interesting, Be Interested in Everything and Everybody

Think for a moment about people you regard as especially gratifying conversationalists. Don't they have unusually broad interests? No matter what subject comes up, don't they plunge into it enthusiastically, either contributing some bits of information and ideas themselves or showing a readiness to learn something from others?

Perhaps you've envied people like that, and wished you had such a store of varied knowledge that you could fascinate any group with your entertaining insights on whatever subject might come up.

The good news is that you can become a much more engaging conversationalist, and you don't have to be a genius or a world traveler to do it. The bad news is that it takes a certain amount of effort on your part to accomplish this; you can't just sit in the corner with your mouth and ears shut whenever the talk turns to some area you're not familiar with.

The Key Is to Open Up

Be willing to learn. Open up your ears, question, exhibit enthusiasm and curiosity about the strange new area to which you're being exposed.

Suppose someone you're talking to turns the conversation to stamp collecting, for example, or the problems of tax accounting. Those subjects may sound like the dullest of the dull. But if you smile instead of scowl, and *throw in a few questions*, you'll discover that people involved in those activities will be delighted to explain them to an interested audience. You'll also find out there's nothing in the world that doesn't have some interesting aspects, if you're willing to learn.

> *Everybody is ignorant, only on different subjects.* WILL ROGERS

For instance, your stamp-collector friend may teach you that, ounce for ounce, rare stamps can be far more precious than diamonds; that Franklin D. Roosevelt was an avid philatelist and that the postmaster general ran off a special issue just for him. He can tell you what a mint sheet and a first-day cover are, explain how stamps revolutionized the postal system, and discuss the latest international auction at Christie's.

The more you learn about a broader and broader spectrum of subjects, the more your friends will say that you're a fascinating, entertaining person to talk with. They won't say, "Here comes old 'broken record,' always prattling over and over about the same old subject."

Just how irritating this can be is exemplified by the actor whose one great triumph was playing the role of Abe Lincoln in a successful play.

As a reminder of this, he began dressing like Honest Abe, mimicked the mannerisms and speech of the former President, and, of course, always got around to some reference to his starring role in the play years ago. One day one of his acquaintances, seeing him coming, remarked to a friend, "If he doesn't stop that Lincoln role, someone is going to shoot him!"

Show Interest with Your Nonverbal Signals

Reading your partner's nonverbal signals is one part of being a skilled communicator. But remember, this is a two-way activity, like a Ping-Pong game, in which sending and receiving are equally important. While observing, you need to keep aware of what you yourself are displaying.

How can you show those with whom you converse that you're vitally interested in them and what they're telling you? If you really are warmed up to them and the subject, some of your enthusiasm will just naturally bubble to the surface. But if you're a reticent person, loosen up and let it surface. Here are some positive signals you can send out:

Approach with Enthusiasm

- *Look bright and alert.*   Look as if you're really looking forward to this talk. Let your face radiate interest.

- *Stand or sit erect.*   Don't slouch, as if you've been dragged to this encounter. And don't wilt as the conversation progresses; that looks as if it's wearing you down. Posture is important.

Give Your Total Attention

- *Keep your eyes on the speaker.*   Nothing is a greater turnoff than to let your gaze wander to other activities or other people nearby. It states unmistakably that you care less about the speaker than you do about others—that you're bored with the conversation.

- *Concentrate on what's being said.*   If you allow yourself to listen to other conversations nearby, this has the same effect as allowing your eyes to wander. You'll lose the thread of the dialogue, and it'll show.

React with Animation

- *Nod your head* from time to time to show you're awake—an active, enthusiastic participant.

- *Smile* when you hear something you agree with. That's a great encouragement.

- *Lean forward,* if you're sitting, to show approval or special interest in some point. Move around a bit, rather than remaining passive and bored-looking.

- *Don't be afraid to gesture a bit.* With our British social customs, we've been taught to appear cold and restrained, to avoid "talking with our hands" as the Latins do. But that doesn't always look friendly. Don't hesitate to slap your hands together, raise a finger, put your hands on your hips...whatever...to show some enthusiasm. It won't kill you! The people you're talking with may be surprised to see this unaccustomed animation in you, but they'll say, "Boy, was Jerry excited about what I told him. He loved it!"

Demonstrating enthusiasm is mostly a matter of energy and animation. That is, if you want the conversation to move, *you* have to move it.

In Your Enthusiasm, Don't Monopolize

A word of caution: In your enthusiasm, don't get so carried away that you monopolize the conversation. Keep the Ping-Pong game in mind; give your partner or partners a 50-50 chance to participate.

An example of what happens when two-way discussions become one-way lectures is provided by a study of public-school students and their progressive loss of interest as they move from grade to grade. Led by John Goodlad, former dean of the Graduate School of Education at the University of California in Los Angeles, it pointed out:

- *Student participation* is high in primary grades. Teachers there use field trips, dramatizations, etc., in addition to talking about the subject. But a typical high school teacher relies *exclusively* on lecturing and monitoring seat work.

- *The average instructional day* in a junior or senior high school includes 150 minutes of talking, only 7 of which are initiated by the students.

- *An excess of teacher talk* creates an atmosphere from which students withdraw, putting their minds on hold. Talky teachers create uninterested students.

No doubt you can find parallels to this in business and social situations. Those who try to inform through monologue or through talk they heavily dominate fail because they turn off their listeners.

Doing What Comes Naturally

As Barbara Walters has pointed out, you're not at your best in conversing when you're nervous, and many times the panic you create inside
yourself is based on false alarms.

Often the alarm bells go off when you're meeting someone of importance. You become so fearful of making a bad impression that you
freeze and everything seems to go wrong.

Don't Let Important People
Frighten You

Maybe you won't get so uptight if you remind yourself that "big" people
can be easier to talk with than the small fry. They're less picky about
little things and less inclined to be critical of you, because they're relaxed and not trying to compete with you. In addition, you may find
them more interested and willing to learn (that's how they got where
they are), so if you're bringing them information or ideas, they'll listen.
They may not always agree, but generally they'll listen. Bring them
something of genuine interest, and they're easy to do business with.

Important people are easy to converse with in social situations too.
We don't always anticipate that. My friend Norman Rockwell, who was
basically a very shy man, once got himself all worked up unnecessarily
because of his fears on that score.

What Norman Rockwell Learned

He was to attend a dinner at the University of
Massachusetts to receive an honorary doctor of arts
degree. This made him one of the celebrities at the
affair, but he was too modest to let it puff him up
much. Instead, he was scared to go because he'd be
seated with the presidents of Harvard and MIT, who
were receiving honorary degrees at the same time.

"Just imagine," he wailed to me, "I'll be sitting with
those two 'brains,' two of the smartest men in the
country...me, a high-school dropout! What in the
world can I say to them? They'll be talking about
things I don't understand, and they'll soon realize
what a dummy I am." I tried my best to allay his
fears.

A couple of weeks later, when I returned to
Stockbridge to go over some sketches with Mr. Rockwell, I asked how
the ceremony had turned out. "Just great," he assured me. "You know,
the thought of being with those two university presidents scared me to

death, but all they wanted to talk about was my paintings and which ones were their favorites. We had a wonderful conversation, and they turned out to be two of the friendliest people I ever met!"

Just goes to prove that once you discover what people are interested in, conversation is a breeze. You can relax and enjoy it.

8

How to Cope with Meetings

If you have enough meetings over a long enough period of time, they become more important than the problem they were intended to solve.   HENDRICKSON'S LAW

When Harry Truman was entrapped in a long, boring meeting, he would sometimes slip out to another room in the White House, take off his shoes, and nap for a little while. He'd time his return so he could catch the last few minutes of the conference and learn what, if anything, had been accomplished in his absence.

Ever wish you could do the same?

Presidents, of countries or companies, have special privileges. Like the rest of us, however, they get fed up with a never-ending succession of meetings that seem to take priority over everything else. No other element of communication causes so much crying, cussing, and confusion. But anyone in management must learn to live with them, sometimes hour after hour, day after day. Somehow, you must learn to cope.

Are Meetings All Bad?

Few people would deny that sitting in meetings can waste more time, effort, and money than any other business activity. They burn up 50 percent or more of many an executive's day, and burn out the executives in the process. *They're the curse of large corporations and other bu-*

reaucracies. Yet they are also one of management's best tools—the key to a smooth-running, enthusiastic team that can move quickly and accomplish great feats. *Meetings can be wonderful.*

Which view is correct? Both, of course. In fact, both can apply even within the same organization. Stanley Marcus has said, "One of the major time wasters in the white-collar world is the meeting." But he has also credited the regular morning meetings at Neiman-Marcus with contributing greatly to the success of that retailer by alerting everyone to the newest merchandise arrivals, up-to-the-minute inventory figures, etc.[1]

Two Obvious Problems

Overkill. It's the assumption that if one or two meetings are good, then formal meetings all day long must be better. Surely you've seen many instances of this, maybe in your own offices.

What does it indicate? Peter Drucker has stated, "One prime indicator of bad organization and time wasting is a proliferation of meetings."[2]

I'd go further: Where you find an overabundance of meetings, you'll invariably find an overabundance of personnel. In lean organizations where the staff is kept busy in productive work, there's no time to waste in unnecessary meetings.

Length of Meetings. How many have you sat through, listening to repetitious haggling and irrelevant nit-picking for an hour or more, when the critical business could have been handled in 10 minutes? In talking and writing to many corporate leaders, a common complaint I heard over and over was, "Meetings last too long!"

> *Regardless of the length of the meeting, all important decisions will be made in the last five minutes before lunch or quitting time.*   CARSON'S LAW

Maybe you concur with the common gripes—too many meetings that run far too long. But griping isn't going to change much. In fact, unless you're a big wheel in your organization, you can't expect to alter greatly either the frequency or the nature of the meetings to which you're invited. You're stuck with them, for better or worse. The question is, "How can you make them work for you, for the better?"

---

[1]From Mr. Marcus's daily radio program, *Another Opinion,* produced and distributed nationally by the Sunbelt Network of Dallas.

[2]From John J. Tarrant, *Drucker: The Man Who Invented the Corporate Society,* Cahners Books, Boston, 1976, p. 97.

I could provide you with long lists of dos and don'ts detailing all possible elements of staging and procedures. But you've probably seen them before, and you know they're widely ignored. Or I could discuss at length the basic procedures of how to manage a meeting. They're widely known, too, but just to refresh your memory...

How Meetings Are Supposed to Be Managed

The basics of managing a meeting are very simple and very few. Entire books have been devoted to explaining them, but they can be boiled down to these fundamentals:

1. *Adequate advance information.* Whoever calls the meeting should give the participants enough time and information so they can come prepared to contribute intelligently. If anyone is expected to bring special data or make a report, that should be noted on the invitation and not sprung as a last-minute surprise.

2. *A clear objective.* Expect to accomplish *one* thing. The meeting leader should state it clearly so that all understand it; maybe write it on a blackboard as the proceedings begin.

3. *An agenda.* Exactly what's to be discussed should be outlined briefly in writing. It's up to the meeting leader to pull the discussion back to the agenda whenever it starts to wander from it.

4. *Brevity.* The maximum time for the meeting should be stated in advance. Start on time—latecomers are out of luck and get no recaps of what they missed. End on the agreed time, or before. It's not a crime to quit early.

5. *A small group.* A discussion-type meeting (I'm not talking about a stage presentation or a report to a large audience) will get out of hand or dribble into nothingness if it consists of more than 10 or 12 people. *Half that number is far better.* Accomplishment is likely to be in inverse proportion to attendance.

6. *Decisions for action.* Come to clear decisions as to any actions to be taken subsequently, by whom they're to be done, and by what dates. Confirm it all in a brief follow-up memo to all participants.

If that's all there is to it, how come you find yourself fretting and fuming during thousands of hours of crummy meetings during a typical career? Several reasons:

For one, you don't run most of the meetings you're involved in—you're an attendee with limited control over the proceedings. This is a fact generally ignored in the textbooks and how-to books, which concentrate on how to manage meetings. Where you really need help is in coping with the 80 percent you don't manage.

For another, the style of meetings in an organization is determined not just by individuals, but by the corporate culture. It may encourage wasteful rituals—the tribal powwows in which form is more important than substance. The culture sets the rules of the game.

A third reason is that the ostensible purposes for gathering in the conference room are often not the real purposes. All may not be as it seems to be.

In addition, there's always the human element to consider. What goes on in meetings is not merely rules and procedures (and common sense), but people reacting with people. And people do the craziest things at times. Let's talk about them first.

Melodrama at the Office

I like to think of the conference room as a theater. A meeting of a couple of people in the boss's office is one thing, but as soon as a larger group gets together—which is what we're considering—the theatrical aspects begin to appear.

Consciously or not, the different characters who enter the conference room (and you'll encounter some characters there) tend to be "on stage." Some hog the spotlight at every opportunity. Some huddle timidly in the wings. Some foul up the director by digressing from his or her script (agenda). Some can be counted on to deliver their lines clearly and effectively. Others get stage fright, causing them to fumble and make a poor impression. Some do well because they've studied for their parts. Others are obviously unprepared. All, from the head honcho to the ingenue who recently joined the company, get a subconscious review from the rest on their performance or lack of it.

Make no mistake about it—many a career is made or broken around the mahogany table where the shows go on daily.

The Cast of Characters and How to Deal with Them

How you view the various participants and what you do about them depends on your role. If you're the meeting leader, the director, it's up to you to control them. If you're one of the troupe, you must adapt your style to complement theirs, or at least not get wounded by the more aggressive characters. If you recognize yourself in the following cast of characters, you may want to reconsider the way you play your role.

The Harpooner.   Could be called the Cross-Examiner, the Inquisitor, the Politician, or several other unprintable names. Pretends to be an impartial searcher after truth, but actually is against everything not proposed by himself or his group. One such person I remember well called himself the Devil's Advocate and took pride in questioning everything that could possibly go wrong with every idea presented—by anyone else. He killed many a good one. In defense, his peers began jumping on all his proposals—a turnabout he didn't appreciate.

The Nit-Picker.   More subtle than the Harpooner, but therefore even more destructive. Always starts out with a compliment that somehow turns into a question that raises nagging doubts. "That plan could have some good possibilities, but I wonder how our dealers will react if we ask them to ..." Before the big picture can be explored, the Nit-Picker will shift attention to some little detail that might be in conflict with the budget, the way it has always been done, or the supposed preferences of the public, the dealer organization, or the Big Boss. If this pimple becomes a subject of early discussion, the beauty of the main proposition loses its luster and is forgotten.

The Droner.   Goes on and on repetitiously. Found especially in informational meetings where an explanation or report turns into a recital of more than anyone wants to know.

Some companies (Dayton-Hudson, for example) set time limits for each speaker in such meetings. Albert Hellwig of Scott-Lad Foods makes a habit of pointing to his wristwatch when speakers drone on too long. At one time, he used to set a timer with a buzzer, but he found this too startling and upsetting to some sensitive souls.

Droners are usually nice people who get carried away with the importance of their duties and activities. If you're chairing a meeting where a droner will be participating, you can avoid embarrassment by indicating in advance that there's limited time for that segment of the meeting. Advise the speaker to send everyone a written summary of the report ahead of time and to use only a few minutes to list the main points and answer any questions.

It can be awkward to cut short a participant who's going to run the clock out, but the meeting leader's prerogative is to call attention to time. It may require: "This is interesting, Jean, and I wish we could discuss it longer. But I see we still have two more topics to cover, so I know you recognize that we must move on. Anyone here who has further questions on this can talk to Jean after the meeting."

The Rambler.   This person wastes everyone's time by wandering afield from the basic purpose. When he or she shoots off into strange new trajectories—often related to the Rambler's own activities and achievements—it's up to the meeting leader to pull the discussion back to the agenda. That's why a printed agenda is essential to even a small meeting.

The Silent One.   Says hardly a word. May be mute because this person is outranked by others, is new to the organization, or is intimidated by aggressive characters present. The meeting leader may need to lend encouragement, addressing the Silent One by name and asking questions related to that person's expertise. Even if you're not leading the meeting, you can do this too. You'll be eliciting information of value (the Silent One should not have been invited if void of it), and you may gain a grateful friend from a reticent person.

If you see yourself as the Silent One, you're doing yourself a disservice. Although you may be younger, newer, or lower on the organization chart than others around you, when you're asked to come to a conference you have not only a right to be heard but a responsibility to contribute. Even the trainee can talk (briefly in proper tones at the proper time) with the top brass at the table; otherwise, they may wonder if they hired a dummy. An invitation to a high-level meeting is a rare opportunity that may have been extended in order to size you up. Don't blow it by identifying yourself as no better than an empty chair.

The Timid Soul.   Talks a little, but apologizes before expressing an idea or opinion. This assures that it will be discounted. Perhaps you can help the Timid Soul by calling attention to a good idea when one is presented, and asking him or her to elaborate on it.

If you tend to be a Timid Soul, be aware that you don't give your contributions a fair chance if you preface them with uncertain words like "maybe…it might be…it probably wouldn't work, but." If you believe in what you're saying, state it with conviction.

The Echo.   Stays quiet and ambivalent during the first part of a meeting, until the Boss hints at some preference. Instantly becomes vocal and enthusiastic about exactly the same course of action. Unfortunately, the Echo is a common phenomenon that thrives and multiplies in many organizations.

If you're the Boss in a group where one or more Echoes materialize in meeting after meeting, you should ask yourself a few questions: (1) Are you encouraging the bounce-back of everything you say because you discourage ideas other than your own? (2) If you want a variety of opinions, shouldn't you open future meetings by saying, "I'm not going to express any views today; I want to hear what *you* think"? That will leave the Echo speechless. (3) If you really don't want to hear a variety of opinions, why bother to hold any meetings? You can save time and money by simply issuing orders.

The Bully. You may recognize this person as the Loud Mouth, the Shouter, or the Bulldozer. This character tries and often succeeds in dominating a meeting by sheer persistence and strength of lungs.

A good meeting leader will not stand for bullying; will gavel down rude interruptions and personal attacks or tirades. When you're battered by a Bully and there is no forceful meeting leader to ensure equity, your only recourse is to meet the attack head on. The Bully doesn't respect politeness or weakness. You might say: "You've had the floor for five minutes. Now give the rest of us a chance to talk." Or, if the problem is loudness: "There's no need to shout; we can hear you. Let's calm down and let everyone express an opinion, quietly."

Those who develop a reputation as a Bully eventually get excluded from many meetings. If shunned often enough, that may have some slight modifying effect.

The Spear Carriers. Where politics are rife, the chiefs of rival factions are prone to bring entourages of henchmen to meetings. This provides volume support if factional differences of opinion arise. Sometimes the appearance of a group from a department when only one representative was expected may be a case of laziness—the idea that if all key subordinates come along, it won't be necessary to brief them later on any matters that concern them.

If you arrange for a meeting for seven, it should not develop into a mob scene for two dozen. When faced with a phalanx of Spear Carriers (which an attendee may consider necessary to supply technical facts he can't handle himself), the meeting leader is justified in suggesting they be seated back around the wall. That separates them from the main participants, who'll still be able to interact in a small group. An invitation for one person is not a sanction for an open house.

The Important Disrupter. Upstages everyone and interrupts the meeting every five minutes by having a secretary or assistant charge in with a letter to be signed or a momentous matter that requires instant attention. Has all phone calls routed into the conference room. The implication is that nothing going on there is nearly as important as the vital activities that require the Disrupter's continuous attention.

There is no valid reason to have a telephone in a conference room. Instead of that jarring interruption to everyone present, calls can be made to a desk outside the door. A secretary there can take a message or, if necessary, quietly call a participant out of the meeting.

Etc., Etc., Etc. The characters I've listed are by no means the complete cast you'll encounter in the myriad meetings in your professional and civic life. You can think of many more: The Doodler, who seems impervious to surrounding conversation while constructing intricate drawings on the margins of the agenda sheet. The Diligent Note Taker, who faithfully records every word spoken. The Whip-Cracking Boss, who does all the talking. The Arguer, who'd rather wrangle than permit constructive discussion. The Miracle Worker, who makes every report a glowing paean of praise to the marvelous work accomplished by his or her group, with any shortcoming or problems carefully whitewashed.

Be prepared to deal with them all as best you can, using the principles of good communication. The conference room is a microcosm of life outside. No better, no worse.

The Plot Is Not Always Simple

Pick up a textbook on meetings and you'll find a list of their purposes something like this:

1. To relay information to a group
2. To analyze and solve problems
3. To achieve group consensus and support for a course of action
4. To reconcile conflicting views
5. To receive reports and review progress, as when a committee supervises and approves an ongoing activity
6. To build enthusiasm, as in a sales meeting
7. A combination of the above

Those are the clearly apparent reasons for holding a meeting. Good reasons, but don't let the theory fool you. Sometimes the plot thickens. If you want to deal successfully with the characters you've just read about and hope to understand what's really going on in meetings, you need to be aware of some aspects often present but never talked about. For example, think about the kind of meeting everyone has attended— the staff meeting.

Throughout corporate and governmental America each Monday morning, millions of managerial workers still traumatized by weekend excesses pick up their coffee cups and coagulate into little groups in their respective departmental conference rooms. There they kill the first tenth of the workweek in talking about the Sunday ball games, in hashing over what they supposedly accomplished the preceding week, and in getting marching orders from the boss for the days ahead.

If you were to ask why this transpires, you'd probably be told that it's essential for everyone to hear all the reports so everyone in the group knows what everyone else is doing. You might also be advised that this is the quickest way for the boss to give instructions to the individuals he or she supervises. If you think about it for a moment, you'll realize that's hogwash. Ask yourself the following:

- "How come everyone still knows what everyone else is doing when the boss goes on a three-week vacation and there are no staff meetings?"

- "Instead of tying up the whole department for the morning, suppose the boss met with each individual for 15 or 20 minutes? Wouldn't that accomplish the same objectives in a small fraction of the employee-hours?"

- "If the above two questions are valid, should staff meetings be eliminated? Or do they have hidden purposes that justify their existence and almost universal popularity?"

Understanding the Hidden Purposes

Some of the most cogent reasons for gatherings of the clan around the big long table are seldom if ever talked about. Here are some of them.

Training the Recruits

Theory and logic might seem to dictate that the weekly powwows should be eliminated and that attendance of junior supervisors at other meetings be held to a minimum. But the costs of meetings must be weighed against their hidden values as training tools. To youngsters and newcomers, meetings are a broadening experience. Someone with little experience can watch and listen as the older hands perform. And what's learned in the group is not just technical skills that can be taught elsewhere, but the nuances of corporate culture that are never verbalized or written down, except in phony platitudes in corporate annual reports and personnel manuals.

Evaluating the Troops

Meetings provide top executives with opportunities to sit back, observe, and compare. At this theater, they can note how well the players communicate and interact with their peers—see how certain promising people present their ideas and handle themselves in a rough-and-tumble situation. The weekly staff meeting offers continuing occasions for the department manager to evaluate the progress of her people, and perhaps to consider where weak spots are developing or who's showing enough growth to take on new responsibilities.

If you're invited to a meeting at a level you'd ordinarily not expect, it may be that someone wishes to observe and judge how you handle yourself. In an atmosphere more rarified than you're used to, you naturally want to exhibit decorum and restraint. *But don't overdo it.* If you sit there with your mouth closed the entire time (the Silent One), the verdict won't be flattering. Remember, anyone invited to a meeting has been extended the right to contribute relevant ideas, information, and questions: in fact, is expected to have something to say. It's up to you to prepare with extra diligence for such rare opportunities so that you can demonstrate quietly but confidently that you've studied the subject and have worthwhile ideas about it.

Building Esprit de Corps

Some meetings have it more than others. The sales meeting may be nearly 100 percent pepper-upper, likened to the war dances that early inhabitants of this continent held before going into battle. But ordinary day-to-day meetings where we work also have the effect of welding the clan together with a feeling of family that can build cooperation and group pride. Just one minute or even less in a departmental meeting can accomplish some of this.

I'll never forget a psychologically perceptive boss who demonstrated this with me and my fellow workers years ago. We were one of several creative groups—writers and artists—in an advertising agency. He was a newcomer with a big reputation, brought in from the outside. We eyed him suspiciously in our first few meetings held informally once or twice a week to review batches of ads we'd prepared for some new campaign. Especially when near the end of each review, he'd single out several examples of copy and layout that pleased him and always say with a broad smile, *"We do good work."* He'd add, "Thanks, and keep it up." We were a cynical bunch of individualists who felt we didn't need this flattering "we do good work" pat-on-the-head hogwash week after week. But despite ourselves, we began to look for it. If the boss left out the accolade, as he did on occasion, we felt downcast—and we broke our butts to make sure he'd end the next review with the familiar phrase. We began to tell ourselves, "We're the gang that does the really good work around here." We believed we were the best, and I think we were.

Providing an Audience for a Monologue

Sometimes it's salutary for one person at a meeting to do nearly all the talking in order to tell others quickly about a new development that requires immediate action. This can be followed by questions and assignments.

However, there's another kind of monologue meeting you may have encountered. (If you haven't, you're lucky.) It's the one that's supposed to be a group discussion, but in which the ranking executive hogs the floor for almost the entire time, rambling on about what he or she thinks. No use trying to tell what you think, because the monologuist doesn't want to hear it. You and the others are there strictly as an audience.

Corporate Culture Writes the Rules

Let me attend a few meetings at an organization—corporate, governmental, or civic—and I'll know more about it than if I read all the annual reports, procedure and personnel manuals, press releases, and speeches by the president. So would you. The style of the convocations in the conference rooms is the mirror of the corporate culture. There are many telltale signs. Here are several.

The Mix of Attendees. In organizations where formality is highly valued, meetings tend to be stratified, with all those at the table of much the same salary range. In free-form companies, often young and smaller, you're apt to see a frequent mixing of those of different levels, invited for a variety of functions and skills regardless of seniority and prestige.

Barriers to Communication

Rigid organizational structures and chains of command are barriers to effective communication. It's important that management be perceived by everyone as accessible and down to earth.

This helps create an atmosphere in which information and ideas can flow freely and candidly.

EDWARD B. RUST, PRESIDENT & CEO
State Farm Insurance Companies

Adherence to the Pecking Order. In formal cultures, the top person automatically selects the chair at the head of the table while the others arrange themselves in precise order down to the foot. Also, everyone knows who can speak freely and often (sometimes only number one) and who'd better shut up unless called upon. Seldom any roundtables here.

The Frequency of Planned-Far-in-Advance Meetings. This is another indication of a tightly structured bureaucracy. Battalions of managers march to the schedules of daily appointment books crammed weeks in advance with meetings that may fill 90 percent or more of each day. At one company of that type, I remember trying to snare a few moments with an always-rushing-off executive and being informed by his secretary that Mr. So and So "is booked up solidly every day *for the next entire month*." When he was canned, I wondered if he was missed at all those meetings he'd be unable to attend.

Decisions or the Lack of Them.   This tells a great deal. If a meeting is held merely to prepare for another meeting, you're likely to encounter many slow-moving people who spend much of their time shining up their 25-year pins and calculating the funds in the retirement pot.

"Sorry, but they're all in the Friday afternoon meeting to plan the Monday morning staff meeting."

The Size of Meetings.   The fact that meetings generally accomplish less and less as they get bigger and bigger is not a secret, even in firms where huge convocations are common. They know it and they condone it.

Hidden Purposes That Relate to Corporate Culture

Whether it be a charitable fund-raising group or a Fortune 500 company, every organization has a personality. It gives rise to certain rituals and acceptable ways of dealing with people that attach themselves to the organization over a period of years.

Like barnacles, these accretions that affect people-to-people dealings, such as meetings, are hidden below the surface but always there. Sometimes, like barnacles, they act as a drag on rapid movement, because they lead to meetings not designed to solve problems but to conform to cultural habits. Here are a few meeting purposes of this kind.

Touching Base with All Surrounding Fiefdoms

In some organizations, the first questions asked before any action is taken are: "Will any other people or departments possibly imagine that we're impinging on their territories if we do this? Hadn't we better meet with them all to make sure no one has any objections before we make a proposal to top management?" In many large companies, this "touching base" is a standard procedure that must be allowed for in scheduling any activity. Skip it at your peril.

Avoiding a Decision

Supposedly, meetings are always held to *make* decisions. Not always. When faced with an unpleasant, hazardous decision, an executive who can create enough meetings with enough people may be able to avoid it indefinitely. Meantime, she's working on it. And hoping the problem will just go away. Sometimes it does.

> When in doubt, hold a meeting. When in trouble, form a committee.
> COOPER'S LAW

When explaining the difference between Electronic Data Systems and General Motors, Ross Perot is reported to have said, "When anyone at our old company discovered a snake, he was expected to kill it immediately. When anyone at GM sees a snake, he forms a committee to deliberate for six months on whether such an animal really exists."

Nailing the Opposition

The textbooks always mention "gaining group consensus and support" as one of the primary reasons for meetings. There is a different aspect of the situation that you'll see in the real war zone when one person knows the other is *never* going to give a full measure of agreement and support.

In corporate cultures where the knives fly freely, it's advisable to nail the opponent to the wall in front of a mutual boss in such situations. If the project under discussion has been approved by management, the foot dragger has two unpalatable options. He can bring his objections out into the open, exposing the fact that he can't be counted on to cooperate fully. (Doing that too often can be fatal.) Or he must swallow his objections and publicly agree to go along—a promise he'd better abide by.

In either case, the nailer has bested the nailee at the old game that psychoanalysts, such as Dr. Eric Berne, the father of transactional analysis (or TA), refer to as "Gotcha, you s.o.b.!"[3]

Observing Reassuring Rituals

There are meetings that take place primarily because they're expected to occur at regular intervals. They give reassurance that all is well in the company; they don't necessarily need to accomplish anything beyond that.

For example, if a board of director's meeting is ordinarily held every quarter, it can't be skipped just because there's nothing special to discuss. Can you imagine the rumors that would start to fly if the continuity of this expected high-level event were broken? Other meetings held year after year on a regular schedule also assume mystical significance.

Throughout a corporation, the annual sales meeting or the periodic deliberations of the executive committee may become established as traditions that always take place. Within a department, there can also grow a regular rhythm of meetings to which people become accustomed. Break the rhythm and the fears of the tribe begin to churn as some ask, "What's happening? Why the change? What's wrong?"

Making Work for the Population of the Empire

Nobody will ever admit this exists, but it's rampant wherever there are empire builders—and they're everywhere. The more people you have in your department, the bigger becomes your job, and your salary. That's decreed by personnel departments throughout the land who may not be sure what everyone is doing, but they can count the heads and assign values accordingly.

The problem that empire builders inevitably face is what to do with all those troops. Can't let them just stand around all the time; they'll get bored and troublesome or, heaven forbid, attract undue attention to their idleness.

The obvious solution is to give them lots and lots of meetings to attend. That moves them around, keeps them happy, and fosters the illusion that much important work is being done. If you wonder why you spend a great deal of time in meetings that could easily be dispensed with, this may be the reason. Either relax and enjoy the situation or leave it.

[3]See Eric Berne, *Games People Play*, Grove Press, New York, 1964.

> Meetings expand automatically without
> limit to absorb any amount of idle time
> and people available.   WALTON'S LAW

Looking at the Bright Side

Some of the meeting practices discussed above may not gladden the hearts of company presidents or of conscientious, ambitious executives, who make up the bulk of the managerial work force. They exist, though. That's why everyone complains about meetings.

But, as you read at the beginning of this chapter, "Meetings *can* be wonderful."

One of the brightest indicators for the future of American business is the emergence of more and more companies—mostly small and midsize entrepreneurial enterprises—where meetings are stimulating rather than stifling. I call this phenomenon...

The Spur-of-the-Moment Free-Form Meeting

Nothing formal about this. It just happens, all the time, in booming small companies and in others—such as 3M, Hewlett-Packard, newspaper offices, advertising agencies, aggressive retailers, new computer companies—wherever innovation and fast action are essentials of the business.

In such places, you seldom arrange to meet through secretaries; you grab a couple of people you need at the moment, enlist their opinions or help (often without bothering to sit down), and split up when the purpose is accomplished. There's no agenda, no notes, and often no prearranged list of participants—they may wander in if the sound of the arguing intrigues them and leave when they've had their say. These are always problem-solving meetings, because in such organizations there's always a new problem (or opportunity) that needs to be tackled right away.

Problem-Solving Meetings Exist in Formal Cultures Too

They are the crux of what productive conferences are all about. *If there's no problem to solve, chances are 10 to 1 you don't need a meeting.* You can disseminate information, initiate an action, or get an agreement via a memo, one-to-one appointment, or conference telephone call, and do it much faster.

But in any organization, you're constantly running into problems where you need help from others. You can benefit from their opinions in defining the problem correctly and arriving at the best solution. You may need their cooperation in attacking it or their OK before proceeding. This is when a collaborative effort with intelligent colleagues who have the guts to make a decision and go into action pays off big. It's the quintessential value of the meeting.

What Can You Do to Make Meetings Better?

The prime reason there are so many bad meetings that waste tons of money and eons of managerial time is that although everyone gripes about them, *nobody questions*. This applies to all management levels in all sorts of organizations. The griping doesn't do any good; the questioning can.

The kind of questions you can ask depends on several variables: whether you're calling the meeting or being called, what other demands there are on your time, your power and position in the organization, and how important the meeting attendees and their possible decisions are to you. Obviously, the person who sets up the meeting and directs it will have the greatest effect on its productivity or lack of it. If that person is you, there are several questions you should ask before you send out the invitations.

What's the Purpose?

You need to ask yourself what fundamental purpose this meeting will serve, and also what accomplishment you expect to see at the end of the meeting that does not exist now. When you figure that out (honestly), write it down in a single sentence. Then keep it in mind during your meeting.

Is a Meeting the Best Choice?

Holding a meeting may not be the only way ... or the best way ... to accomplish your purpose. For example, if your need is to convey information, can you do that today with a memo instead of next week in a meeting? If you need an urgent decision on some matter, can it wait for a meeting, or is it appropriate for you to take executive action immediately yourself? If group consensus is required, can you get it simply by telephoning one or two people or by a conference call, instead of an in-person meeting that pulls people away from other work?

How Long Must the Meeting Last?

In too many organizations, the one-hour meeting has become the standard minimum, even though 30 minutes or even 15 would be adequate on many occasions. If you set the time limit on a brief schedule rather than a leisurely one, you'll be surprised how the pace quickens. Everyone realizes they're gathered for action—not a coffee klatch. The brief meeting stimulates prompt attendance; those who show up 15 minutes late find the meeting is over. A brief businesslike meeting also elicits gratitude from busy people. And it demonstrates to the boss that you're not a time waster.

How Many People Need to Attend?

Check your tentative list of attendees and ask yourself how many of them are really needed. If it's to be a decision-making session, can they all make decisions? If not, what other circumstance requires their presence? The more you pare the list to active, necessary participants, the more you're likely to accomplish.

Is Your Agenda Specific Enough?

It should be concise and focused on a single subject. Send a copy to all participants ahead of time, so they'll be prepared for that subject. Also, let them know in advance what action, if any, should be decided upon in the meeting.

Your Questions as a Participant

If the person who invites you to a meeting has done his or her job perfectly, using all the questions above, you shouldn't have to ask any. But, of course, you can't count on perfection. If you've been "meetinged" to death and shudder at each new invitation, a few questions may help you decide whether to attend or to try to skip the impending session. Don't just go automatically.

What's In It for You?

Consider what you can gain or lose at the forthcoming meeting. If it will involve information you need or decisions vital to you or your department, that's fine. But often you may discover that the benefits are likely to be marginal and that your contribution to the discussion is apt to be slight. If this seems to be the situation, check it out. Ask the meeting holder politely what he or she had in mind in including you. Sometimes you'll discover that not much thought was given to making up the list; you're on it just because you've been on other lists. If so, you can ask to be excused, saving yourself time and also freeing the meeting leader from at least one nonproductive attendee. Whether or not this is possible depends on the next question.

Do You Dare to Decline the Invitation?

This depends on your position on the corporate ladder. If the myriad invitations come from your boss, you're going to be hesitant in turning them down. Even in that circumstance, however, you could be doing yourself a favor by pointing out, "I'd planned to work on the new proposal you need next week; do you want me to stick with that or go to this meeting?" When meetings become so prevalent that they begin to hurt your job performance, as sometimes happens, you'd best get on record that something has to give.

Can You Leave Early?

This is a logical question that's seldom asked. Often a participant is needed only to answer a few questions or to discuss only one item of the several on the agenda—an activity that may require but a few minutes. Yet that person often stays on through another 40 or 50 minutes of merely warming a chair.

If you surmise from the agenda you get in advance that your participation will be needed for only one small part of the session, check this with the leader. Advise that you'll be happy to sit in on that part of the discussion but would like to time your arrival and departure to miss the bulk of the meeting that won't really benefit from your presence.

During a meeting, you may often find that the discussion is getting farther and farther away from your area of expertise and interest. It's appropriate then to excuse yourself and leave quietly. Your colleagues aren't going to be offended by such a logical action. They're going to recognize that you're an intelligent, busy person and that maybe they'd be smart to start emulating you in similar circumstances.

What's Your Objective?

You should always ask this before you go into a meeting, just as you do before you enter into any other activity. If there will be an opportunity to sell a certain viewpoint, you should have a plan for doing this and should take along the facts that may be needed. If you anticipate that there may be some decision you won't like, you need to plan the best way to forestall it. If the meeting presents a chance to learn important information, go prepared with the questions that'll help you get it.

Those who walk blindly—without questioning—are bound to stumble. Those who look ahead are the winners in the conference room. They make meetings a tool for success, not a boring waste of time.

Questions from the Top

Throughout corporate America today, the top executives are looking for ways to whittle away at bureaucratic bad habits and improve efficiency. I can't think of any better step to take that everyone will applaud than to bring unbridled "meeting mania" under control. In fact, since meetings eat up such a huge portion of managerial time, it's almost impossible to improve productivity significantly without tightening up in that area.

In talking with senior executives, I've found this to be a sore spot with many. The questions they ask are:

- Are all these meetings really necessary?
- Couldn't they be smaller?
- Couldn't they be shorter?
- Do they accomplish as much as they should?

These questions aren't unlike the ones we've just considered—the ones you should ask. The perspective is different, though, because the upper echelon is looking at costs, while you're more concerned with the drain on your personal time and energy.

Charles J. Pilliod, Jr., who was chairman of the board at Goodyear Tire & Rubber Company for many years, epitomizes the executives for whom myriads of meetings have become a symbol of white-collar inefficiency. Here are some thoughts he sent me:

Ideas for Better Meetings

In 40 years of participating in meetings, I have become convinced business could save millions if its meetings were conducted with the same efficiency as the production and distribution processes. I believe that:

- Advance announcement of the meeting's theme or purpose helps participants to come prepared and avoid conversation not germane to the subject at hand.
- Unless what might be said is relevant to the subject of the meeting, don't say it.

- An important point can bear repetition. It is better to make a point succinctly and repeat it than to make it just once in a windy and convoluted manner.

- An idea should not be kept unsaid just because it might seem obvious; it might be obvious only to the person conceiving it.

- Although business meetings have serious purposes, a dollop of humor here and there can relax the participants and perhaps encourage them to open up.

- All businesspeople are not great communicators. So, spoken ideas should not be tossed aside merely because they are not skillfully presented.

- Most business meetings take twice as long as they should.

CHARLES J. PILLIOD, JR., CHAIRMAN
Goodyear Tire & Rubber Company

I agree with all the points Mr. Pilliod makes; he states the problems well. One of his points intrigues me especially; I believe it underscores your need to be a good communicator. As Mr. Pilliod indicates in his second-to-last point, all businesspeople aren't good communicators and their ideas shouldn't be tossed aside because they're poorly presented. But, of course, this very statement highlights the fact that *poor communicators do get tossed aside*—in meetings and in other business interchanges.

The Pendulum Is Swinging

Years ago there weren't enough meetings. Commanders and their lieutenants didn't bother with such things as consensus. They simply barked their orders and expected them to be passed down the line without comment.

In more recent times, as the popularity of participative management has grown, meetings have proliferated—sometimes to the point where no one can make a decision without extensive and protracted hand holding. The need to break that sort of gridlock is what's pulling the pendulum back a bit.

Viva la meetings! They're necessary and wonderful. But let's view them wisely—as one useful element of successful communication—not as the main purpose of our day that pushes all else aside. Let's try for fewer, shorter, and *better* meetings.

9
Presentations That Sparkle

Be a craftsman in speech that thou mayest be strong, for the strength of one is in the tongue and speech is mightier than all fighting. Maxims of Ptahhotep *(circa 3400 B.C.)*

Webster's dictionary defines a *presentation* as "something set forth for the attention of the mind; a descriptive or persuasive account." That covers a tremendous amount of territory—most of what you say or write. In business, however, the word takes on a narrower meaning. If you're required to make a presentation, it usually means that you, perhaps aided by one or more associates, will be allotted a specified period of time *to stand before a group to explain, report on, or sell something.* You may do this within your own company—maybe to a group that supervises your activities—or to executives of an outside company to whom you hope to sell products or services.

Salespeople make presentations all the time. You do, too, in the sense that you're always explaining, selling, or reporting on something in your daily meetings. These are generally brief, informal "minipresentations." Right now, let's consider those of a more formal nature where you don't just talk extemporaneously when an opportunity arises, but are scheduled to occupy center stage, uninterrupted, for an appreciable time. Not the quick interjections in meetings, as discussed in the previous chapter...nor a long speech before a large audience, as covered in the next chapter...but something in between.

Why So Many Presentations Are Disasters

Does the following modus operandi sound familiar?

The presentation team opens the show with a handout folder delineating all the main points they'll be talking about. Those receiving this written exposition immediately begin reading it so they'll be a step ahead of the presenters. They zero in on the summary at the end so they'll be prepared for any requests for money or approvals and can fortify themselves against being too easily persuaded.

Throughout the session, some continue to browse through the folder, rather than pay attention to what the speakers are saying. They don't miss much, because the verbal presentation is almost a duplicate of what's in the folder. So are the visuals shown on charts or a screen. These consist mostly of words, which the presenters read to their audience. This may be done on the assumption that those watching are illiterate, or because the wording is so small that only people with exceptional eyesight could possibly discern the characters.

If the session is lengthy, those sitting in a darkened room during a slide show may doze, since they already know what the presentation is leading up to. If the meeting is cut short (which may happen when previous meetings or unexpected crises upset the schedule), the presenters have to skip some crucial elements of their buildup and jump to a hasty climax.

In the question period at the end, someone raises a point not covered. No clear, forceful answer is given by the presenters, so others take over the discussion, introducing their speculations and arguing as to the facts.

That's the worst sort of scenario that can occur. What steps should you take to make sure your presentation is one of the best?

Three Important Questions

What Does Your Audience Really Want?

Before starting to write anything, or even to gather material, it's wise to reflect on who your audience will be and what their primary interests are.

This may not be difficult for an in-house presentation. If you must report to the finance committee, obviously they'll be interested in all the figures—not in a lengthy exposition of your wonderful marketing plan. Obversely, the marketing committee will want all the details of your selling plans, before you discuss costs. Just get yourself pointed in the right directions before you get rolling too fast with your preparations.

However, if you'll be facing outsiders, the most important step in your entire project may be solving the question, "What do they really want?" Remember, they don't care a damn about you, your firm, or the products or services you hope to sell them. A long exposition on the merits of your company and what you're offering is likely to draw nothing but yawns. But just one fact about how you can solve a difficult problem for your listeners can bring you success.

Problems Are the Key. Everyone has problems. Everyone is looking for help with them. Your starting point should be to look for the problem of concern to your listeners that you can alleviate.

For example, if you're trying to sell something to a company, have you talked to any of their customers? Have you visited their dealerships? Compared them with competitive dealerships? Listened to what competitive salespeople say about them? (You can be sure they'll know of any problems.)

Instead of beginning by talking about how good you are, suppose you start your presentation with a tape recording of what consumers are saying about the products or services of your prospects and their competitors. That'll get them on the edges of their chairs.

Or suppose you show comparative graphs of what you learned in a field survey? Or how about photographs of dealerships you visited, of customers you talked to, or of your own satisfied customers you've helped with similar problems?

It's not slick words that make a presentation sparkle. It's the use of shoe leather to go out after all the facts that may be vital to your audience. Do that, and you're halfway home to a successful conclusion.

What Do You Really Want?

You should be able to state it in one sentence. If you can't, you haven't yet thought about it sufficiently. When you begin your outline, write that one prime goal across the top of the paper, so you'll be sure to keep focusing on it. And *repeat* it throughout your presentation.

What Action Is Desired?

In a sales presentation, the action is obvious—you want an order and you need to ask for it, probably several times. But most other kinds of presentations are selling something too. Whatever it is you want your listeners to do, make sure they've committed themselves to it before you step off stage.

Often the purpose of a presentation is to *explain* something—a new program or procedure, for example. In such a case, you may assume no action is called for from your audience. But that's not always true. You'd best ask your listeners if they understand all aspects of the new program you've described, and if they agree with it. Unless you get that concurrence, and everyone knows it, the time may come when your new program bogs down because of a lack of understanding at the beginning.

Sometimes your purpose is to *enthuse*—perhaps to introduce dealers or salespeople to a new product. Again, you're selling. And you need to ask for action by calling on your audience to join in applause for the new arrival. If you can't stimulate an enthusiastic response at the moment of introduction, you'll never see much zeal down the road.

Even when your purpose is merely to *report* on some activity, you may be wise to ask for action before you sign off. Suppose it's a periodic report on what your department is doing. Such reports to higher management often present opportunities to request support for new plans; they may, in fact, be the best opportunities you'll ever get. So don't pass up any bets.

If your routine report can be the vehicle for sending up a trial balloon on some new idea you'd like to try, ask if your listeners agree that it has good potential. You may get lucky and receive a go-ahead, or at least permission to carry it forward to a more complete proposal. If you don't, you're no worse off than before.

Whatever type of presentation you're making—one to explain, enthuse, report, or plainly to sell—some sort of action is generally the payoff. No matter how smoothly the show goes, if you don't get *action* at the end, you've struck out!

Timing Strategies

A specific amount of time will probably be allotted for you to make your presentation. To be on the safe side, assume you won't get it all. Factors that can cut your promised time allotment are many: The meeting may start late or may be forced to end early because of some unforeseen crisis. There may be interruptions that will eat up your allotted time. Even if you go the full distance, the key listener (the person you really must influence) may leave early.

What can you do?

Bring in Your Main Points Early.   Structure your material so it won't be catastrophic if your show is cut short. Stating your main points early, you won't lose everything; then, time permitting, you can repeat and elaborate on them later. Also, this helps make your presentation concise—a good approach in any communication.

Stay Ahead of Schedule.   This gives you more time for questions. Or it could let you end early—a welcome surprise for your listeners!

Get on the Schedule Early.   Another thing you can do to avoid being hurt by a time squeeze is to get on the schedule as early as possible if you're one in a series of presenters at your office. Usually the secretary to the Big Boss draws up the schedule and doesn't care who comes first. If you ask for an early spot, you stand a good chance of getting it.

"You can all go in with the presentation now, but you'll have to finish by noon."

The advantages? In a meeting-packed day when time runs out just before noon, or before quitting time, who gets canceled or short-changed? The last one on the schedule. Also, when the top brass have to sit through many hours of reports, etc., they can't help becoming fatigued and a bit less attentive during the final sessions.

When to Try for the Last Spot.   Go the opposite way and try for the last spot if you're making one of several presentations to an outside company. For example, when a firm considers a change in major suppliers, such as a new advertising agency, it may invite as many as half a dozen contenders to make complex proposals. Because of their length, such presentations are often spread over a period of several days or weeks. By the time the last team unleashes its barrage of facts, figures, and visuals, the panel of judges is so groggy it can scarcely remember the groups who put on the earlier performances. You don't want to be one of them.

The Setting

Sometimes you can't do much about the conditions under which you perform. But, especially on your own turf, there are some things in the environment you can control:

- *Interruptions play havoc with a presentation.* In your own conference room, you can instruct your secretary that even though important guests may be expecting phone calls, messages should be routed to a receiver outside the room so people can be called quietly out of the session. (Phones don't belong in conference rooms anyway.)

- *Adequate light and ventilation are requisites.* A common mistake is to turn all the lights off when showing slides. Keep at least one light on; it's disconcerting to sit for any length of time listening to a voice from the darkness. Also, that takes the emphasis away from you, the key figure, and transfers it to a slide or movie machine.

- *Too much glare behind you isn't good either.* Try never to stand in front of a window when you're presenting. You can usually find some pretext to move away from backlighting, even in another person's office. When an audience looks at you for 10 minutes or more with sunlight glaring into their faces, their eyes recoil and so do their minds.

The Mood

Never, never start a presentation with an apology—about your lack of time for preparation, about missing information, the quality of your slides, anything. If something's deficient, *fix it* before you step in front of your audience.

You must start out upbeat and stay that way. Unless you indicate confidence and capability, why should anyone listen to you? Remember, it's not just what you say that determines your credibility, but *how you say it*. The best beginning is to indicate that you've brought interesting things of special relevance to your audience. Then deliver them.

Never, never hand out a printed folder at the start of a presentation. It's an interruption that destroys the mood. Put such material in the hands of your audience too soon, and they'll ignore you while they read it. If that's all you want, you might as well skip the meeting and just send them the folder.

And never to be caught stammering and apologizing at the end of a presentation, prepare for the nasty questions you hope will never arise. Sure, you've dug up all the information you want to reveal, and the script, visuals, and handout folder you've put together are beautiful. But don't stop there. Ask yourself what the most dreaded questions are that may come flying at you at the end of your performance—and figure out how to answer them. If you end up empty at that point, all the brilliance you've shown earlier goes down the drain. So do your homework thoroughly. Like a good scout, be prepared.

The Hardware

Don't let it dominate. *You* are the star of the show, so don't allow the machinery of a presentation to steal the spotlight. There's a wealth of audiovisual equipment available today, and all types have their useful supporting roles. No need to dwell at length here on the mechanics of using them; their sellers can give you advice on operating details if you require any. Just a few general comments that may be helpful...

The visual is not your audience. Don't talk to the projection screen or the flipchart; keep your face to your listeners as much as possible, which should be most of the time.

Slides.   Slides are great, but you should have a remote control on the projector so you can stand in front of the room where your audience can see you. There should also be some light near you (an overhead spot is best) so you're not in the dark. And stand at an angle—mostly toward the audience, slightly toward the screen. This allows you to follow the slides out of the corner of your eye without turning away from your listeners.

Movies.   They're intriguing, and invaluable in some situations, but they require a substantially darkened room. Also, they shut you out of the presentation entirely. They're best used only as a brief interlude to break up and enliven a very long session, or to provide dramatic on-site coverage of some distant action.

Overhead Projectors.   These have many advantages. You needn't darken the room for them. You can interject yourself into the visuals by drawing on the cells as you show them, moving graph lines, etc. The more of this action and motion you introduce, the better. The cells are inexpensive and can be prepared quickly. (The 3M company has an abundance of excellent folders that give not only ideas for using their projectors but also practical advice on the mechanics of meetings. I suggest you get them.)

Rear-Screen Projectors.   Available in small portable size with screens about a foot square, they're great for salespeople, especially those who sell big products they can't carry to prospects. Even a novice salesperson can make an impressive, accurate presentation with a professionally prepared strip film. No room darkening is required; you merely set the machine on a desk away from direct light and start the pictures (audio can be provided too). Your sales department may have these projectors. Maybe you could borrow one sometime for a different kind of presentation to a small group.

Writing Boards.   Whether the old messy chalkboards or the newer white plastic surfaces you write on with an erasable colored pen, writing boards are available in most conference rooms. They're informal, user-friendly, simple. In a short presentation, you can make your points interestingly with these basic visual aids.

Just remember, you don't want to do nothing but writing, which will keep the back of your head toward your audience. And you're not limited to words on the board; you can pen in such things as a line graph, a pie chart, a giant dollar sign. Even if you're not much of an artist, a simple chart or picture can be outlined on the board ahead of time with a faint yellow pencil line invisible to your audience. At the appropriate moment, you can sweep your pen over the guidelines as you talk.

Flipcharts.   Flipcharts are also old standbys that are simple and inexpensive. They, too, avoid the complications of screens and room darkening. Some people regard them as old-fashioned and unsophisticated for the modern age, but that depends on how you use them. Apply imagination, and a chart can rival slides in color and interest.

As with other visual aids, you should *keep words to a minimum*. Instead, put symbols, drawings, or photos on the pages, along with a few key words and phrases. There's no reason why an entire flipchart page can't be a big photo print, but how often have you seen such a simple, obvious graphic used? A chart will be as interesting, or as dull, as its designer.

For example, I recall a flipchart I once used as a teaser buildup on the benefits of a new packaging device. After a dozen pages of information, the final page was flipped up to disclose the colorful package itself, nestled in a recess built into the back of the chart. I pulled the small package out of its niche, placed it in front of the key person at the conference table, and proceeded to demonstrate how it worked. This dramatic (and successful) presentation would not have been possible with any of the other visual equipment discussed so far.

Posters.   Posters or other cardboard displays are simple devices with wide potential. A series of cards on an easel can be the most flexible of visual aids. They can be of various sizes and shapes, providing visual variety not possible with flipcharts, slides, or overhead projectors. They can be moved around, hung on walls, made free-standing, picked up and waved to emphasize a point. With such flexibility, cards can serve as "exclamation marks" you insert into a presentation to liven it up.

At the end of a dramatic presentation—perhaps one to introduce new products and/or programs to a sales organization—you might pull a cord to cause a giant cloth poster to unfurl on a back wall. That's effective showmanship at minimum cost.

Another example of flexibility is the fact that cards have two sides. Obvious, isn't it, but have you ever seen any use made of this? Suppose you want to emphasize that a new plan, product, or service offers the solution to several difficulties. On the front of a card, you can show what the problem is; then flip the card over to disclose the solution. Do this several times ... problem with gloomy picture, solution with bright cheery colors ... and you not only tell your story, but also repeatedly implant a strong subliminal image that your proposal will solve existing troubles.

This simple idea could be applied to almost any kind of problem-solving situation. It's not difficult at all, just different, which makes it attention-getting and effective. It even cuts in half the amount of cardboard you need to lug to your show.

Models or Samples. These can provide an excellent climax. For instance, after showing slides of the development and testing of a new product, there's nothing more dramatic than to let your audience see the real thing. Anticipate, however, that after you hand out samples of a small product or provide an opportunity to examine a large model, your presentation is over. You'll never recover the attention of your audience.

The Graphics

The kind of hardware you select—projectors, flipcharts, display cards—is not of prime importance. Any of them can enable you to produce a superb presentation, or a putrid one. What's really crucial is *what you put on the slides, charts, or cards*. It's the quality of the graphics that adds power to your words, focuses attention, provides dramatic impact, aids understanding, increases memorability.

The biggest mistake presenters make is to waste the power of their slides, etc., by filling them with words. *Words are not graphics*. Your audience doesn't need and doesn't like to see your audible message duplicated word-for-word on a screen or chart. That puts them to sleep! You need to wake people up with exciting visuals, with picturizations of your thoughts, with something they can *see*.

Example 1.   You need to present many statistics—dull stuff to look at if you just type them out. But they're always more interesting, and understandable, if you translate them into bar, line, or pie charts. And don't throw all the figures at your audience at once; reveal them one at a time in a sequential buildup.

You can also add motion as you reveal a bunch of statistics. On an overhead transparency, add the bars or pieces of the pie one by one. On a line graph, you can draw in the broad colored line as you report the changing figures. And if the sales figures are rising rapidly, make an issue of it by sketching a rocket at the end of the skyrocketing line. Your listeners may forget the exact figures, but they'll remember that simple, lively graphic.

Example 2.   You need to talk about markets, customers, or employees. All these relate to people. So instead of restricting yourself to words on slides or paper, why not introduce pictures of the people you're discussing? That requires a little work, but it can produce dramatic results.

Instead of hiding in your comfortable office and playing guessing games when you put together your presentation, get out and do some real research by talking to the customers, dealers, or employees on which the proposal is based. And take a camera (and maybe a tape recorder) with you. Your premises will be much more believable if you authenticate them with photos of actual people—the long-time customer, the first-time buyer, the dealer who refuses to carry your products—accompanied by quotes of what they said. Photographs make wonderful graphics; it's a pity they aren't used more often in presentations. And it's also a pity more research of this type isn't done at the start of more proposals; it might change some of the premises set forth.

Sizzle versus Fizzle

Presentations that fizzle may not be bad from an informational standpoint; they simply lack what it takes to hold attention and move an audience to some sort of mind change or action. If they can't do that, what good are they?

An interesting, stimulating manner of speaking is one of the things it takes to hold an audience. You'll get ideas on that from the next chapter, which is all about speaking. It'll suggest ways to control voice and tempo, how to employ opening grabbers and eyeballing, and how to get audience participation. Right now, let's concentrate on other elements that can add sizzle to a long, complex presentation.

Break It Up

Divide your presentation into segments of different kinds. Consider breaking it up with different presenters; instead of a one-person show, bring others into the act. Or break it up with different display devices. For example, if you use slides early in a presentation, don't go back to them later, but switch to a flipchart or display boards.

Change the Style and Color

Too many presentations are a dull gray in tone. After a series of graphs or charts, introduce a few photos or drawings. Don't be afraid of color either; it can provide a jolt of energy to stir a weary audience. For example, a flipchart doesn't have to be all black type on white paper. At an important point, slip in a couple of pages solidly covered in bright colors with a few big white words or symbols on them. Smack your audience to attention!

Keep the Visuals Simple

Just the first glimpse at some flipcharts or slides is enough to make viewers wince—line after line of small type. Remember, words are not visuals. A slide, chart, or card shouldn't have more than a dozen words on it. Ideally, they should be limited to such things as titles for key points, a listing of important items, or a few figures to spell out the highs and lows on a graph. You supply all the other words verbally.

Talk, Don't Read

You'll find more about this in the next chapter, because it's the essence of speaking successfully to any audience. You should know the material you're presenting well enough that you can tell it to your audience either standing up alone or in synchrony with visuals (which will serve as notes for your subject matter as you glance at them). You shouldn't need to read from a script or, God forbid, from a screen or flipchart on which you've transcribed 30 minutes of conversation.

Dramatize

Dramatize at least one memorable point. The previous pages have suggested several ways to add drama: photos, big graphics, bold color, three-dimensional models, adding a cartoon to a graph, unfurling a giant poster, flipping a card over to show the back, introducing a tape recording. Anything to break the monotony and add a bit of sizzle.

The best dramatic touches can emerge naturally if you think about the one idea you want most to implant in your listeners' minds—and what can symbolize or focus attention on that key point. Here are a few examples of how to work out simple dramatizations in common situations.

A Change of Size Can Provide Emphasis. Suppose you're using a stack of display cards and want to emphasize one particular point. Just use a bigger card. From behind your easel, pull out a giant card with your key idea on it. Not complicated at all, but it'll focus your viewers' attention where you want it.

Picturizations Can Do the Job. Suppose you want to emphasize a rapid growth rate in a certain activity—one that deserves increased support but may not get it because of budget tightening. (Sound familiar?) As you present your figures, you could tie them in with a growth symbol—perhaps a picture of a flower in a pot. With each succeeding statistic, you make the flower larger. Your final slide or page would be filled with a huge flower picture as you estimate the growth achievable *if* your project gets all the nutrients it requires.

You could go still further by handing out jars of Rapid Grow plant food at the finale and expressing the hope that your listeners' gardens will flourish, as you expect your project to do if properly nourished. Corny? Of course. But I'll bet your audience would go away smiling and remembering they ought to support you so you can bring in a bumper crop.

There are many other ways to symbolize growth. It could be pictures of a child being measured for height while standing next to a series of bar charts.

Add a Human Touch. Most things you talk about in a presentation—markets, sales, corporate organization, factory operation, customers, dealers, competitors, employees, etc., etc.—involve people. So bring actual people into the act.

As suggested earlier, you can accomplish this with photographs. Or with tape recordings of interviews.

Another way to make those people coplayers on the stage with you is with life-size cardboard displays. Your local display company can make up two or three full-size standup figures, similar to the Bartles and James posters you may have seen in your neighborhood liquor store. They can mount some of your photo faces onto drawings of men and women. You can introduce these realistic people to your audience and move them around to follow your script. Realign them in order of importance ... tell what their interests are ... set them up on a higher or lower level ... turn them around ... knock them down.

There's no rule that requires all presentations to use the same kinds of visual aids and all look alike. Nothing except a lack of imagination.

Help! Help! Help!

Only a fool is afraid to call for help. Get all you can.

Computer Graphics

The computers in your office are one source of assistance when you're trying to create an impressive, professional-looking presentation. No doubt you're familiar with the kinds of charts, graphs, distinctive headlines, drawings, and stock cartoons they can provide for desktop publishing. Computer-generated graphics are adaptable not only for your handout folder, but can also be made into slides or transparencies and blown up for flipcharts and cards. And they cost you nothing.

If you're not a computer expert, many others in your company must be. Ask for their help.

Outside Sources of Help

Art studios can create outstanding designs and visual ideas. There's cost involved, but it's modest in relation to the difference it can make in the looks and effectiveness of your production.

The people at your advertising agency are a versatile source of help. If you have authority to enlist their aid, and depending on your budget, they can supply a smorgasbord of services—ranging from basic ideas and research to writing, photos, artwork, finished slides, charts, movies, staging, etc. One agency at which I worked even maintained a department to create and stage annual new-product introductory shows that were Broadway-type extravaganzas.

Whatever the size of the project, an important advantage is that a good ad agency has in-depth knowledge of your business. Its staff can provide valuable counsel as well as technical expertise for a major presentation.

10
Our Speaker Today...

What is this? An audience or an oil
painting?   MILTON BERLE

What do most Americans fear most of all? In the *Book of Lists,* you'll find that the thought of making a speech is more likely to cause clammy hands and terror in the heart of the average person than are thoughts of death or physical danger.[1] It's number one on the "fear" list.

Of course, you're not the average person, so you're not going to be terrified if required to get up in front of an audience, but you might have some qualms if speechmaking is new to you. In any event, you want to come off at your best, because a public appearance of this sort is a great opportunity—a chance to show many people that you're a winner when it comes to communication.

The difficulties are not insurmountable; the techniques you need to follow are mostly common-sense approaches, simple enough for anyone to use. They are all listed in this chapter. If you'll just follow them, and do some practicing, you'll do OK. On the platform, you'll perform like a pro.

---

[1]*Book of Lists,* compiled by David Wallechinsky, Irving Wallace, and Amy Wallace, Morrow, New York, 1977.

Keep Your Cool

Just in case you're a bit squeamish about addressing an audience, let me set your mind at ease about the nervousness that public speaking can cause.

It may make you feel better to learn that even professionals get a little tense before a performance. For example, theater people refer to the malady known as "stage kidneys"—the urge to run to the bathroom one more time, just before the curtain goes up.

Pavarotti and His Handkerchief

If you're an opera lover, you may know about the handkerchief twisting of Luciano Pavarotti when he gives a solo concert. The man many regard as the finest singer today gets nervous when he must stand alone on a stage. He's gotten in the habit of holding a handkerchief in his hand; it's his security blanket. But he performs superbly well.

So you see, a bit of tension is normal. In fact, it's even beneficial because it keeps you alert, not careless.

I've been speaking before sizable audiences since I was 16 and now make part of my living as a speaker at conventions. I still feel the adrenalin during an introduction, but even when the unforeseeable happens—the public-address system going haywire, a projector malfunctioning, or a preceding speaker who won't finish on time—I've learned to go on with the show calmly. Maybe that's because the worst calamity I've ever encountered on stage happened to me early in life. I'll never forget it.

The Ultimate Embarrassment

I was 17 years old and a member of our high school's debating team. We had reached the finals of the citywide tournament and were to appear at a downtown auditorium, where a local radio station would air the championship debate. It was my first broadcast appearance—the big time!

That didn't make me too nervous. Waiting in the wings, I felt good and looked good, too, I thought. I was wearing a new suit of creamy-white linen for the occasion.

Everything was fine until I decided to get a quick gulp of water before going on stage with my partners. That was my undoing.

I had neglected to notice that the fountain worked two ways. Twist the handle one way and the water burbled up toward your mouth; a twist the other way (which I mistakenly chose) shot a strong stream *downward* so you could fill a cup. Only I had no cup there. The water splattered all down the front of my ice-cream-white trousers, creating a spectacular dark stain on the pale fabric.

I froze in horror as I stared down at myself. It looked exactly as if I'd wet my pants. My feet didn't want to move, but my partners pulled me on stage. I tried to hide behind them as we moved forward, and was able to sit down for a while, hiding my accident. But when it came my turn to speak, I had to walk front and center where there was only a slim microphone between me and all those faces staring at the dumb kid with the wet pants. Fortunately, no one snickered.

I didn't die, though I wanted to. And yes, we won the decision. (Maybe the judges felt sorry for me.)

Many mishaps on stage have happened to me since, but nothing has bothered me half as much as that adolescent embarrassment. And I know now that the audience takes far less notice of irregularities than the speaker does. The people out there just want the show to go on, so keep cool and give it to them.

Your Role as a Teacher

When you speak from a platform, as a businessperson, your main role is likely to be that of a teacher, a bringer of interesting and useful information. Like any good teacher, you should be well supplied with that information, bubbling over with your subject.

 When the heart is afire, some sparks will fly out of the mouth.   THOMAS FULLER

You Can't Have Too Much Material

If you're scheduled to give a half-hour talk, it's best to have a full hour's supply of material to work from. Or more! All too often, it's the other way around: The speaker tries to stretch a few minutes worth of information into a long harangue. It doesn't work. You don't fool an audience that way; you put it to sleep.

The most important part of any speech is the preparation that precedes it. Doing a thorough job then is the all-important foundation for everything that follows.

You're Giving a Talk—Not a Reading

An effective teacher doesn't read from a textbook. The same principle applies when you're trying to impart information or ideas from a platform. You can't hold your audience's attention—or gain its respect—if you read all your material.

You encounter a lack of attention when you read to an audience, because you can't maintain eye contact. There's no rapport. And there's a lack of respect if you read everything, because your audience assumes you don't know the material very well—you can't really be an expert.

You Don't Need a Crutch, but a Helping Hand Is Fine

A speaker who uses a manuscript as a crutch to be grasped tightly throughout an exposition, from start to finish, is doomed to give a miserable performance. I've heard executives of major companies drone on from a sheaf of papers—so have you—and they don't realize what an awful spectacle that is. It makes them look stupid, because the audience assumes that someone else wrote the speech for them (which probably is the case), and they can't even read the script smoothly in many instances.

If you are a senior executive, there's nothing wrong with conserving your time and benefiting from some other people's ideas by getting the assistance of a speech writer. That's an intelligent thing to do. But take the script, give it your own input and special emphases, and turn it into a conversational talk you can give without bobbing your head up and down from a piece of paper.

That's not as difficult as it may seem.

A TelePrompTer Is the Ultimate Aid

With the miracles of modern science, it is possible to follow a detailed script without appearing to do so. You can use a TelePrompTer if you're in a theater setting or a TV studio that will permit such mechanics.

Many a time you've watched a skilled performer like Ronald Reagan read from the moving band so smoothly that you never even see his eyes twitch as they scan the words. If you go this mechanical route, though, be sure the machinery is properly installed and in good working order; if it slips a gear, you've had it.

The TelePrompTer You Hold in Your Hand

You don't really need a mechanical device to help you keep your speech on track. A simple procedure is to read it a few times to get it in mind; then transfer the main thoughts to a couple of small cards you can hold inconspicuously in your hand. You may not even need them if you get your talk well memorized, but they'll be there for a peek if necessary.

All you put on these cards is a few crucial signals. These consist of one word, or a brief phrase of not more than three or four words, to signal you the main ideas you want to be sure to cover.

All You Need Is a Couple of Cards. A couple of cards will suffice to hold the key words for a half-hour talk. And if you really know your subject as you should, these signals will enable you to stay on the track and not forget anything crucial. Sure, you'll leave out a few words of your script, if you started with a written speech, but that's not nearly as important as the spontaneity you gain. You won't have to be bobbing up and down from a manuscript. You'll be free of the confinement of a podium, and you can look at your audience instead of at a piece of paper.

Color-Key Your Notes. When you write out your note cards, you'll find it helpful to use pens of different colors. If you have a dozen lines on your card, for example, break it down into color bands of three or four lines each. Then when you glance down at your reminder card, your eye doesn't have to sort out the whole array. You can quickly spot the green area or the red area that identifies a certain subject.

Suggestions for Practicing

Practice before a Mirror. When you rehearse your speech, do it before a mirror. This enables you to become at ease not only with the words but also with the facial expressions and gestures you'll be using. It should be a full-length mirror so you can see your entire body language.

Keep on Practicing. After you think you know your speech well, rehearse it some more. Get so familiar with it that you won't have to worry about what comes next, and can speak with assurance without constantly looking at your notes.

Use a Tape Recorder. While you're practicing, tape your speech and play it back. You'll get a better idea of how your voice sounds, and you can analyze where your speech is weak or rough. If you have access to a videotape camera, that's ideal. It will enable you to study the visual effectiveness of your facial and body movements, as a mirror does, only you can rerun it as many times as you wish.

Estimate the Length. You'll want to time your speech before making your appearance. Remember, you tend to talk faster when by yourself than you will on the platform, so figure that in front of an audience (with a few gestures and pauses) you'll go a trifle longer.

If you're not used to free-form speaking and have a manuscript all typed out, you can figure that the average person talks to an audience at the rate of about 125 words per minute. Count your words and divide by that number.

How to Hammer Your Message Home

Don't be afraid to repeat. You can't underestimate the ability of an audience to miss or forget your most precious gems of wisdom.

Surely you've heard many times about *the rule of three* in speechmaking: First tell them what you're about to tell them. Then actually tell them. Then tell them what you told them.

That's a good format for any speech. I'd like to go further and suggest that the main points you're going to emphasize and reemphasize be kept extremely simple. Even if you repeat, people can't remember more than three or four simple points, at the most.

If you want the brutal truth, you'll be lucky if your audience can recall even *one* central idea the next day. Figure out what that one most important thought is. Crystalize it into a memorable phrase, if you can. You may supplement it with a variety of supporting facts and stories, but try to point them all at your one big central point.

Centuries ago, Marcus Cato conducted his successful campaign of rhetoric with the phrase "Carthage must be destroyed," repeated over and over in speech after speech. That's what it took to persuade his compatriots. The persuasion process hasn't changed any since that time.

Your Role as an Entertainer

Whether you like it or not, whenever you're on stage, *you're in show business*!

Yes, your primary mission may be as a teacher bringing important information. But even in our educational institutions, the best teachers know they must liven up their presentations if they expect to hold attention and get their messages across. So make it easy on yourself; make use of the proven techniques of professional entertainers; make your audiences perk up and maintain rapt attention. You can do it.

Take a Tip from Johnny

Do you ever watch the Johnny Carson show? If so, you may agree with me that he makes the first few minutes of it the most interesting part, or tries to. The rest of the program may be filled with vapid chitchat from dull guests you've seen several times before, but Johnny gives it his best shot when he walks through that curtain.

He may appear dressed in some outrageous costume that gets a laugh. If not, he'll be wearing a suit you've not seen before—never a standard outfit from week to week—so you have something new to look at. Near the opening of the show, he may go into his "Swami" act, donning a huge feathered turban while he thinks of the questions to go with the answers picked from sealed envelopes. That's a popular routine of his that everyone seems to listen to. Or he entertains you with his popular takeoff on the day's news: "There were heavy rains in Santa Barbara yesterday. How hard did it rain? Well, I'll tell you."

Don't Ever Forget the Grabber

Carson is a gifted entertainer—far better than you or I will ever be. Why, then, does he strain so hard to start off each show with a bang? Because he knows that even with his charisma and popularity, he must *grab you* right at the start. Otherwise, if the opening doesn't look lively, you may click the dial of your set to some competing program, and that isn't what NBC is paying him several million a year for.

Readiness to Move Up the Ladder

We certainly believe in communication at The Coca-Cola Company. It has helped to make ours the world's most widely known trademarked product. In addition to our corporate communicating, what our people say and the way they conduct themselves in the communities around us have played an important role in the high regard Coca-Cola enjoys around the world. Those contacts may be as small and informal as the conversation at a PTA meeting, or they may involve one of our executives addressing a large group, but whatever the occasion, that person speaking represents Coca-Cola to his or her audience.

We encourage our people to communicate effectively by being themselves, by knowing their subjects and audiences, and by speaking directly and listening attentively. The ability to do these things well is definitely a factor in how we judge the readiness of our managers to move up the corporate ladder.

ROBERTO C. GOIZUETA, CHAIRMAN & CEO
The Coca-Cola Company

The First Minute Is the Most Important

Remember, you're assuming the dual roles of teacher and entertainer. Like Johnny, you're walking on stage, and you'd better start out with something interesting. Otherwise, you'll lose your audience.

No, they can't switch channels, and they'll be too polite to get up and walk out, but they can tune out mentally if you give them the all-too-usual dull fare. That means stepping behind a lectern where they can't see you, shuffling a bunch of papers, and opening the festivities with thrilling remarks about how pleased you were to be invited to this august gathering.

You can do better than that—a lot better. Without trying to be a comedian (don't tell any jokes, please), you can take a tip from Johnny and use some of the simple basics of showmanship to let your audience know right off that this is going to be an interesting program.

In that first minute or so, you either get off to a running start or you cause your listeners to slump down in their chairs. And it's slow, hard work getting them perked up again.

How to Start the Show

You're not an actor or comedian, and shouldn't try to be one, but by now you've surmised that you're in show business when you agree to speak to a large audience. At least, some of the principles of the theater (and of selling) are going to help you present yourself and your company in an effective way.

Look 'Em Over and Let 'Em See You

It pays to mix with the audience before the program starts. Usually, you'll be speaking in a large meeting room, perhaps at a luncheon or dinner. Get there early. As soon as you've checked any mechanical aids you may have (such as a microphone or projector), use the time to mix with the people you're going to address. Walk around to shake hands and say hello to as many as possible. This accomplishes four things:

1. It Prepares You Physically. Limbers up your body as you move around. Warms up your voice as you talk.

2. It Helps You Mentally. Gives you a chance to size up the audience and determine the sort of people in it. If it's a business group, are they mostly managers, a lot of salespeople, many dealers or jobbers, factory supervisors or engineers? How many women versus men? What's their vocabulary like? You may want to make some adjustments to your talk if you've misjudged the group in some way.

The mental benefits also include giving you a chance to feel more at ease because you'll get a warm response in such a pretalk get-together. You'll meet some nice people and build confidence that this is going to be a pleasant and successful experience for you.

3. It Breaks Down the Initial Barrier between You and the Audience. You're a strange animal coming into the midst of a new group when you prepare to mount the platform. Just as animals circle each other warily at first, an audience sort of sits back and sizes up a speaker who first appears before them. Sometimes this chilly period lasts for quite a while before an audience warms up. By giving a lot of people a chance to look at you beforehand, you can greatly reduce the warm-up period.

4. It Plants Friends throughout the Audience. Brief as your hellos may be, they establish you as a friendly, likable person. You're a celebrity of sorts, as a speaker, yet you've gone out of your way to make a gesture of friendship to Mary and Jennifer and George. They like that; they like you, and in a few minutes they're going to be seated throughout the room with their smiling faces pointed at you. You'll have a warm audience right from the start; they'll want you to succeed.

Create Your Best Setting

If your presentation is to be given in an auditorium—as in a commencement address or a new-product introduction—you're lucky, because a stage eliminates many of the distractions that other settings pose. You have room to move around and there's no competing noise.

However, let's assume you're making a talk to a business or civic group in a hotel meeting room, possibly right after a meal. Let's hope you're the only speaker on the program, or at any rate the first one, because if your audience has been subjected to a previous speaker for half an hour or more, your listeners may already have foggy minds and sore bottoms. That's a handicap for you. So is a situation where a dining-room staff is clearing away dishes while you're being introduced. You should realize that hotel waiters and waitresses hate after-dinner speakers and always clunk china dishes together as loudly as possible when they're clearing tables. How do you deal with such hazards?

Don't Fight the Noise

Many a good presentation gets off to a bad start because a nervous speaker feels it's obligatory to start into his or her talk instantly on being introduced, even if the situation makes that a disaster. That's not the thing to do. If there's a problem, the only sensible thing is to alleviate it as best you can.

For example, instead of trying to drown out noisy waiters, it's better to stand up and say, *"That was a good meal. I'm full, and I'm glad I have a chance to stand up now and stretch a bit. Why don't you do the same? Let's all stand up for a minute while the waiters get the dishes cleared away."*

Call for a Seventh-Inning Stretch

You can do something similar if you've been preceded by one or more long-winded speakers. You might say, *"Well, you've heard all about our new products. Now let's get prepared to think about marketing them. While we make that transition, how about standing up for a few minutes and stretching our legs and other places? Etc., etc."*

Better yet, of course, there should be a break between speakers.

For whatever reason you do it, the pause that refreshes is a good gambit. It not only gains time for you in a bad situation, but it also does your audience a favor, and any salesperson will tell you that it establishes a receptive frame of mind. It also aids in the following.

Let 'Em Look at You

As indicated previously, an audience needs to look you over for a few moments before those people really tune in to what you say. They start looking when the introduction begins. So realize you're "on stage" as of that moment. Don't fuss with papers or watch the introducer at that time; instead, look out at the people. Look alert and pleasant.

Don't Hide Behind the Lectern

Most after-dinner or after-luncheon speeches take place, unfortunately, back of a table with a lectern on it. This situation doesn't allow your audience to see you very well.

The only redeeming feature about a lectern is that it's a crutch for speakers who need to read from a manuscript. If you're a novice speaker, unsure of yourself, you may require that assurance of having all the words in front of you in black and white. If so, you won't be any worse than the average nonprofessional speaker, but try to get away from a script as much as your self-confidence will allow.

Move to the Side When You Say Hello

Stand *beside* the lectern for a minute, even if you're going to get behind it for a reading during most of your allotted time. Usually an after-dinner speaker is seated right next to the lectern, so you can just stand up in front of your chair for a while. That'll give people their opportunity to see you better, at least at the start. During that period, you can make your first few remarks.

If you must read, practice doing it with as little looking down as you can. Eye contact is very important, as I'll discuss later.

Highlighting a Manuscript Builds Confidence

One thing that will help you avoid a word-for-word reading is to highlight a few words or headings on each page with a colored pen. With some practice, you'll find that you start to use your manuscript pages much like brief notes. You just glance down from time to time at the key words, proceeding with the reassurance that you have those pages to cling to, but not needing to bury your nose in the script.

Once you get used to speaking enough that you can do it with no more than a note card in your hand, you can get away from a lectern altogether. Sometimes you're still locked in behind a table. But even then you can move around a bit, use a few gestures, and give your audience at least a waist-up view instead of their seeing you only from the chin up.

About Microphones

Wherever possible in a "banquet" setting, I like to get around in front of the table. Generally, a lectern microphone can be lifted out of its bracket and hand-held, so I can stand where I wish. Generally, if arrangements are made ahead of time with the meeting organizers, a lapel mike can be provided with a long plug-in cord.

In either case, I can free myself from being locked in behind that wooden stand. I can walk around to the front of the speaker's table where it's possible to move about, gesture freely, and get closer to the audience both physically and psychologically.

Your First Few Words

There are a couple of things you should do very early in your talk, and they go together. One is ...

You Must Establish Credibility

Probably whoever introduced you will already have outlined your expertise in the field you're discussing. Yet during the initial time when your listeners are sizing you up, it's good to reinforce the impression that you really know what you're talking about.

You don't do this with any braggadocio. It must be low-key—perhaps transmitted in the form of a story that relates to your experience. A bit of humility may even add to its effectiveness.

For example: *"I thought I knew something about economics, just because I had a graduate degree in that field. But during the eight years I lived in Brazil and Argentina, and the four years at our international headquarters in Switzerland, I found I had to change a lot of my ideas about how the world operates. Let me tell you about three things that really shocked me."*

Notice in this example that the speaker is admitting in a likable manner that she wasn't as smart as she thought at first, but is nevertheless transmitting to us that she (1) has a graduate degree in her discipline, (2) learned much more after leaving graduate school, (3) has had many years of international experience, and (4) discovered three momentous economic facts that, if they were shocking to her, are likely to be revelations to us.

Hit Your Listeners with a Grabber

The other thing you want to do in the first couple of minutes is to hit your listeners with a grabber—some sort of statement that's controversial or unusual enough to grab their attention. It should illustrate or lead into the key theme of your speech.

This grabber may follow immediately after what you say to establish your credibility and/or your similarity of experience with your audience's. Or the grabber may be part of it. In the example just given of the economist with worldwide experience, the talk might continue: *"One thing I learned is that what's happening today in a back alley in São Paulo or Sri Lanka can have as much effect on our business as what's happening in the laboratories of our biggest competitor."*

A Prop Can Be Your Grabber

Let's suppose you're addressing the subject of increased government regulations—dull stuff. In this case you might hold up a fat volume of the *Congressional Record* and say, *"Do you know what's in this book? It contains 3168 new laws and regulations, all created last year. I'll bet at least 100 of these new laws and government rules affect your business— maybe could even land you in jail—and you probably don't even know what most of them are."*

Now that you've grabbed them, you can go on to explain at length what you mean and what you propose people should do about it.

The Worst Way to Start a Talk

Never, never begin by saying you're sorry—about anything! Unfortunately, nervousness in a speaker often expresses itself in the form of an apology.

Don't tell the audience you're sorry your voice is raspy today. It probably sounds fine to them ... until you call attention to it.

Don't apologize for your lack of expertise in public speaking, or in any phase of your subject. If you do, you're telling your listeners ahead of time that you don't belong on the platform and that they're going to waste their time listening to you.

Tricks of the Trade

Signals from the Rear Can Be Helpful.   Sometimes you're able to put a friend in the back row. If you have that opportunity, ask him to sit at the back of the auditorium or meeting room and signal you about the acoustics.

If he gives you the "OK" sign when you first start speaking, you won't have to go through the distraction of asking the audience as a whole if the microphone is working. And if anything goes wrong during your talk (perhaps you're not speaking directly into the mike), he can signal with a wave of the hand to bring you back on track.

If You're Nervous, Take a Deep Breath. Everyone gets nervous at times. Don't let it throw you. The quick, easy way to ease the jitters is simply to take a few deep breaths.

This calms you down. And slows you down. The latter is important because people tend to talk too fast anyway when they're on stage, especially if they're uptight.

So remember, *breathe deeply, talk slowly*. And everything's going to turn out fine.

How to Introduce a Personal Touch

Don't be afraid to use personal pronouns. Tell the listener, "This will help *you*." Tell what *we* know and what will affect *us*.

You needn't hesitate to use the word "I" either. You're not being conceited when you tell about yourself. That's what the people came to hear—your experiences and your knowledge.

Stories about you and your friends are especially useful. They let you get a point across in a palatable and memorable way. One of the most successful, spellbinding "speechmakers" of all time, Jesus of Nazareth, mostly just told stories or parables. A parable is a brief story illustrating a moral attitude or a religious principle.

How Funny Are You?

Funny stories are another thing. When the speaker of the day starts out with, *"I just heard a funny story,"* much of the audience isn't likely to believe it, either before or after the story has been told. Maybe you're an exception; maybe you're another Steve Martin or Roseanne Barr. But if you're that good, you don't need to read this chapter.

And if you aren't, don't try to be a comedian. Just concentrate on being a sincere professional, business, or civic leader who has some interesting stories and provocative facts to transmit in an informal, chatty, friendly manner.

The Importance of Eyeballing

Eyeballing is a vital personal factor in successful speechmaking. Throughout your talk, you want to make eye contact with people throughout the audience. That's why I've made such a point about the negative effects of constantly looking at a script instead of at the people before you.

Eyeballing establishes a magical electrical contact between you and the one person you're making eye contact with at that moment. It draws that person to you, and it relaxes you. Look at her. Look at him. And *talk to just that one woman or man at a time, as if the two of you were all alone.* That takes your nervousness away, and it gives your talk warmth and friendliness.

How to Get Audience Participation

Once you've progressed to the point where you can get your audience to participate in your presentation, you know you're becoming a good speaker. This helps in both of your functions—those of a teacher and an entertainer. The most effective way to teach is not to stand up and lecture the pupils, but to use the Socratic technique of having them participate in the exploratory process. And the best way to get an audience on your side is to make the members of it feel a part of the act.

I believe that encouraging some audience participation at the very beginning of a presentation is especially good because it warms people up quickly. For example, when I was promoting my last book, a biography of Norman Rockwell, I discovered that if I asked my audience to recollect some of the artist's paintings and tell me about them, I could readily get replies from all over the auditorium. And the people warmed up instantly as they remembered favorite works by an artist they loved. After two or three minutes, I'd call a halt to the outpouring of recollections. By then I had the audience with me, and could go on to point out why people could recall details of pictures created 20 or more years ago.

The Value of Questions

The technique of audience participation is not difficult to master. In essence, *all you do is ask a question or questions.* I merely asked people to describe their favorite Rockwell paintings. You can ask questions about some aspect of the subject you're addressing.

Audience participation through the use of questions is also a great way to emphasize a point in the middle of a presentation. After covering a certain problem or precept, you stop and quiz someone about it. The question you throw out at someone in the audience reiterates your point. And the brief quiz breaks up your monologue.

Keep the Juices Flowing with the Three T's

Energy is an important part of public speaking. Believe me, it's hard work if you do it right, because to hold an audience you must keep an electric flow going between you and your listeners. Otherwise, your presentation dies.

We've already covered some ways to keep the juices flowing between you and your audience: eyeballing first one person and another, audience participation, starting out with an exciting grabber, telling stories.

There are three other elements to utilize. I call them the three T's.

Tone.   You want to alter your tone of voice as you go along. A monotone is soporific. Start out in your average, strong voice. After a while, when you come to something you wish to emphasize, drop your voice almost to a whisper. Yes, a lowering of the voice is a good attention-getter; we don't want to miss anything that might be a whispered secret. And of course, let your voice rise and expand too. Build to a crescendo, and then drop back to the middle tone again.

> *People will believe anything if you*
> *whisper it.*   THE FARMER'S ALMANAC

Tempo.   Just as you want to vary the tone of your voice, so should you alter the tempo at which you speak. Shift gears once in a while. And pause. The amateur speaker is afraid to stop when talking, but a brief silence...or even a long one...will often get more attention than anything else you can do. A pause is often effective after a question or when you repeat an especially significant point.

While we're talking about tempo, remember that the novice speaker tends to talk much too fast when addressing a large audience.

- **The larger the room you're in, the longer it takes for your voice to reach the far corners.**
- **If you rattle on at great speed, half the people won't know what you're saying.**
- *Slow down, slow down, slow down!*

Tactics.   These are the maneuvers or devices you use to attack the problem by a different route. Throwing out a question to the audience is one. Another tactic is to switch from voice alone to the use of a visual—a chart or slide, or a prop of some sort.

Interjecting gestures is another basic tactic. You can point at someone in the audience. You can throw up your hands, spread out your arms, shake your head, move around.

How to Handle Interrupters

If you're lucky, you won't ever have any out-and-out hecklers in your audience, but sometimes you run across an ill-mannered person who wants to interrupt with a question or comment in the middle of a talk.

When you spot people who seem to be bouncing up and down and indicating a desire to interrupt or disagree (perhaps starting to thrust a hand up), don't focus on them. Don't give them eye-to-eye contact, because once you look straight at them, they'll interpret that as permission to speak. So if you don't want that, keep your gaze moving in other directions.

Sometimes you'll get an interruption or unfriendly comment whether you want it or not. In that case, don't encourage that person further. You can say, "Thank you for your comment (or opinion). Now I see someone else over on the right side who wants to say something. Let's hear from her."

How to Handle Questions

At the end of a talk where you're offering a lot of information, it's customary (though certainly not obligatory) to ask if there are any questions. This can be a lively and stimulating period. It can also be a dull letdown.

It's a downer if you ask for questions and receive in response only blank stares and silence. Don't let the silence drag on too long; that's no way to end your presentation—with a period of nothing. After your invitation, pause just three or four seconds for a response. If you see no hands go up, say, "Well, I guess I must have covered the subject thoroughly. I thank you for your attention, etc." And leave the platform.

Repeat the Question

Sometimes the questioner will speak so softly that few people can hear what's asked. Or the question will be so rambling and involved (maybe two questions strung together) that it can be confusing to the audience and maybe to you as well. In such instances, you should repeat the question. You may want to rephrase it, perhaps saying, "I believe what you're asking is [state it]. Is that right?"

Besides clarifying the question, this rephrasing or restating also gives you a few extra seconds to formulate your answer. So you may use this technique even if the question is clear, but difficult. It's better than hemming and hawing.

Always End on a High Note

Although a question period may be necessary, it's not a lively way to end your presentation. After all, the dying down of the questions is a placid situation. Give your audience another shot of energy and enthusiasm when you close off the questions. You want your viewers to go away remembering that this was a lively, interesting session.

In just a sentence, repeat your main theme—that one key thought you hope they'll retain. And tell 'em you want them to remember it.

> *A mighty thing is eloquence. Nothing so much rules the world.*   POPE PIUS II

Some Dos and Don'ts

Do	Don't
• Talk to people in the audience before the program starts. It will warm them up, and you too.	• Don't panic. Always remember that your audience wants you to succeed.
• Start off with a grabber.	• Don't read a speech word for word. Even if you must use a script, just glance at key words you've marked. Look up at the audience most of the time.
• Slow down, slow down, slow down when you speak. Take a few deep breaths before you begin.	
• Be as natural as possible.	• Don't be afraid to repeat your main thoughts. Several times.
• Eyeball your audience. Talk to one person at a time.	• Don't put your hands in your pockets. Use them for at least a few simple gestures.
• Pause for emphasis from time to time.	
• Vary your tone of voice, tempo, and tactics.	• Don't stand immobile. Move around a bit. Look energetic.
• Tell stories—about yourself and others. People like to hear about people.	• Don't try to be funny unless you're really good at it.
• Get personal. Use personal pronouns.	• Don't apologize.
• Be lively and energetic.	• Don't run on too long. Say what you have to say, and then quit.
• Keep coming back to a central theme.	

11
Your Interview on TV or Radio

Imagine the light above the TV camera is
your mother, and talk to Mom.
Donald Walton

As you move up in your career, you'll gain visibility. Sooner or later, you're likely to be invited to appear on a talk show or special-interest program to be interviewed about some newsworthy business activity or civic involvement. An interview on TV or radio is always an important event—even for someone of high established stature—because it provides an intimate close-up that will reach a wide audience.

When your turn comes to face the camera and microphone, you want to make the most of this opportunity to project your specialized knowledge and likable personality in the most favorable way possible. And you can. There are several steps—simple, but too often overlooked—that can help you avoid common mishaps and assure that you come across like a pro in the electronic media.

First, don't forget the basic principles discussed in the previous chapter; they apply to a broadcast audience as well as to a live one:

- Be as natural as possible.

- Speak clearly and slowly.

- Don't try to be funny if you're not.

- If asked a question that's the slightest bit confusing, clarify it before answering.

- Decide on one central thought you'd like to leave with your audience. Come back to it repeatedly as opportunities arise.

If you follow these basic principles of communication, just as you do when making a speech, you're well on your way to a successful broadcast. However, there are some peculiarities in interviews and in the electronic media, especially in television. Here's what you should know...

How to Look Your Best

Bright lights and extreme closeness are two elements that make you look different on TV than you do when facing an audience in a conference room or auditorium. The brilliant lamps in a TV studio wash some of the color out of your face and create glare against certain materials. Instead of being several feet or many feet from a live audience, you are brought almost nose to nose with your TV audience when the camera zooms in. Here's how to compensate for those factors.

Avoid White Garments.   They act as reflectors to the bright lights. On TV, a pale-blue shirt or blouse will appear to be white, but without the glare. So will a light-cream or beige garment.

Avoid Bulky Jewelry.   Metallic necklaces or earrings are a no-no for women. Any reflective jewelry creates distracting flashes of lights as you move before TV lights and cameras. Keep it small and simple.

Use Makeup.   Women need just a little more makeup than usual to avoid a washed-out appearance. A touch of makeup is not unthinkable for men either (the professionals use it). If you have a skin blotch or blemish that may not look good in a close-up, just a bit of pancake makeup can cover it. And if your eyebrows are thin and pale, a couple of light strokes with an eyebrow pencil can prevent your looking as if you have none.

Avoid Bold Patterns and Colors.   They stand out terribly on TV. Forget the jazzy tie or jacket, the fancy dress. If you're representing your business, look businesslike. You won't go wrong with solid-color clothes or subtle stripes.

Subtle Colors Are Best. A compromise between bold and blah. Not red or other bright hues. But I feel that businesspeople shouldn't come across to the public as stodgy either. On TV, black is worse than red; remember, this is a color medium. If you choose a blue suit or skirt—an excellent choice—don't select the ultraconservative midnight blue, much like your father or mother wore, but a slightly warmer tone. Maybe with an inconspicuous stripe of soft color blended into it. Or perhaps a conservatively patterned shirt or blouse with a solid-blue or solid-brown jacket.

Watch the Whiskers. If you're scheduled for an afternoon or evening interview, don't forget that the camera can magnify a man's beard. So be prepared for a last-minute once-over with your shaver.

Use the Restroom. As soon as you arrive at the studio or other filming location, head for the restroom. It can relieve the kidney pressure that sometimes accompanies tenseness. It also gives you a chance to check your appearance. If your hair is windblown, you can slick it back into place. And you can brush off any dandruff flakes that'll look like snow on the shoulders when the bright lights go on. Don't figure on doing these things later, because when you meet the interviewer and are introduced to the studio and its technicians, you may not have a chance to get free before show time.

How to Sound Your Best

The peculiarity of a broadcast interview is that it's a three-way conversation—between you, your host or hostess, and that mechanical device called a microphone. You can't ignore the mike, because it's a sensitive instrument that plays an important part in the process. Here are a few things to keep in mind.

Don't Touch the Mike. If your hand or anything you may be holding brushes against a lapel mike, or a table mike at a radio station, it'll send a crackling thunderstorm of sound over the airwaves.

Take Care with a Table Mike. Distance and direction can be critical. Your radio host or hostess should show you the proper distance to maintain from the microphone. If not, you can just watch what the interviewer does and follow suit. Keep your mouth at a constant distance from the instrument.

And *don't turn sideways* to talk if the interviewer is not directly facing you. You're not talking to that person; you're talking to the mike. Directly into it.

Keep Your Voice Low.   Without being aware of it, you may sometimes raise your voice when talking on the telephone or into a mike to a live audience. Both radio and TV are intimate media. The microphones pick up every whisper. It's as if the people listening out there are just a few inches from your face, and you're having an intimate conversation with them.

So keep it on the quiet side. But be animated. Try to vary your tone and rhythm (remember the advice in the previous chapter) so that you come across not as monotonous and dull, but as a lively and interesting conversationalist.

Above All, Be Cool

As Marshall McLuhan pointed out, the medium is the message, and television is a cool medium. Therefore, the impression you make during a broadcast may depend more on *how* you talk and look than on what you say.

So much for the theory. What does being cool on TV really mean? What should you do during a broadcast so you'll be perceived as a cool character who's really with it?

Examples are the easiest way to explain what goes over well on the air waves. Think of your favorites. Do they include Cosby, Carson, Walters, Donahue, Oprah, Rukeiser? Who else? They're examples of cool. Things they do, which you should try to emulate, are these:

- They speak quietly, intimately. In a relaxed tone.

- They move in a relaxed way. No quick, jittery movements. No sweeping gestures.

- Somehow they always manage to give the impression that they're talking just to you. They look right at you, with a smile. You feel that they like you, and you like them.

These are simple things, but not so easy to copy, especially if you're at all tense during your interview. However, there's one simple little trick I've found helpful when on the air. It could help you to be more relaxed. To feel as if you're at home, talking intimately to someone you like. It's to talk to Mom.

Talk to Mom

As in any kind of speaking, you want to eyeball your audience, but you can't see the people out there in TV land. All you see is the interviewer, so you tend to look exclusively at that person. That's a mistake! Even though you must turn to the interviewer, as a matter of courtesy, when he or she questions you, remember that *the camera is your primary audience*. If you constantly keep your nose pointed toward the interviewer and don't swing toward the camera after a question, you're ignoring your audience. The people out there won't like that.

In a studio setting where you're encircled by a jungle of wires, lights, and equipment, it may not be easy to keep track of the camera. There may be more than one; they move around on wheels; the bright lights blind you. Before you go on the air, however, ask your host or hostess which camera or cameras will be used. Then you'll know approximately where to look. And as a camera goes on, so does a red light right above its lens. You can spot that red light, follow it as the camera moves from side to side or in and out, and note if it goes off and a light appears above a different camera.

You may be facing the interviewer both at the start and when new questions are introduced. But in giving answers of any length, which you must try to do, pivot your head away from the interviewer and *talk to the red light*.

Imagine the red light is your mother out there in the haze. Talk to Mom! Relax. She loves you and loves to hear your confidences. Forget the rest of the world while you lean forward a bit, smile, and tell Mom all about the interesting information and wonderful thoughts you want to impart, confidentially, just to her. That's a way to achieve true person-to-person communication. That's cool.

How You Can Help the Interviewer

On a national program, a great deal of preparation goes into any broadcast. The host or hostess of a show has a staff of researchers and writers to uncover information about the project, person, or institution to be presented to the public. That creates the raw material that should result in perceptive questions for an interesting show. On a local program, where preparation time and staff are minimal, you need to help. And even with the most skilled of interviewers you can make the show better. Here's how.

What You Should Know in Advance

Probably the most important thing you'd like to know in advance is the host or hostess. This person will be calling the shots, so the more you can learn about her personality or his style of program, the better.

If you're on a multicity promotional tour, as I've been several times, the best you can hope for is a few minutes just before air time to shake hands, look each other over, and briefly discuss what the interviewer is seeking and what you can provide. Sometimes this discussion is com-

Advice from Barbara Walters

If you're going to be interviewed on radio or television, never script your answers in advance—all interviewers dislike that because it destroys the naturalness.

Interviewers rarely go over their questions with guests in advance of the interview for the same reasons. Without the element of the unexpected, interviews get a stale, stilted flavor. Most interviewers, however, do discuss with the guest the general areas to be covered in the questions. I sometimes do this by telephone the day before the program, or else I take the guest aside for a few minutes just before we go on camera.

It is often a help if you write a short note to the researcher or writer preparing the questions and tell him what general areas you would most like to discuss and possibly a sample question or two. I welcome this kind of material because it makes my job easier.

Most interviewers will respect your request not to ask personal questions which may prove embarrassing. If you are concerned about something in particular, or perhaps prefer not to have a family reference, tell the interviewer frankly how you feel.

Ask the interviewer how much time has been allotted, and ask for some sort of time signal so you'll know when to wind up what you are saying. You don't want to be cut off while making your most important point. The system I use is to touch the guest out of camera range, with a hand on his knee or my foot against his, when we're running out of time. I warn him in advance about this, and instruct him not to be flustered when it happens—just finish his thought as succinctly as he can and let me end the interview by thanking him.

The trick has failed me only once. The program was in California and I was assigned to interview the veteran actor Leo G. Carroll. I explained my time device to him before the interview but Mr. Carroll isn't a young man and he promptly forgot. As I got my cue from the floor manager to wind up the interview, I reached over and touched Mr. Carroll lightly on the knee.

He drew himself up sharply. "Young woman!" he snapped. "What are you doing crawling up my thigh?" I explained weakly that it was my prearranged signal, and the interview mercifully ended, with the crew and cast of the show almost prostrate with laughter.

Reprinted with permission from
How to Talk with Practically Anyone
about Practically Anything. (© 1970 by Barbara Walters.)

pressed to three or four sentences before the producer yells, "You're on."

Setting Up the Advance Meeting

On a local broadcast, you have much more opportunity to get acquainted. Take advantage of it, because it's always better (for both of you) to have a conversation between friends than between total strangers. If you've never met before, make every effort to do so before the broadcast.

Always try to set up the meeting at the station, not at your place. This saves time for the broadcast person, who always works on a rush schedule, and it precludes the possibility of a cancellation at the last minute on the media person's part.

Maybe someone at your company or the civic organization you're involved with—perhaps the public relations director—knows the interviewer and can arrange an advance meeting.

What Interviewers Like

Always request a prebroadcast meeting not on the basis of its helping you, but because you can bring to it something that may be of help to the interviewer. Your request will be hard to turn down, for the host or hostess of a show needs information to put on a really good program, and at a local station there's likely to be little or no research staff to assemble it. There are various ways to state your request; for example:

- "I have some background information about [me, the organization, the campaign, etc.] that you might find helpful. Could I drop it off at your office tomorrow afternoon and say hello at the same time? Or when would be the best time?"

- "I found several newspaper clippings [or a magazine article] about [the subject] that I'm sure you'd like to see. They'd be a big help in developing your questions."

- "I have an idea for some interesting visuals I'd like to bring to the interview. Of course, I want to find out what you think and get your suggestions."

During your prebroadcast meeting—or, if you can't arrange one, during a phone call—you must get definite answers about a few parameters. Here are four critical questions to ask:

1. What specific areas do you (the interviewer) wish to talk about?

2. How much time will be allotted to this segment of your show?

3. Will I be the sole interviewee? If there will be others present, who are

they? What areas will they cover, and what part of the subject will you direct principally to me?

4. Is there any particular point which interests you especially and which you expect may be the main focus of the interview?

Prepare to Keep the Ball Rolling

An unskilled interviewer may feed you questions you can answer with a simple yes or no. Don't. These aren't answers—they're barriers that halt the flow of an interview. Your aim must always be to keep it rolling. That's why you need to know as much as you can beforehand about the kinds of questions to expect, so you'll be prepared with informative, intriguing answers.

You'll want to try to guess some of the questions you're likely to be asked, and how you'd answer them. Not just factually, but what interesting bits of information such questions could allow you toss into the conversation. Of course, you'll also want to be prepared with appropriate answers if the questioning gets into touchy territory you'd prefer to avoid.

The Simulated Interview

The best way to prepare for both good questions and bad is to have a friend or friends assist you in a simulated interview. You shouldn't coach them as to what you expect; let them hit you with whatever questions come to their minds. They may come up with some you'd never have thought of. Be prepared for the worst and you'll come out best when you're on the air.

If you tape a simulated interview, you can study it and figure out how to improve your performance. A videocamera is ideal for this, since it allows you to replay visual mannerisms as well as your voice. But just an audiotape will allow you to analyze your responses and figure out what you should have said to various questions.

The Advantages of Show and Tell

Television is a visual medium; more than half its impact is wasted when there's only talk and nothing intriguing for viewers to see. That's why program producers are pleased when a guest offers to bring something attractive for the audience to look at. Very few guests think of this. If you provide a "show and tell" possibility, you improve your chances of being allotted more air time and decrease the risk of being bumped off the schedule in a last-minute reshuffle.

What you show doesn't have to be complicated. There are numerous possibilities in almost any situation if you and your colleagues give it a little thought. Here are some examples.

Ways to Dramatize Money.   Instead of merely saying, "Our company is contributing $000,000 to the Community Fund," you could have a giant check made up for presentation on the air. Or you might bring along a pair of bank guards lugging a huge sack of currency to be dumped on the table before the interviewer. I guarantee that this would create far more interest and be remembered 10 times longer than a flat statement.

Ways to Dramatize Products.   If the interview includes some reference to your company's products, there must be at least one new or unusual item you could show or demonstrate. In a big, complex product, this could be merely one small but key part in it, such as a fingernail-size computer chip that does wonderful new things for its function or expands capacity a thousandfold. An antique product versus the latest model is another possibility. So is some indication of unusual product-line range: "We make 5000 different bolts, from this one you can barely see with the naked eye to this one that weighs 100 pounds."

If there's to be a new building mentioned, don't just talk about it. Bring an architect's rendering so people can see what it'll be like.

Alternatives to Words or Numbers.   A chart, a graph, a map. And photos—they can be a delightful adjunct to your words. Photos of the three original employees of your company in front of the plant in 1908, contrasted with an aerial shot of your sprawling corporate complex today. Pictures of people. Of the space shuttle for which you make components. Of an Ugandan wearing the sunglasses or clothes you manufacture or using your products. You can hold up mounted 8 × 10 photos (matte finish to reduce glare) for the camera. Or the camera operator can use color slides if you alert him to this ahead of time so he'll have the proper equipment at hand.

Get the idea? There are many things you can do to make your broadcast visually interesting. That's what you want it to be.

Beware of Tape in Hazardous Interviews

Most interviews are pleasant experiences and great opportunities, whether the show is live or taped. But if the subject matter is likely to be controversial and you may face some sharp questioning by a not-too-friendly person, be careful. *Insist that the interview be live*—not taped.

Even if you're the greatest when it comes to rough-and-tumble argument, you can lose disastrously in a taped broadcast. The reason is simple. You have absolutely no control over the finished product; you've given your antagonist (if that's what the interviewer is) the power to cut, rearrange, and possibly even distort what you say. You may talk brilliantly for 15 minutes in the studio and end up viewing only a minute or two on the air the next day—all of it consisting of words taken out of context that you'll scarcely recognize.

Many a self-assured eloquent spokesperson has been bushwhacked on an exposé-type broadcast. If the sharpie has the scissors, you can't win! Don't try. It's much safer to "just say no."

PART 3
Writing

12
Think It Through

Learning to write is learning to think. You don't know anything clearly unless you can state it in writing.   S. I. HAYAKAWA

Thomas B. Watson, Sr., who headed IBM in its formative years, was obsessed with one bit of advice. If you visit the offices of the giant computer company, you'll still see signs all over the place that carry his favorite exhortation: "THINK." Judging from what's happened to IBM over the years, that couldn't have been too bad a guiding principle.

What does it have to do with writing?

In searching for outside opinions from the very best experts, as I've done throughout this book, I decided that Andy Rooney would be the ideal person to give succinct advice on what a real pro keeps in mind when he or she writes. As you may know, Rooney has excelled in many fields of communication—as a journalist, a TV and radio writer for such people as Arthur Godfrey and Gary Moore, a widely read syndicated columnist, an author of several diverse books, a writer and producer of TV shows that have won him three Emmys and numerous other awards, and the creator and star of the weekly *60 Minutes* segment "A Few Minutes with Andy Rooney."

I asked Rooney if he could give me one dictum he'd put above all others for those who hope to write well. He said it wasn't easy for him to come up with such gems, but he finally settled on this as the most important thing for any writer to keep in mind:

"Unclear writing comes from unclear thinking. If you can't put an idea down on paper, the chances are you don't have an idea."

So you see, it isn't style, grammar, rhythm, or fancy words that count most, contrary to what you might have imagined. It's what you get clear in your head *before* you reach for the pencil or typewriter or dictating machine. You know that when you speak before you think, you get into trouble. The same applies to writing.

Start with the Facts—All the Facts

The biggest mistake you can make in a report, letter, proposal, or other important message (and it's made all the time) is to write without first getting and correctly analyzing all the facts. It's the one unforgivable mistake. Your boss or customer can overlook a slip in grammar, but not bad advice that results when factual preparation is sloppy and incomplete.

This doesn't mean that you have to put everything into your final missive. First, you gather material indiscriminately. Then you do your *thinking* to winnow out what's important, which may be a small part of what you found and considered. Let me give you a personal example.

On my last book, a biography, I spent about three years in research before I began to write; the research included organizing hundreds of notes, clippings, and transcripts of interviews. For this present book, I gathered enough notes to make a pile a foot high and enough books on its subjects to fill several shelves.

That's the hardest part of writing, whether it's a book or anything else. It gives you a *choice*, to pick what's best and throw out what's not so good. It has been my experience that...

You Need a Choice to Make Your Writing Choice

In business writing, the extra facts you gather allow you to verify your ideas, or to question them, and to consider alternative courses of action. A good proposal, for example, should recognize that there may be more than one choice possible; it may even indicate those alternatives and tell briefly why they're less desirable. That's *thinking*, as opposed to fast and fuzzy writing.

Zero in on the Core Idea

One evening at about 6 o'clock, I was in the office of a man who headed a large manufacturing company. As I finished my conversation with him, he was gathering up a day's supply of memos, letters, etc., from his in box and dumping them into a briefcase for reading at home. He didn't look happy about the huge stack of material that needed some type of perusal before the next day's supply arrived.

I asked him, "How long are you going to spend tonight reading all that?" I knew that he was headed for a civic gathering and dinner from which he'd get away late and still more tired.

He answered, "I don't know. Not more than an hour, I hope."

I thought about that afterward, and many times since, when I've been writing to people like him. He must have had a hundred pages or more he intended to skim through. An hour would allow about half a minute per page, so I'm sure many of those missives would get just one quick glance before hitting the wastebasket.

The question is, which ones would he stop and read carefully? Which messages to any harried executive like him manage to get attention and hold attention?

Those which instantly present *one idea* of interest to the reader have a chance to be noticed.

Those which stay on the track of that core idea, developing it rather than shooting off into haphazard directions, have a chance to be read thoroughly ... and remembered.

So, after you've collected all the facts and stirred them around to separate the pertinent from the peripheral, it's time to start putting them together into a pattern in your mind. It's up to you to do the thinking—to put the pieces of the jigsaw puzzle together so they present a coherent picture. The busy people I know aren't going to take the time to do that for you.

Do the Pieces All Fit?

This piecing the puzzle together into a valid core idea is the crux of thinking before you write. Because if the pieces don't go together to form a complete, logical picture, *you don't have an idea.* Some of the parts are missing, or your basic premise is faulty. You'd better find that out before you start to write and make others aware of the deficiencies.

Once you have the important core idea, then express it succinctly, put it at the top of your message, and repeat it as needed. If by chance you should come up with two basic but unrelated ideas, write two memos or reports, etc. It's difficult enough to get a single thought from one mind to another; don't double the odds against you.

Outlining Helps You Organize Your Thoughts

Even if I'm writing something as brief as a one-page letter, I like to jot down some sort of outline. It may consist of no more than three or four words or phrases: the essence of the thought I want to get across and the order in which I intend to build my message.

> You've got to be very careful if you don't know where you're going, because you might not get there.
> YOGI BERRA

That simple outline helps me focus on what I want to do. It clarifies my thinking, and it keeps me from forgetting something or getting off the track.

The Advantages of Index Cards

For a longer piece, such as a business proposal or complex report, you might like the index-card method used by many professional writers for major projects. It's easier and safer than working from an accumulation of papers, clippings, and notes that get out of hand when they get voluminous enough.

Get yourself a stack of 3 × 5 cards and a file box. As you gather data and ideas over a period of weeks, you write each item on a separate card. When the cards begin to pile up, you can classify them into groups and put them behind various headings in your file box.

The original nonelectric thought processor.

The file-card system of thought organization is like using a personal computer, only very simple and flexible. You don't have to figure out your programming ahead of time. You can rearrange the cards within each group to get them into logical order for your presentation. As you develop and change your thinking, you can shuffle the groups around. Finally, it's easy to check off each card as you write your proposal, so you don't forget anything.

However you do it, *simplifying and organizing* are the essence of thinking. Get it all straight in your mind and you're ready to transmit your ideas clearly to others.

> *Few people think more than two or three times a year. I've made an international reputation for myself by thinking once or twice a week.*
> GEORGE BERNARD SHAW

Questions to Ask

Now you know what's needed to think out an effective message before you start to write it out. It's just common sense:

1. Get *all* the facts.
2. Zero in on the important *core* idea.
3. *Simplify and organize* your presentation.

While you're doing that, I suggest you ask yourself the following three questions to make sure you're headed in the right direction. They're just common sense, too, but since that's a rare commodity, these questions are often overlooked.

Do You Need to Write?

Could the question in your memo be handled better and more quickly if you asked it in person? Japanese managers generally prefer to deal with their cohorts face-to-face rather than through the paper route. That saves time by providing an immediate response. And the brief face-to-face interchange provides not just a cold answer, but a chance to uncover nuances of enthusiasm or doubt, and maybe some additional input or guidance.

Instead of taking your time and that of your secretary in preparing a formal response to a memo or letter (which efficiency experts tell us costs at least $10 or $15) could you simply write your answer on the margin and send it back?

The blizzard of paper that I mentioned before has enough garbage in it now without your adding any unnecessary poundage.

What Does the Recipient of Your Message Want?

I admit that my view of writing is influenced strongly by a couple of decades in creating advertising. But the fundamentals required for success there could do a lot to enhance the careers of nonprofessional writers, especially when it comes to sizing up the person you hope to influence.

No advertising writers who expect to keep their jobs would dream of starting a new campaign without first giving much thought to the people at the other end of the message. They'll consider many things about the readers of the magazine or the viewers of the TV show: age, sex, social background, etc., and what they're apt to like or dislike. They'll consider what *benefits* of the product or service advertised may appeal to the prospect, and to what degree.

You have a great advantage over the advertising writer; you don't have to guess about the prospect for your ideas or depend on general information from a research report. If you're in business, you have first-hand knowledge of the controller, the product manager, and the senior vice president who'll be reading the proposal you've labored over so long.

Are You Using Your Intimate Knowledge?

Do your facts about the new Widget proposal justify the start-up-cost figure the controller will worry about the instant she sees "new product" on the paper, and does it pointedly mention the low distribution cost because Widgets can be sold by your present dealers and sales force? If you know that the product manager has had a long hard struggle in building up his present line and consequently is very protective of it, will you quickly indicate that Widgets will help and not hurt existing items? If you know that the senior vice president is unhappy with the southeast district, will you be sure to headline the fact that they'll love Widgets in Dixie?

It's a Matter of Viewpoint

Keep in mind at all times that nobody (except you) cares a hoot about what *you* want.

The people you're writing to care only about what will be good for them. You have to figure out carefully what that is, and then tell them about it.

If you do that consistently, they'll like you. Also, they'll think you're smart. Because you are.

13

Vigorous Words Have Bite and Power

All managers, like it or not, are in the business of words.   ROBERT HELLER

How much is a word worth?

A one-minute TV commercial may contain 100 words, never more than 125 or 130. To put that 100 words on the telecast of the Super Bowl at the end of the football season costs $1 million. That's $10,000 per word.

Costs can also be high to distribute words in print media. For example, campaigns I used to be involved in to introduce new automobile models required budgets of many millions for space in newspapers and magazines. They contained a few words, along with a picture or two. We took infinite pains to try to find the most effective words: writing, discarding, judging each one.

What about the words *you* write; what value do you place on them? It doesn't cost a business executive anything to get a few hundred words typed, copied, and distributed. That's the danger: no budget needed, so maybe no thought given to how crucial those words can be in the daily job of selling you and your ideas. That's worth a great deal to you, isn't it?

Words Are the Building Blocks

If you want your writing to come alive and motivate people, you must choose words that are vigorous and incisive. Build with mush and you end up with mush. (The next chapter discusses this "spaghetti" factor you want to avoid in your writing.)

There's no problem in having ample choice. English offers you about *a million words* to choose from—more than any other language. It's so voluminous because modern English is really two languages in one. After the Celts were driven out and the Roman legions returned to their homeland, the basic language of England was Anglo-Saxon, a Germanic tongue introduced by tribes from the North Sea coast who had invaded and colonized the island. But the invasions weren't over; in 1066 the Normans took over and imposed a whole new vocabulary of French words duplicating the Anglo-Saxon speech the peasants retained.

The peasant ate; the Norman lord dined. One sweated in a hut; the other perspired in a mansion. The farmer raised pigs, cows, and sheep so his French masters could enjoy porc, boeuf, and mouton, which we still call today by very similar names. Talk became conversation. Nearly all our polysyllabic English words are of Norman origin (French-Latin), while most single-syllable ones are derived from Anglo-Saxon. When we attempt to write in a refined manner, we tend toward the longer, more *pretentious* (from the French) words.

Don't Be Afraid of Little Words

One reason we speak with more vivacity than we write is the length of the words we choose. Short, staccato Anglo-Saxon words in speech; ostentatious polysyllabic Norman ones in correspondence.

If you're going to *write more like you talk*, that's the wrong route to take, isn't it? Don't be afraid to use the direct, short word. There's good precedence for it.

Shakespeare, the greatest writer in the English language, chose words even the simplest fellows in the stalls could understand. Probably the most widely quoted phrase in our language is Shakespeare's "To be, or not to be, that is the question." The Bard of Avon used only 30 letters in that memorable 10-word phrase. That's an average of only 3 characters per word. So why should you hesitate to use short words?

Ernest Hemingway, considered by many the finest of all American authors, also pared his prose to the bone. He searched for short, direct words that would hit home hardest. His *The Old Man and the Sea*, which won a Pulitzer prize, is one of the most beautiful novels ever written. In its style, it may be the exact opposite of what you were taught in composition classes, but it's a perfect blueprint of how to convey thoughts and images powerfully. Following is a brief excerpt describing the lonely battle of the tired old fisherman who has just hooked his last and hugest marlin, while the sharks hone in on the catch lashed to the side of his small skiff:[1]

The next shark that came was a single shovelnose. He came like a pig to the trough if a pig had a mouth so wide that you could put your head in it. The old man let him hit the fish and then drove the knife on the oar down into his brain. But the shark jerked backwards as he rolled and the knife blade snapped.

The old man settled himself to steer. He did not even watch the big shark sinking slowly in the water, showing first life-size, then small, then tiny. That always fascinated the old man. But he did not even watch it now.

"I have the gaff now," he said. "But it will do no good. I have the two oars and the tiller and the short club."

Now they have beaten me, he thought. I am too old to club sharks to death. But I will try it as long as I have the oars and the short club and the tiller.

He put his hands in the water again to soak them. It was getting late in the afternoon and he saw nothing but the sea and the sky. There was more wind in the sky than there had been, and soon he hoped that he would see land.

"You're tired, old man," he said. "You're tired inside."

The sharks did not hit him again until just before sunset.

The old man saw the brown fins coming along the wide trail the fish must make in the water. They were not even quartering on the scent. They were headed straight for the skiff swimming side by side.

Short words? Almost every word in this passage from Hemingway has only one or two syllables in it. Specifically, in the entire 273-word passage there are *only four words of more than two syllables*. They are "shovelnose, fascinated, afternoon," and "quartering," each having three syllables; not exactly long or complicated, are they?

So, if it's good enough for Hemingway,...

Verbs Are the Engines That Power a Sentence

Verbs express action and supply the zip that moves a sentence along.

For that reason, they're the key to forceful expression. Vigorous, active verbs generate vitality; weak, passive ones make your writing limp and sluggish.

There is some action inherent in almost every thought; all you need do is express it in a direct way. This produces a simple, forceful sentence—*subject, verb, object*. Here are some examples, taken from newspaper headlines, of direct declarative sentences using the active voice. Following them are rewrites in the passive voice.

ACTIVE   Major banks *cut* prime rate.
          Business groups *push* spending freeze.
          Stocks *ignore* retail sales increases as industrials *decline* 6.29 points.

PASSIVE   The prime rate *has been cut* by major banks.
          A spending freeze *is being pushed* by business groups.
          Retail sales increases *are being ignored* by stocks, *resulting in a decline* of 6.29 points in the industrials.

In the passive-voice examples, note that the forceful verbs (*cut, push, ignore, decline*) have been replaced by various forms of "to be" (*has been, is being*). These are low-horsepower verbs. They make the sentences longer. And they invert them, pushing back to the end of the sentence the thing that is *doing something*, and moving forward as subject the thing that is *having something done to it*.

In the last example above, note that the word "decline" is changed from a verb form into a noun. This is another way in which strong active verbs are neutralized, replaced by nouns and weak linking words such as "resulting in, will become, is expected to be," etc.

Don't misunderstand; there's nothing wrong with using the passive voice. (Notice that I used it in the preceding paragraph.) One of the beauties of English is that it enables us to express our ideas in a variety of ways. But when you want your writing to be as forceful and straightforward as possible, lean strongly toward...

Active Verbs—Active Voice

Look analytically at your daily newspaper, the source from which I extracted my examples of direct prose. You'll observe that newspaper writers and editors employ every grammatical form, to give their stories variety, but that they favor strong verbs and to-the-point sentences: "Man bites dog." They know that hurried readers want the news fast and want it straight, very much in the style that people talk. If you believe you face a similar situation, you'd do well to tailor your professional messages more like those of the daily press.

Unfortunately, that's not the pattern you find in much of the correspondence, reports, and literature that cover the desks and occupy hours of each day of businesspeople.

Do You Use Weasel Words?

The habit has been around a long time. Theodore Roosevelt warned against weasel words. Sometimes they're so bizarre they make you laugh.

My eyes popped when I picked up my morning newspaper and read the statement of a government spokesperson that there had been *"A pre-dawn vertical insertion on the Island of Grenada."*

To my unsophisticated mind, that sounded like an introduction to obscene humor. I read on eagerly, but was disillusioned to figure out, not without some difficulty, that the writers were referring to a military maneuver. They didn't want to say it, but they had to announce the sensitive news that U.S. Marines had invaded Grenada by dropping paratroopers onto the island early that morning.

Other spokespeople have similar problems and try to weasel out of them in like manner. You read about airplanes that have *"near misses,"* never *"near hits."* The nuclear power industry has invented the phrase *"an unscheduled event"* for an event no one likes to think about. They also call it *"a rapid energetic disassembly,"* which is much less scary than suggesting what happens when the uranium starts to blow. Attorneys (for the defense) have used the phrase *"therapeutic misadventure"* in relation to a physician's treatment. In case that isn't clear to you, it refers to medical malpractice.

"Members of a career offender cartel" appeared in a report to the New Jersey Division of Gaming Enforcement. They meant *"Mafia,"* but, of course, that doesn't exist around the Atlantic City casinos. New employees at the U.S. embassy in Budapest were warned against *"available casual indigenous female companions."* Translation: *"The local hookers are spies."*

Evasions Don't Fool Anyone

Such spokespeople have difficult problems. Yet their weasel words don't really solve them. You see through the subterfuges and laugh at the writers.

Trying to weasel around the facts, often when there's nothing to be timid about, doesn't fool anyone in business correspondence either. And you don't want your colleagues to laugh at what you write, do you?

The evasions you encounter in business writing sometimes take the form I call...

The At-Arm's-Length Style of Writing

You know what I mean. Sounds as if someone else wrote the memo; it comes from some vague third party who presumably should be held responsible if there's any criticism generated or if anything goes wrong.

The writer of this type of corporate prose never, never says, "I recommend." Instead, the report generally states, "It has been recommended that...." This puts the onus on an unidentified flying object beyond the scope of responsibility. Besides the use of third-person pronouns as the subject, such memos are invariably couched in the passive voice, and they are replete with generalities. A typical example might be:

> It has been determined that a new inventory system has the potential to provide a clearer overview of the necessity for parts ordering, and therefore could result in closer controls with subsequent reduction of warehouse stocks and consequent economies in investment. It is therefore advisable that the adoption of such a new system be considered for installation within the earliest feasible time frame.

How much better to boil such fluff down to:

> A new inventory system can cut lead time in parts ordering by 30 days and reduce stocks by 25 percent. We can install one in six months. We should.

Even if your colleagues tend to use an indirect, involved style of writing, it makes no sense to follow them. When you seem to be distancing yourself from what you write, you destroy its credibility. If you have no confidence in it, who will?

Modesty, carried to extreme, is one basis for the wide growth of third-person corporate style. It stems from the fear of seeming too forward if you say "you" or "we" in a business memo when formality seems to be the accepted mode of the organization. If you don't hesitate to sign your name to a memo, why be afraid to write it in the first person? Be proud to be the author; the meek do not inherit the executive suite.

Although third-person, at-arm's-length writing *has become standard corporate style in at least half of all U.S. firms,* many chief executives spout fire when they see it. One of these is Harold Geneen, who sent this message to his managers when he was chairman and chief executive at ITT.

Who Is Responsible?

Many reports prepared in the company are inadequately put together for the purpose of decision and for understanding how the recommendation was arrived at and who is responsible for the recommendation.

A professional report must start with a brief summary that gives in clear factual language (1) the action recommended; (2) the problems; (3) the reasoning behind the recommendation; and (4) the position taken by the writer of the report or memorandum. Evasive language taken at this point is a sign of poor preparation or poor sense of responsibility.

Let's have none of this!

HAROLD S. GENEEN

Personal Pronouns and Contractions for Warm Informality

Along with active verbs and the active voice, two other characteristics help give your writing a conversational tone.

Personal Pronouns. These loosen up the style. Use them rather than repeating names. For example:

> Jones and Walton contacted Lloyd Wilson at Superior Stores in Minneapolis. *We* presented the new variety display package. *He* told us...

Once you've identified the cast of characters, it sounds stiff and formal to repeat them continually. Go to personal pronouns, such as "we, he, they, it." And don't hesitate to draw the reader in occasionally with that all-important "you." I haven't counted, but I'll bet you'd find that word used a thousand times in this book.

Contractions. These are the second handy tool for making your writing more like your speech. Words such as "it's, she's, haven't, won't, you'll, I'll, doesn't," and "aren't" reduce the formality and stiffness. They make your writing sound more like you.

Take a Tip from *The Wall Street Journal*

Look at your newspaper again, and you'll find an abundance of both personal pronouns and contractions. You'll also find numerous examples of how to make dull subjects interesting. I noted a couple in *The Wall Street Journal*. That's a fairly conservative paper, wouldn't you say? But here's its approach to two dry subjects—the potential for industrial chemical accidents and a divergence between the stock market and retail sales. Here's the first subject's lead-in:

> TEXAS CITY, Texas—"For God's sake, send the Red Cross. The city has blown up."
> It was the last desperate message from the telephone exchange here after a French freighter brimming with ammonium nitrate exploded with such force it registered on the Richter scale in Denver....

And in the stock market summary column, I read this opening sentence:

> Consumers are buying, but the stock market isn't.

No beating around the bush there. I hope you like this kind of straightforward approach as much as I do. But would you use a statement as direct, attention-getting, and informal to start out one of your business memos?

If not, why not?

Important Words

Whether you're writing or talking, some words have universal appeal. They're probably the strongest words in our language. Don't be stingy with them.

The six most important words:
  I was wrong—please forgive me.

The five most important:
  You did a good job.

The four most important:
  Can I help you?

(Continued)

The three most important:
  What's your opinion?

The two most important:
  Thank you.

The one most important:
  You.

The least important:
  I.

Try to get into the habit of using these important words and phrases frequently. They're the keystone of the vocabulary of success.

14
Skip the Spaghetti

We love to pump air into our language
and make it soft and gaseous.
                          Edwin Newman

I'm fond of pasta; you may be too. But writing that resembles it causes indigestion in the human message system.

Writing can get as convoluted as a plate full of overcooked spaghetti—mushy, tangled, a squiggly slippery heap you simply can't ingest. To illustrate, here are some examples you may find amusing as well as instructive.

I didn't make these up, nor were they intended to be humorous. Believe it or not, they were written in all seriousness by college freshmen doing their best to demonstrate their knowledge of history. Over a period of five years at McMaster University and the University of Alberta, Professor Anders Henricksson collected these startling statements from his students' papers. (Perhaps they had some bearing on his decision to forsake teaching for a career as a research analyst.) He assembled these gems into an essay for the *Wilson Quarterly*. Here are a few brief excerpts from it:[1]

---

[1]Excerpted with permission from the *Wilson Quarterly*, Spring 1983. Copyright 1983 by the Woodrow Wilson International Center for Scholars.

During the Middle Ages, everbody was middle aged. Church and state were co-operatic. Middle Evil society was made up of monks, lords and surfs. After a revival of infantile commerce slowly creeped into Europe, merchants appeared. Some were sitters and some were drifters. They roamed from town to town exposing themselves and organized big fairies in the countryside.

In the 1400 hundreds most Englishmen were perpendicular. A class of yeowls arose. Finally Europe caught the Black Death. The bubonic plague is a social disease in the sense that it can be transmitted by intercourse and other etceteras. It was spread from port to port by inflected rats.

The French Revolution was accomplished before it happened. The revolution evolved through monarchial, republican and tolarian phases until it catapulted into Napoleon. Napoleon was ill with bladder problems and was very tense and unrestrained.

See what I mean? But you may say, "Those examples are the product of semiliterate youngsters. They're far removed from me and my world."

Really? Here's a directive to bankers regarding the deposit of taxes withheld from interest payments:

A timely deposit with respect to a specific eighth-monthly period is treated separately from deposits with respect to subsequent eighth-monthly periods and should not be aggregated with such subsequent eighth-monthly deposits for purposes of determining when taxes with respect to a subsequent eighth-monthly period must be deposited.

What, exactly, does that mean? Is it any clearer than the college students' descriptions of historical events? Bankers may not think so. And they are not the only ones subjected to confused communication. It's endemic to every profession and business, no doubt including the one you're in.

The Lure of Jargon

For centuries, the clergy of the Roman Catholic church used a different language to elevate itself above the laity. The clergy (from a French word meaning knowledge, learning) spoke Latin. This was unintelligible to the laity (meaning the mass of people, unskilled). And that's the way the hierarchy wanted it.

Within our spheres of expertise, we're tempted to do the same thing—to set ourselves up as a clerisy beyond the understanding of yokels who labor with their hands or in disciplines other than ours. Our particular Latin serves a purpose in pinpointing precise technical meanings among ourselves, but it serves us poorly when we arrogantly carry it over into communicating with customers or others who may come from different backgrounds. In a letter to me, Rawleigh Warner, Jr., expressed his concern about that:

Specialization versus Clarity

Ours is an age of specialization. As each field of specialization increases in sophistication, it develops its own vocabulary. Within a given field, such a vocabulary is useful and in many cases essential, but it militates against an easy interchange of information and beliefs among individuals in other fields.

Mobil interfaces with many different publics, both in this country and abroad. We engage in all phases of the oil business and in coal, chemicals, retail merchandising, packaging, and real estate as well. We span a wide range of languages, laws, customs, cultures, in addition to numerous disciplines.

This compels a common denominator of clear, unmistakable communication...clarity and brevity in speech and writing, along with careful reading and listening.

RAWLEIGH WARNER, JR., CHAIRMAN
Mobil Corporation

In complex situations such as Mr. Warner describes, not uncommon today, it's hard enough to communicate clearly without muddying the meaning with arcane jargon.

In some professions, obscure jargon is a tradition of centuries. If the legal and medical fields come to mind, you're right. Dr. C. Rollins Hanlon, director of the American College of Surgeons, has said, "Law and medical schools indoctrinate their students in stilted and verbose language to impress the unfortunates they are going to lay a fee upon."

My attorney admitted to me, "Lawyers like to write in words few people, even lawyers, can readily understand. That's what causes lawsuits and keeps them employed." He cited an example of a legal term designed to confuse. "The word *demise*," he told me, "can mean either *death, lease,* or *grant*. So if you say 'the date of the demise was January 5,' no one—not even a lawyer—can be sure what you're talking about."

Fortunately, some of our leading educators are attempting to clarify the language of the law...and of medicine too.

The law colleges at Notre Dame, William and Mary, and the University of California at Los Angeles are among those telling their students that legal documents need not be indecipherable. And Baylor College of Medicine in Houston, for example, now offers courses in scientific

"Of course no one can understand it. If they did, they'd never sign it!"

communication. Professors Lois and Selma DeBakey, who conduct them, teach their students to avoid the confusion, ambiguity, and misinterpretation arising from jargon they call "medicant." You'll never hear them saying anything like this to patients: "You have idiopathic symptoms, but the etiology of your febrile condition may be a sequella involving no sepsis. It may respond to two antipyretics Q.I.D."[2]

Common Business Buzzwords

Just as every occupation and industry has its own peculiar jargon, American business also uses words and phrases not always readily understood by the general public.

Some are coined words. One such is "GIGO," created from observations that when you put *garbage in* (to computers), you get *garbage out*—and this applies to other situations as well. They may be pickups from electronic slang, such as the "glitches" that occur when a sudden surge of current fouls up the operation of a machine. Some from sports—"blindsided, hardball, touch base"—are more easily deciphered. Many are nouns converted to verb forms, such as "to prioritize" and "to stonewall."

I've called them *buzzwords*, which is a buzzword in itself. They've been termed *business slang*, which isn't an especially apt name either, because many are standard English words or phrases, but used in a new or specialized context.

---

[2]Translation: "You have symptoms the doctor doesn't understand. But your feverish condition may be the aftermath of a previous illness involving no bacteria in your body. It might respond to two aspirin taken twice a day."

The Pros and Cons of Neologisms

To be more precise, such words and phrases are *neologisms* (there's one for you!), which means a word or expression that's new or used in a new way...and which may be disapproved of for that reason.

Journalists and academics frequently lament the popularity of neologisms and advise that they're always to be avoided. I disagree. New words, like new ideas, are stimulating.

Some expressions that gain quick popularity in business (and sometimes fade just as quickly) indicate exactly what we mean, but in a fresh way. Only when they're thrown into every conversation and memo, to show that the author knows what's "in," do they bother me. Then they become ridiculous.

What Executive Vice Presidents Say

Jeanette Gilsdorf of the College of Business at Arizona State University surveyed executive vice presidents at 300 of the nation's largest industrial companies and found them "not hostile" to such expressions. They regarded them as "useful in a number of ways," such as providing "more precise, more amusing, or more comfortable ways to say a thing." She did uncover some negative attitudes, however: 45 percent of the executives thought that people who use a great deal of business slang tend to be pretentious, and 40 percent considered such people unoriginal thinkers [as reported in *The Journal of Business Communications* (ABCA), Volume 20, 1984].

My conclusion is that if a current buzzword seems right for the occasion, use it, particularly among people close to you. In a formal report to top management, you'd be advised to be extremely sparing. But in either case, don't replace your standard, easily understood English vocabulary with a constant barrage of neologisms that have long since lost their "neo" because everyone is mouthing them. That's not in—that's out.

Pretentious Words Bury a Thought

Even simple thoughts can become abstruse (or maybe a better word is absurd) when expressed in overly long, overworked words and phrases. Below are four truisms you've read and heard many times, but never in the form presented here. Perhaps they sound like some of the memos you receive. See if you can recognize them.

1. The parameters of an aqueous environment mandate that the only viable alternative to heading in a nether direction is immediate implementation of a vigorous, ongoing orchestration of one's limbs.

2. Exposure to an insignificant magnitude of instruction, education-

wise, leads to a mindset with potential for creating perilous glitches at some point in time.

3. Preservation of 1 percent of a dollar is analogous to acquisition of a similar aggregate through the application of remunerative exertion.

4. Voluntary disbursement of legal tender to those in impecunious circumstances may require a midcourse correction for orientation within the confines of one's own domain.[3]

The Baldrige Solution

Perversion of language by government is what English novelist and prophet George Orwell warned against in his book *1984*, written in 1948.

His prediction certainly has come true. Our government departments and bureaus are experts in the "doublespeak" that Orwell foretold. The Pentagon has created such thought twisters as calling peace "permanent prehostility," describing civilian casualties as "collateral damage," and naming war "violence processing." Alexander Haig, who at one time brought the linguistic style of Howard Cosell to the State Department, gave us such gems as "to definitize how the procedural aspects of American assumptions can be met."

A rare and refreshing change occurred in the halls of government when Ronald Reagan selected Malcolm Baldrige as secretary of commerce. Baldrige, a maverick who had been a cowboy, rodeo rider, and head of Scovill Industries before coming to Washington, declared war against gobbledygook when he arrived at the Commerce building.

Word Processing Joins the War against Gobbledygook

Baldrige told his people to communicate in simple, lean language that gets the meaning across directly—not to take 17 words to say what they could in 7. In fact, he put together a taboo list of the worst bureaucratese—confusing and redundant words and phrases. *And he had word processors in the Commerce offices programmed to reject any words on this taboo list.*

He said, "We have these computers that go through copy. When they hit a word on my blacklist they begin to smoke, and fire comes out, and they *get* the writer."

---

[3]Answers: (1) Sink or swim. (2) A little knowledge is a dangerous thing. (3) A penny saved is a penny earned. (4) Charity begins at home.

Maybe someone in your organization ought to try the Baldrige solution, setting up your computers to spout some fire when they sense an input of gobbledygook?

Overused and Abused Words
from Baldrige's Taboo List

actualize	optimize
articulate (as a verb)	parameters
bottom line	politicize
climate (other than weather)	posture (for attitude)
comfortable with	prioritize
concept	quantify
conceptualization	ramifications
dialog	replicate
dichotomy	scenario
dynamics	structure (as a verb)
finalize	substantive
impact (as a verb)	viable
interface	-wise (tacked onto nouns, as in
maturation	*resultwise*)
maximize	

Cut, Cut, Cut the Windy Words

The infatuation with long, redundant phrases blossomed way back in the days of Watergate when John Dean blabbed his confessions on television. He repeated his favorite vacuous phrase over and over. Remember it?

It was "at this point in time." You must have heard it a hundred times or more if you listened to those hearings. For that alone, he should have gone to jail. Instead of simply saying, "now," as Lincoln or Hemingway would have, he dinned that stupid five-word circumlocution into the skulls of millions of Americans, who began to use it themselves.

Many other redundant phrases clutter our communication. Especially our business language. In the following list, you may recognize some you're inclined to use.

Which Words Do You Use?

This?	Or this?
Notwithstanding the fact that	Although
In regard to	Regarding
In consequence of	Because
In accordance with	By
In the event of	If
Along the lines of	Like
In the nature of	Like
For the reason that	Because
With a view to	To
On the basis of	By
At the present time	Now
At this point in time	Now
At the earliest possible time	Soon
In proximity to	Near
Make a recommendation that	Recommend
After the conclusion of	After
During the course of	During
Until such time as	Until
Reduce to a minimum	Minimize
In the vast majority of	In most
Have a belief in	Believe
By means of	By
For the purpose of	For; to
On the grounds that	Because
Due to the fact that	Because
Despite the fact that	Although
In reference to	About
In advance of	Before
Take under advisement	Consider

The phrases you've just read are based on prepositions and conjunctions. These basic elements of grammar serve useful purposes; they connect thoughts.

The trouble arises when a writer wrongly supposes that if one word is good, a long string of them must be better. The result is the cumbersome grammatical gimmicks you just saw, which contain compound prepositions and conjunctions tied in with nouns. You needn't remember all that. Just keep in mind that such windy connecting phrases foul up your writing and destroy your true image as a decisive, to-the-point sort of person.

Double Images Add Confusion

We also clutter up our language by tying together two words meaning the same thing. Here are some examples:

If and when

Unless and until

Exact same

First and foremost

Deeds and actions

End result

In the twin words above, either one or the other will serve your purpose. Pick one and drop the redundant twin.

Similarly, we sometimes add redundant adjectives. Many not only fail to add meaning but also inject a ridiculous note. Here are a few:

Untimely death   (It's never time.)

Serious crisis   (Ever have one to joke about?)

Final outcome   (How many outcomes can there be?)

Future plans   (Do you ever plan for the past?)

Personally reviewed   (Hard to do otherwise.)

Very unique   (Either it's unique—one of a kind—or it isn't.)

The word "very" is redundant most of the time. Very often it's very, very much overdone by most of us. Try to avoid it.

Clichés and Prefabricated Phrases

Clichés are phrases that start out as fresh expressions. They become popular—so popular that you hear and read them constantly. No longer fresh and interesting, they become boring because they've been beaten to death (a cliché).

William Paxson, who operates a business- and technical-writing service in Sacramento, wrote a spoof on clichés that explains them better than I can. With his permission, it's excerpted here. It purports to be an interview with a cliché expert.

Q: Tell us of your research.

A: I've left no stone unturned but only discovered the tip of the iceberg, I fear.

Q: What have you found out?

A: That clichés have become the state of the art, or the state of science. I'm not sure which.

Q: Who helped you?

A: I touched base with the experts.

Q: Were they all experts?

A: No, some weren't up to speed. Others were too laid-back to understand where I'm coming from, where I'm at, or where I'm going.

Q: And the rest were?

A: People with whom I had a meaningful relationship.

Q: You talked it over with them?

A: We had meaningful discussions.

Q: As groups?

A: No. We went one-on-one.

Q: Is that the best way?

A: I felt comfortable with it.

Q: What did you do?

A: We verbalized our posture, per se.

Q: To accomplish what?

A: The thrust of a new program.

Q: Which is?

A: Expressed in an operative proposal.

Q: What will it do to clichés?

A: Stonewall them.

Q: Is that all that can be done?

A: There is no viable alternative.

Q: Really?

A: That's the bottom line.

What more need be said? We all use clichés at times, but the fewer the better. No doubt you have your own pet examples. Are they to be avoided? *Like the plague*, if you'll pardon my cliché.

Don't Write as Your Grandparents Did

A specific type of cliché was the mainstay of correspondence a generation or two ago. Unfortunately it still crops up in business correspondence. This outdated style is built around *phrases to suit all occasions*; the phrases can be picked up with little thought to form a prefabricated missive. Problem: The lack of thought is evident in the resulting correspondence, which is lengthy and lacking in information. Here's an example:

> In regard to your inquiry of August 20th, receipt of which is hereby acknowledged, with respect to your order of 10 gross of Super-Whatzits, we regret to report that shipment of same was delayed by unforeseen circumstances beyond our control. We are pleased to advise, however, that according to our records, said order was able to be filled with all due speed as soon as our stocks were replenished, and that you may expect delivery of the aforementioned merchandise within the month.

What the customer wants to hear is:

> We're sorry we were out of Super-Whatzits when you ordered them on the 20th. A new supply has just come in, and you'll have your shipment in a day or two. I'm sending it air express at our expense. Please forgive us.

Double-Talk in Annual Reports

Annual report time is often ulcer time if glowing sales and profit forecasts made 12 months earlier haven't quite materialized or have crashed through the subbasement. That's when language is called upon to make painful figures look not so bad, or even to look like the prelude to a rosy tomorrow—without actually lying, of course.

One of my favorite newspapers, *The Wall Street Journal*, observed this phenomenon with this headline:

> DOUBLE-TALK GRIPS BUSINESS REPORTS
> AS FIRMS TRY TO SUGARCOAT BAD NEWS

The *Journal* went on to say that understatement, overstatement, non-statement, buzzwords, and the use of the passive voice are means used by "troubled firms to depict themselves as victims of sinister forces beyond their control." One sentence in the article particularly caught my attention. It pointed out that investment advisers view unclear writing in such reports as a cover-up and quoted one as saying, "The amount of pontificating a company does varies in direct proportion to how screwed up it is." Evidently the double-talk doesn't fool the investment community.

Iris A. Varner of Illinois State University made a comprehensive analysis of 35 letters to stockholders that had to convey disconcerting news. (She selected those from companies listed in *Fortune* magazine as big losers for the year.) Dr. Varner's report verifies the feeling of the security analyst about the relationship between the degree of pontificating and the depth of the disaster. Three brief examples:

> "This year, we began climbing out of a valley and moving on to new heights."

> "I would like to thank the men and women at _____ for their contribution in helping see that the performance met the promise."

> "We are proud to report a great deal of accomplishment in our program of restructuring our company."

Remember, these are the *biggest losers of the year*. The firm that thanked its employees for their great performance suffered a drop of $360 million in its profits.

What are Dr. Varner's conclusions? That those few letters which were clearly misleading were not likely to fool stockholders, and could do a disservice by showing the company as dishonest and deceptive. Those letters at the other end of the spectrum which *faced the facts directly* made the best impression on the people surveyed. Since the negative statistics had to appear in the accompanying annual report anyway, it was best to admit them up front and then go on to point out planned improvements.

Double-Talk in Memos

The annual report is only one form of business communication in which people sometimes try to cover up facts with fairy tales. You've seen many examples in classified ads for used cars and in realty ads that glowingly describe rickety homes as "a handyman's delight" or "a cozy, rustic charmer."

I'll bet you also come across phrases to be regarded with skepticism when you read memos at your office. See if you agree with my translations of the following phrases that frequently interlard business memos and conversations:

Double-Talk	*Translation*
Your suggestion is very interesting.	You must be kidding.
Under active consideration.	Should be in the files somewhere; we'll keep searching.
Will advise later.	Don't count on it.
In line with our policy,...	If it hasn't been done before, don't expect me to be a pioneer.
Let's get together sometime.	You'll never hear from me again.
Keep this highly confidential.	Everyone knows it, but don't put it in writing.

Please note and initial.

I'm not sticking my neck out unless you commit yourself to some of the responsibility.

Looking at the big picture,...

Have no facts whatever, so let's stick to generalities.

What's Your Personality on Paper?

Sometimes even the simplest things that should be explainable in a sentence or two are presented in a way that allows for misunderstanding. That's especially prevalent in government writing, often labeled "governmentese."

An example of this, made famous by Franklin D. Roosevelt during World War II, was a memo he received intended to instruct federal employees on what they should do in an air raid. It read:

Such preparations shall be made as will completely obscure all Federal buildings and non-Federal buildings occupied by the Federal Government during an air raid for any period of visibility by reason of internal or external illumination. Such obscuration may be obtained either by blackout construction or by termination of the illumination.

When the President read this, he was irritated by the circumlocutions and feared many people wouldn't understand what action they should take. He sent this note:

Tell them that in buildings where they have to keep on working, to put something over the windows; and where they can stop work for a while, to turn off the lights.   FDR

The two memos you just read indicate different personalities. FDR was a straightforward man of action. The bureaucrat who first described the blackout procedures was more concerned with how he might be perceived than with giving clear instructions. He thought he'd show himself as educated and important by using long words and an impersonal authoritative tone. Instead, he sounded pompous and confused.

In person, he may have been altogether different from that, but many people exhibit a dual personality. They're sincere and easy to understand when they talk, but evasive and ostentatious on paper. Recognize the type?

Straightforward guy   **But a pompous ass**
when he talks...   **when he writes.**

This raises an interesting question: When you write, do the people who read it picture you like the air raid security officer, or more like Franklin Roosevelt?

Think about that. Better yet, take a few minutes to dig into the files of your recent memos, letters, and reports, so you can read them with that question in mind. Read as if you were a stranger—someone who had never met you and was forming a picture of you based solely on your words on paper. Someone who didn't know what a charming, forthright person you really are.

What you write is what you are to many people! That may include people of considerable importance to you. If you're a middle manager, you're not likely to have much direct contact with top executives, so they'll have only a vague image of you based on verbal communication. But reports or memos with your name on them may get to top people's desks with some frequency. You want to be sure they'll make the right impression.

How to Present Your Best Image

One of the best ways to judge the things you've written is to *read them aloud*. How do they sound? Would you walk into the president's office and say something in that way? If not, don't say it on paper! Almost invariably, if your writing presents a different image than your speaking, it's a poorer image.

The lesson is obvious. If you talk better than you write (and most people do), you'd better learn to write more like you talk.

There'll be some differences, of course. When speaking, we tend to repeat ourselves and throw in extraneous words, such as "well, ummm, oh," as we stop and start. Those aren't necessary when you write (and needn't be so omnipresent in speech either). But if you imagine your reader sitting across the desk from you, you'll naturally refrain from stilted, formal language in your writing.

One simple change can greatly improve your writing. Just remember this...
Write more like you talk.

Many find this a difficult switch to make, because in our formative years we were taught that writing is supposed to be different. Fancier. Utilizing (instead of using) longer French-derivative words instead of short Anglo-Saxon words. Structured in a different way—in long sentences and paragraphs, allowing few changes of pace such as we put into our speech. Avoiding personal pronouns—you talking to me—in favor of impersonal references and passive voice.

Forget it!

If that's the style you discover when you reread those papers you've been sending out, it's time to forget everything you were taught about writing. Wipe the slate clean, because people don't talk in a stiff, stilted way anymore, and you shouldn't write as they did in the nineteenth century.

The Secret of an Easy, Conversational Style

Suppose you have an idea or information worth transmitting. You've thought about your audience; you know what they want and how best to approach them. You've sorted out the facts and prepared some sort of outline. Now, how can you put it all into words that'll present the kind of personality on paper that you achieve face-to-face?

Here's my secret—one that's shared by many professional writers who are always striving for clarity, warmth, and interest: *I talk to myself silently before I begin to write and while I'm writing.*

That's why professional writers often keep the doors of their offices closed. When passersby notice them sitting quietly with a faraway look in their eyes as they mutter to themselves, they conclude that the lucky stiffs at the typewriter have time to kill, so they either make snide remarks or pop into the office for a leisurely chat.

Actually, that quiet period when a writer thinks, and talks over with herself what she's about to put on paper, is 90 percent of the job. Operating the typewriter or computer, which most other people view as the key step, is merely a mechanical chore of low importance. Writers give up trying to explain this. How can you tell your envious coworkers, "No, I'm not loafing, I'm thinking" or "I'm talking to myself"? We have a reputation for being strange, without that sort of explanation, so it's easier to close the door.

Talking to myself silently accomplishes several things. It saves me time, because I can try out different phrasings in my head in just a second or two. It keeps me from producing spaghetti, because speech, even though silent, tends to come out in short, easily digestible pieces. It enables me to listen to the tone of what I intend to write. If it doesn't *sound* right in my head, chances are it won't read well either. And in getting that desirable sound of language, I end up with writing that's close to the personality and style I project when I talk.

Here's what I try to do to achieve an easy, conversational writing style:

1. *Use the right words.*   Simple and clear, not pompous or evasive. The kind I use in everyday speech.

2. *Keep it brief.*   I don't run on endlessly in my writing any more than I'd babble on when talking to someone.

3. *Be specific and accurate.*   People want facts—correct ones— especially in business.

4. *Add some interest.*   Visual as well as verbal. Because readers become bored easily.

Those characteristics will add clarity and force to your written messages.

15

Be Brief, Specific, and Accurate

I put a premium on brevity and accuracy.   J. PETER GRACE

If you want those businesspeople who receive your messages to love and trust you, remember three things when you write. I'll try to be *brief, specific*, and *accurate* in telling you why.

Be Brief

Why? Because the people to whom you write have neither the time nor inclination to wade through pages of unnecessary crud.

Because you don't win any brownie points for hard work when you produce a large poundage of paper. On the contrary, it shows *you haven't taken the time* to boil down ideas and facts to the essence—to pan for the gold instead of shoveling a lot of gravel onto others and expecting them to do the sorting.

Because trimming your writing down to the lean hard core causes you to *think*. You sharpen your ideas as you sharpen your prose.

At the start of World War II, Winston Churchill was one of the busiest men in the world. He had no time for nonsense or verbosity. He sent this directive to the First Lord of the Admiralty:

Pray state this day, *on* one side *of a sheet of paper, how the Royal Navy is being adapted to meet the conditions of modern warfare.*
WINSTON CHURCHILL

How'd you like to get a request like that? Can you imagine the consternation such a directive would cause in our Pentagon, and the reaction it would get?

The commanders of our complex corporations have no time for nonsense or verbosity either. More and more of them are embracing Churchill's view of the form that messages should take. Proctor & Gamble has outlawed memos longer than a single page; so has United Technologies; Harold Geneen demanded single-page memos at ITT. Do such demands for brevity mean that complete facts and comprehensive analysis should be eliminated? Of course not. Their *essence* is to be summarized in a page, while all the details are to be made available either in an appendix or from the author when requested.

The demand for brevity was carried beyond the "one page" dictum by Joyce C. Hall, founder of Hallmark Cards, Inc. When I went to work for that company, one of the first things I noticed was the popularity of 3×5 file cards. Ideas, notes, reminders were jotted on these small cards; they were pinned up on bulletin boards; used for memos.

I was told that when Mr. J. C. was still active in the operation of the company, he insisted that any idea submitted to him be written on a card. His view was that "*any idea which can't be typed on a small card hasn't been sufficiently thought out.*" Like other successful entrepreneurs, he was a man in a hurry.

Ways to Achieve Brevity

Skip the Preamble; Get to the Point.   Business messages, whether they be letters, memos, or reports, don't need a chatty introduction. In fact, any sort of general preamble creates a barrier to the basic business of telling someone something quickly. Once you decide what your most important idea or bit of information is, put it in the first sentence or a headline; then proceed immediately to explain it or back it up.

Don't Use 20 Words When 5 Will Do.   Once you get in the habit of cutting lazy words and trite phrases, you'll be amazed at how much more concise your writing becomes. And how much clearer. (For example, I could have written, "And how much clearer *it becomes too*." But those last three added words wouldn't have accomplished anything, except to lengthen the sentence and waste the reader's time.)

"*That*" is a word with which we tend to pepper sentences too liberally. Often it adds nothing to the meaning. Example: "We believe that you'll like our products." Eliminate "that." Same meaning, but a more direct, forceful statement, isn't it?

"*Which*" is a similar redundancy at times, often used in place of "that." Example: "I put down the book which I'd been reading." Strike out "which" and the sentence flows better.

Test yourself. Look at the last memo you wrote, and pencil out every word or phrase that serves no purpose. Maybe you can turn some passive-voice sentences into shorter active-voice ones too. How many words were you able to cut; does the new version read better?

> The most valuable of all talents is never
> using two words when one will do.
> THOMAS JEFFERSON

Eye Long Sentences Suspiciously.   Whenever you have a long sentence in your writing, ask yourself why it's so long. Maybe it needs a period to cut it into two easier-to-assimilate bits. But maybe the reason for its length is that it's padded with one or more trite, useless phrases. If so, cut 'em out!

Replace Words with a Chart or Graph.   When you need to convey facts about a business operation, one simple bar chart or pie chart may convey more information than hundreds of words, and do it better, faster, more memorably.

Get in the habit of using charts and graphs in your memos and reports. You can use them in letters too. Why not? Who decrees that such correspondence must be limited to words alone, when a simple visual device can transmit your message more efficiently and add interest at the same time?

Strive for the One-Pager.   If you set a goal—a single page for a memo or letter—you'll automatically write more concisely to achieve it. Then you'll have less cutting to do when you edit your work. If you feel you need to go longer on special occasions, that's fine, but start with brevity in mind.

Stop When You're Finished. Just as some people can't stop talking, others don't know when to stop writing. As soon as you've dealt adequately with your subject, that's when to quit. You don't need to add any "tail" to your message any more than you need a preamble to introduce it.

Some long memos get that way because the author tacks on a few paragraphs about an entirely different subject. That's worse than just being wordy; it introduces a new, confusing thought. If you have another matter to bring to your reader's attention, do it in a separate memo. It deserves that.

Trivia on Brevity

- The Lord's Prayer contains only 56 words.

- Abraham Lincoln made his memorable address at Gettysburg in 268 words.

- It took only 1322 words in the Declaration of Independence to get our whole country started.

- A survey of 74 federal agencies showed they issued 102,000 publications over 18 months. The *Monthly Catalog of U.S. Publications* listed 66,000 for the same period. One official's explanation: "The government is putting out printed material faster than it can keep track of it" (from *U.S. News & World Report*).

- George Washington delivered the shortest inaugural address of any President—only 135 words to state his aims for the new nation. The undistinguished William Henry Harrison was our wordiest President. His inaugural speech contained more than 9000 words. Standing in the rain during this lengthy harangue, Harrison caught pneumonia and died soon after. Moral: Be brief and you can claim to be like the father of your country; get too windy, and it may be the death of you, in one way or another.

Be Specific

Dick Hodgson, an international expert on direct marketing, told me of testing two ads that were identical except for headlines. He said, "The one with a specific promise in the headline pulled 52 percent more orders than the other which made a general statement. That's the difference between a profit and a big loss."

Such examples are not uncommon in the mail-order field, where it's possible to put exact dollar values on differences in wording. Experienced writers in that business know they can't afford to be vague in their mailing pieces. Not ever.

You can't afford to be vague in your business either. It causes misunderstandings, wastes time. Peter Grace is one businessperson who demands specifics.

What Does "Substantial" Mean?

We have a saying at Grace that "numbers count." They count in terms of precision, accuracy, and giving you the facts. To me, one fact is worth a thousand words, and by "fact" I mean numbers.

I look at everything on a spreadsheet basis. No matter how large your business, all of its key elements can be summarized on a single sheet of numbers arranged in lines and columns. We have spreadsheets that run 20 or 30 feet in length, but all the facts are there.

When I give a speech, I use 30 or 40 charts to get my points across. Each chart is like a mini-spreadsheet. We even use charts and tables in our advertising, and it's been proven effective.

In my experience, words are inefficient and imprecise. Even worse, they are often misleading. This is especially true of adjectives and adverbs, whose use is frowned on at Grace. Take, for example, a word like "substantial." What does it mean? How "substantial"? Is "substantial" life-threatening to your business or just a serious danger—or neither? How do you quantify "substantial"?

Instead of words, give me numbers. Numbers are reality.

J. Peter Grace, chairman & CEO
W. R. Grace & Company

Beware of Vague Modifiers

Mr. Grace asks, "What does 'substantial' mean?" There are many other vague modifiers that permit a wide latitude of interpretation—words such as "appreciably, much, very, slightly, somewhat, far, little." Beware of those generalities; replace them with specific information whenever you can.

Vague	*Specific*
Slightly behind schedule	Ten days late
Appreciably better sales	Sales up 15 percent
Let's meet *soon*	Can we lunch together Friday?
Deadline is *quickly* approaching	Deadline is June 1
Very good response	230 inquiries received
Far costlier	Costs $100 more per unit
Frequently used	Used daily
Prices *little* changed	Rising 2 percent annually
Essentially the same product	Only the container is new
Marked increase in costs	Costs doubled last year
Highly recommended	Recommended by Jones
Extremely fast service	Next-day delivery

Let's look at an example of how generalities can confuse, while facts and figures clarify. There's no specific information in a memo like this:

> The latest economic forecasts indicate a very strong likelihood of continued escalation in the prices of basic materials required for the manufacture of products like ours. An area of special concern is the potential substantial future increases anticipated in the cost of cuprous components which have been highly sensitive to the effects of inflation throughout the preceding 12 months, and which we purchase in substantial volume to fulfill our scheduled obligations to our customers. It would seem advisable, therefore, to consider augmenting as rapidly as possible our inventory situation, which at the present time is at a lower level than the norm for this period of the year.

If you were talking to someone, you'd say:

> Copper wire doubled in price last year, and it probably will again. We'll need 80 tons of it just to fill the orders on our books. And our wire inventory is only two-thirds of normal. We'd better stock up now with at least 100 tons.

Be Accurate

The only thing worse than having no information is proceeding with the *wrong* information. If you get your facts wrong, no amount of experience or brilliant reasoning can avert a disastrous decision.

Unfortunately, decisions are all too often predicated on shaky facts. So you have to question the sources of what are presumed to be facts, and view with a very critical eye any information you have the slightest reason to suspect may be flawed. Only when you have all your facts straight are you ready to communicate them to others.

At first glance, this may seem like an obvious procedure that's always followed by everyone. But if you'll reflect on your own experience for a moment, you'll surely recall instances when you've been fed incomplete or distorted information.

You may have run into characters who bristle when their facts are questioned, giving you an injured look and loud assurances instead of the specifics that are really needed. Isn't it true…

> *The degree of one's emotions varies inversely with one's knowledge of the facts. The less you know, the hotter you get.*   BERTRAND RUSSELL

Beware of those who act that way.

When Harold S. Geneen was chairman of the board at ITT, he established a dictum that only "unshakable facts" were acceptable in management reports. His views on that subject are still circulated to new executives at the company. Here's an excerpt from one management folder:

Unshakable Facts

There is no word in the English language that more strongly conveys the intent of incontrovertibility—i.e., "final and reliable reality"—than the word "fact." However, no word is more honored by its breach in actual usage. There are:
- Apparent facts
- Assumed facts
- Reported facts
- Hoped-for facts

Professional management requires the literal ability to "smell" a *real fact* from all others—and moreover to have the temerity, intellectual curiosity, guts, and/or plain impoliteness, if necessary, to be sure that what you have is indeed what we call an "unshakable fact." That is the only kind of fact you can accept or submit.

HAROLD S. GENEEN

For the good of your company (and your own self-preservation), develop a healthy skepticism about any facts that seem to have a hazy origin. Ask questions. Track down the source of your facts. And if you can't identify a reliable source you agree with, always state your doubts or objections. Once you quote another authority, whoever it is, the data you pass on becomes *your* responsibility.

Finding the True Truth

In our society, we are bombarded with information constantly. Some of it good. Some of it bad. All of it used in some way by individuals making decisions about what they will do.

Without straightforward communication, anyone can begin to believe that what they are thinking is absolutely true. But truth often falls somewhere between one person's perception of an event and another person's perception. Give-and-take of communication is necessary to shape and polish individual ideas and discover truth.

A manager who does not express his own thoughts and ideas abandons the opportunity to contribute to discovering truth. He abandons his responsibility to manage.

Keep communication simple and make sure it expresses your own ideas. Use the communication process to formulate your own "truth" but, when you say something, be certain to use your own thoughts—avoid "committee" writing.

RICHARD FERRIS, CHAIRMAN & CEO
United Airlines, Inc.

Careless Writing Can Be Costly

Finished manuscripts need to be checked and double-checked before you sign and distribute them—for as you know, there can be many a slip of your pen or your secretary's typewriter.

An apocryphal example often cited about the high cost of careless writing concerns the misplacing of a hyphen. This jumbling of a simple little punctuation mark took place in the office of a nuclear power plant. Supposedly, a supply of lengthy uranium rods was needed for the reactor of the power plant. The purchase order was supposed to call for a number of "10-foot-long" rods. Instead, it asked for "10 foot-long" rods. Note the slight difference; only a hyphen was dropped. But when 10 short pieces were received, they all had to go back for reprocessing at huge expense and with a long delay.

Could something as small as a hyphen or a comma or an incorrect word cause a great deal of trouble? It probably has, more than once, in your organization. Don't let it happen to you.

Checklist for Accuracy

Here's what you need to do to ensure accuracy:

- *Know the source.* If the information came through a succession of people, where did it begin?
- *State the source.* Let those who read your message know precisely

where you got your data. (Notice that newspaper stories always identify the source.)

- *Question the reliability of facts and figures.* Are you absolutely certain they're correct?

- *Proofread carefully.* It's so easy to transpose or skip a figure. And *you* are responsible for the accuracy of anything you sign—not the secretary who typed it.

> To err is human, but when the eraser
> wears out ahead of the pencil, you're
> overdoing it.   ANONYMOUS

In Sum

This chapter is about writing, but its examples could just as well have involved speaking.

Whether writing a memo, making a speech, or talking to someone, you can get in just as much trouble if your facts aren't correct. You'll come off as vague and uncertain if you deal in generalities rather than getting down to specifics. And you'll leave your audience yawning if you don't know enough to stop when you're finished.

> When you say less, and say it more
> clearly, people remember more of
> it—and longer.
>   QUENTIN E. WOOD, CHAIRMAN & CEO
>   *Quaker State Oil & Refining*
>   *Corporation*

One of the biggest pitfalls in communication is to become enamored of your words, written or spoken. That's when you get carried away with your eloquence and desire to appear witty, profound, or important. That's when you forget that, in business, it pays to "get down to business"—to be brief, specific, and accurate.

To avoid that temptation when you're preparing a report or presentation, you might imagine that you're going to give it to former President Johnson. Remember Lyndon B. with his piercing gaze and chilling scowl. He was of the same ilk as the toughest, most demanding of the bosses and customers you deal with. And like them, he was impatient with any communications that were not straight to the point. His dictum to White House staff and government department heads bringing in reports:

> Cut it in half, get it straight, and leave
> out the damn jokes!
>   LYNDON B. JOHNSON

16

How to Make Writing Look Inviting

Every style that is not boring is a good one. VOLTAIRE

Does your writing scare people off or draw them in? The way it looks can determine that. The layout of a written page can also make it easier to absorb and remember information.

Think of your own reactions when you're plowing into a pile of correspondence. When you come to pages packed solidly, margin to margin, with huge paragraphs, your eyeballs shudder and resist. You say to yourself, "This is going to be hard work." And you may push that memo or letter aside, temporarily, which means it may be buried forever.

Here's how you can make your writing easy to get into, easy to assimilate.

Flag the Reader with a Headline

Make it easy for the reader to determine instantly what you're writing about. Put some sort of label at the top of every memo or report, and atop the text of all but the briefest letters.

Save the reader time in determining what you're writing about by identifying the subject in this manner. Make it easy to file your missive. Make it easy to find it again when the reader says, "Now where did I put that memo? I know it's somewhere in this pile."

You don't want to get cute with this identification, but it always helps to be interesting—as newspapers and magazines are with their headlines. Take the most significant or most interesting bit of information and make that your headline. Instead of

> RE: NEW TAX LAW PROVISIONS

maybe you can say,

> WHAT WE NEED TO DO TO CLAIM
> FASTER DEPRECIATION

Use Subheads

One or two subheads on a page breaks the monotony. Like a headline, a subhead enables you to flag the reader's interest with some significant bit of information.

A subhead can be typed either in caps and lowercase or in all caps.

Break Up Long Paragraphs

Several lines of solid type look hard to read, because they are. Break them up into short paragraphs.

The page will look more interesting if your paragraphs vary in length. Some can be three or four sentences long; some longer; some a single sentence. You may want to use a one-line paragraph to spotlight a significant thought.

Indent to Bring the Eye In

Another way to break up solid chunks of type is to indent significant items.

Key facts won't be buried if you pull them out of the text into a list with numbers or letters (or asterisks or dots) in front of each item. For example:

1. Indentation makes the text look more inviting.

2. It calls attention to significant facts.

3. You may want to use a variety of indentations to put your message into outline form, rather than the usual paragraphs.

Underline or Capitalize for Emphasis

One or two words IN CAPITALS will stand out.

To emphasize phrases or sentences, use underlining. Besides calling attention to something of importance, <u>underlining adds visual variety to the text.</u>

Write in the Margins

Leave ample margins on each side of the text. If you want to really emphasize some point, take a pen and jot a note in the margin next to it. Maybe with a little arrow. Or a circle around your note.

Highlight with a Spot of Color

Don't be afraid to use a bit of showmanship. Your messages are fighting to get attention against all those others in the blizzard of paper.

All it takes is a note written with a colored pen. Or a yellow underline with a felt-tip highlighter. Or a yellow or blue arrow in the margin.

Any reader is going to look at the line you highlight in color. If it's important and interesting, that'll lead to the reading of the rest of your message. That's what you want, isn't it?

Consider Pictures or Graphs

Words are not the only means of communication. Don't forget that in certain circumstances a picture or graph may do a better job.

More quickly. More memorably.

Instead of taking hundreds of words to explain a complexity of related facts, can you picture it instead? With a simple bar chart? A graph? A pie chart? Maybe that's all you need, along with a sentence or two.

Don't forget photographs either. It's not impossible to use them in business messages. Nothing's impossible if you're willing to exhibit some ingenuity in order to be more effective.

Early in my business career, I had to develop a lengthy report based on interviews I was making in several states with dealers of a potential advertising client. I soon realized how difficult it would be for my colleagues to visualize what I was seeing on my trip. So I took snapshots of every dealership, inside and out, and mounted small prints throughout the couple of copies of my report that went to our key people. They saw exactly what I was talking about. They liked it well enough to give me a raise in pay.

Don't Forget a P.S. on Letters

The letter experts, the direct marketers who send them out by the millions, have proved that the postscript gets more attention than any other part of a letter.

So if you're writing a sales letter of any kind (and a lot of our letters are selling something), don't forget to add a sentence or two in a post-script. That'll give your reader another reason to agree with your thoughts.

To make a page look interesting...

◀ Not this...

but *this.*
▼

October 5, 1922

To: Deshvkex Xrstuvbn
Mqwert Yuiopasdf
From: Ghjkl Mnpiuytr

Qweet yuiop aasd fg hjklzx mnop ious uiopqweet asdf ghjklm
qwert yuiopa sd fgh jkl;zxcvbn mqwert yuiop as dfgh jklmnb
asdfg ikjhg gfdsamnbv. Xzpoiu uytre ew qlkjhgfd sazxcc bnm
poiu uyttree ewq poi lkjhhg gffdsa lkjh lkjhg mnbv lkjhg
poiunty tyuiope Hiow. Lkjhgf hgf dsamnbvc vcxz mnbvcx lkjhgv poiu
youiop rewtyuhgf jklhnoip uiop werthuiop, yuioplkjh cayhio
uiop. Hjklmnuio uiop wert yuiop wert yuio gffds.

Uiop uiop opiuyt ghbnmnkl. Mnbvvcxz kjh gfdasewqrt iopuiop
iopp uiop iop klllijhuygtred hngvfredser yuytre yuuy iopgh
iu hui uioopkjjh hgfdret ytred wqart er tyrrew yui uiiopp
ytuihjgr fdewr mnyutrews ftyres-;uj kujliop hyreer ui.

Wertfgdc hgvbfrt yuiop hnbgty juiop hjkliuyt tyred
huynt yuh yuioplk kjhngbvf fdsertyuiop gredw qwert'
yuiop kuhjuiop lokijhyt ghty ghjkll fgde. Mehy hgt
uiopkljnh mnhjuiop hjkl ghyfttred tyri-tryuioe gft
kljui sfweqart zxcadsq ,frtedtyuis uiiopr pfiodf.

yuirphar huiepp ausoojsjw thuushe hysuehdyetra dg
huiop wgsyweurt wheyettjaland jhauhs hsuwkeorjaie
huweishe agwfwretyu yuroiappsk hjsuend hsujenndf
hujenderhn. Hjksmeisnw, kjuwidlw sneiwjksm swert
shwerty yuiprps hjkalmcnb anlisnwm, wleduidsnns
gsueiepep wheuebdsnd, smklwmsiopp wertta shwuiwr
shuwiwoo psomsnxbxhwsl hsjwueip hjuls hye sheel

Hunskwj sheuwye ahqyweu ahauowp shuwwpp ahslwif
hnwjskn zcxbanmsdl lkjshag oeieyryaba peoeutja(
losiisjqj. Huwjisnds jsssuwt justhaksl lmanhsk
ispwpskk snsuwnshs qksisppa anhsiwnw asjwiw s
lamansjkqwl; jsklwmno iospw hsjuuwpwna,s nasl‹
hajnsklq. Hjwuaislwna askipans jahsbavcczz as‹
jansklw shwioans, nahkancla halandhuqnan man‹
asghjkamsn laksnshkla, manahkcinzcqt qgqtauac
namsk;quiops whayusoso shuisnshuu aahsjlakah

To: Deshvkex Xrstuvbn   October 5, 1922
Mqwert Yuiopasdf

From: Ghkl Mniuytr

FOUR MAIN REASONS FOR SALES
INCREASE IN SEPTEMBER

Qweet yuiop fg hjkslms nkopow yuiwpepk shueip ghklmn
manu nusipeo jiden nsjeoun nhieoe:

1. Fghjd kldj nh jduiep jeudd hsuiep
   fgeyuie jsuie.

2. Ghsj whueiep sjueipe ju jsuieo.

3. Gduiep mwjuwiep sjue jsuei.

4. Gydueie jsuek dfjud ioepe skieop
   sgeyui. Nhduei nsu e jsuei jduieo.

Desrt we wheyeu sue, keipe sjeui ui. Huei asuei seioe
hsuei sheui sheui.

Comparison with Competition

Wentyu hu i jshbsje hsuei sheuie. Huiwn kanbzc hndh jl
tuuio. Iosjw ui sjklw sheu hu skle shei shekep ks jkll
hui.

Smith

Jones

Zilch

Note improvement by Smith

Ascvbn sehyu wyeui io j jkuip juidp jduie kiop s klsl
shey. Je hsue jsuei kslamdn a,nhe jeio.

P.S. Bdccfg chjkl lo im mopuytre as do meel nopiu yuio sdfg sd s
asdf dfer gh hjuiop kl⁺hn mno op iuy.

17
Your Critical Role as Editor

Most writers slough off the most important part of their trade—editing their stuff, honing it and honing it until it gets an edge like a bullfighter's killing sword.
ERNEST HEMINGWAY

Writing is a three-part process. Thinking out your message and putting it on paper are the first two parts. The final part, which is just as essential, requires you to switch roles.

You must become the Critic, the Editor. Your job isn't finished until you assume this critical role, because it can *always* improve your writing. Keep in mind that your first draft is a starting point; succeeding drafts (one or several more) will make it better. And anything important you send out deserves to be crafted carefully so it hits its goal and reflects favorably on you.

Shape Up the Rough Draft

Your first draft should be double-spaced with wide margins so it's easy to make corrections or additions. Don't spare the pencil! I don't know any writers who can assemble their words perfectly the first time. The better they are, the more likely they are to make revisions, again and again.

Here are the initial steps that you, the Editor, must take in this first whack at your writing:

- *Cut it.*

  Cut unnecessary words.
  Cut meaningless phrases, redundant sentences.
  Cut irrelevant thoughts. Aim for one objective and stick to it.
  Could you cut the entire first paragraph to start out faster?

- *Check it.*

  Check all facts and figures, and tell where you got them.
  Check spelling, especially of names.
  Check grammar.
  Have you left out anything important? Refer to your outline.

- *Package it.*

  Break up long sentences.
  Break up long paragraphs.
  Use subheads if the text is long.
  Consider some of the techniques described in the previous chapter—
    indentations, lists, typographic devices such as underlining—to
    make the text easier to assimilate.

Put Yourself in the Reader's Place

Once you've trimmed and tidied up your first draft, get it retyped. Then put it aside for a while. If possible, stay away from it at least until the next day. If deadlines preclude that, get a cup of coffee and clear your mind of your writing for a few minutes, because you need to come back for the second step of editing with a fresh viewpoint, the viewpoint of a reader.

Imagine a critical reader—one totally uninformed about your subject and just as uninterested in it. One who'll surely garble the meaning of your sentences if you provide the slightest opportunity. One who'll toss your message in the wastebasket at the first yawn.

Looking at your precious writing from the viewpoint of this super-critical klutz, ask yourself these questions:

1. *Does it grab the reader and hold on?*

   Is there something of interest in the first sentence, or in a headline?
   Is there a "zinger" buried in the text you could move up front?

Is everything throughout of interest to the reader, and presented in terms of reader benefits?

2. *Is it easy to read, conversational?*

Is it built with short words, short sentences, active verbs, active voice, personal pronouns, contractions, somewhat like people talk?
Is the language right for the reader? Not over the reader's head, but not talking down?
Is there anything that can possibly be misunderstood?

3. *Does it flow logically and easily?*

Are your points in the right order? Do you start with the key idea and carry the reader along step-by-step to a logical conclusion? If not, you'd better rearrange, because your reader isn't going to jump back and forth to reach the goal you have in mind.

4. *Does it sound like you at your best?*

Sincere: Did you say what you mean with no weasel words or evasive third-person phrases?
Likable: No pompous jargon or gobbledygook?
Businesslike: Specific statements and provable facts? Direct and to the point?

5. *What will the reader carry away?*

If it's *information*, will it be all the reader wants?
If it's *persuasion*, will the reader reach exactly the conclusion you hope for?
If you seek *action*, will the reader be fired up to take it? Did you spell out in a request at the end the precise action you desire?

Let Your Ear Be the Judge

One of the most helpful things you can do as an editor is to read your writing aloud. Listen to it. Your ear can spot phoniness, pomposity, and dullness where your eye may have overlooked it.

Keep the supercritical reader in mind. Imagine you're sitting across from that person, talking; then read your message aloud. Could you use those same words and expressions in conversation, or would they embarrass you?

If it sounds OK, chances are it'll be OK. But if the sound doesn't seem right or the message doesn't come across clearly, heed the warning.

Get a Second Opinion

If something you write is extremely important, test it before you send it on its way.

That's done all the time to professional writing. Every newspaper and magazine, for example, has an editor who must OK every piece of copy before it's set in type. Until it passes the editor's test, it doesn't go.

Advertising copy also gets the once-over (or twice-over) by an editor or copy chief. And the ad or commercial may be shown to a consumer panel, a group of typical buyers whose reactions to a variety of approaches are tested. You can do somewhat the same thing in a limited way, to determine if you're leading your readers where you want them to go.

> *I sometimes think that writing is like driving sheep down a road. If there is any gate to the right or left, the readers will most certainly go into it.*
> C. S. Lewis

A patient spouse is the handiest sounding board. Have your spouse read your message quickly; half an hour later, ask what was remembered. That'll give you a realistic, often sobering, view of what your ultimate reader is likely to derive from your writing.

You may be able to get helpful suggestions from those who work for you. Don't ask them if they like your creation; you don't want flattery. Ask them to question anything that bothers them and to indicate improvements wherever they can.

You may not agree with the suggestions; you don't have to. But you may get an indication of the ultimate reader's reaction, and you may spot weaknesses or omissions that should be fixed.

The Search for Excellence

How much editing should you do? A hurried polishing job? A careful rewrite of a second draft, or many drafts? That depends on how important a piece of writing is to you.

If you want it to be good, expect to sweat a little. Even those who are masters of this art can't always spew forth jewels from their typewriters. They create flaws aplenty, which they must spot and polish away. Just as you and I must.

In his correspondence with me, Andy Rooney admitted that he's never quite satisfied with his writing and is always trying for something better.

Even a Pro Has Doubts

When I got to college I looked back on what I'd done with such pride in high school, and wondered how I could have been so young. When I went to work for a newspaper and started cleaning out boxes of things I'd written for the college newspaper, I burned them hastily so no one would ever know how bad I'd been as a writer. Over the years, whenever I've looked back at things I wrote in the past, they seem...how shall I say...jejune.

That's okay for high school, college, and early newspaper pieces I wrote, but now I notice I look at things I wrote last week and decide that this week I'm finally growing up and writing better. What am I going to think of this next week?

ANDY ROONEY

So you see, writing that's excellent is the result of hard work. But it's satisfying and can be very rewarding, especially if you're building a career in business or the professions—because few business and professional people have even adequate writing skills.

You can stand out from your peers with writing that's clear, natural, concise, modern, vital. Like you. Destined for success.

18

Personal Chemistry Is the Catalyst

Friends come and go, but enemies accumulate. ANONYMOUS

How well you react personally with other people has a powerful effect on how well they're going to listen to you. Developing the right chemistry with others can determine your success in social life and in business. Often it outweighs everything else.

You can talk until you're blue in the face and write the most persuasive memos and letters, but all your elaborate words and brilliant ideas are apt to be ignored if the spark of rapport is missing. You've seen it happen. People may seem to be attentive, but you can tell from their eyes that there's no warmth of response. They may even nod or say yes to a request, but if they dislike the individual it's coming from, there's little likelihood they'll follow through. The souring of personal relations negates communication.

If you have any doubts about the role that personal rapport, or the lack of it, plays in business, recall the incident that shook the automobile industry a few years ago. It was a matter of chemistry between Henry Ford II and his chief lieutenant, Lee Iacocca. Remember?

Even the Mighty Can Tumble

Iacocca, now chairman of the board of Chrysler Corporation, was then president of Ford Motor Company—an eminence achieved by 32 years of spectacular performance at the company. Starting as a lowly engineering trainee, he'd distinguished himself in one sales and marketing assignment after another. He'd developed and introduced the Mustang, Ford's hot seller of the decade. During his presidency, profits zoomed to an all-time pinnacle of $1.8 billion. He was raking in one of the highest salaries in the world as crown prince of the Ford empire. *He had it made*. Right?

Not entirely. The crown prince began to notice some signs of coolness from the king of the Ford empire, known in Detroit as Henry the Deuce. One fateful morning Henry called Lee into his office and bluntly told him he ought to resign.

Iacocca demanded a reason. Did Ford cite any dissatisfaction with sales, administration, finance, production, profits—the things business textbooks cite as the quantifiable factors that determine success in the corporate world? Not at all. After some hemming and hawing, Iacocca relates, Mr. Ford could cite only one reason. His explanation, in the traditional style of monarchs, ignored such mundane details as performance or results, but it went to the heart of the matter. All he said was: *"Sometimes you just don't like somebody."*

What more can be said about the role of personal chemistry in our careers and in our social life?

Scattered throughout this book, you'll find a variety of suggestions about nurturing rapport with others. Here are some additional ones to think about.

Do You Indulge in Omphaloskepsis?

In the temple of Apollo at Delphi, there was a huge round stone that was thought to be the center of the universe. It was called the "omphalos," the center point.

Early physicians who wrote the first medical books liked that Greek word. It sounded fancy, so ordinary people wouldn't understand it, and it seemed appropriate to designate the center point of the human body. So they selected "omphalos" to be the medical name for the navel.

A few people who are into Yoga and other eastern religions go in for contemplating their own navel (omphaloskepsis) because they believe it'll help them concentrate on the center of their being and discover the meaning of life. There's a danger of your becoming an omphaloskeptic at times, because, like the ancient Greeks, you may think you've found the center of the universe.

Where to Find the Secret of Life

If you ever allow yourself to assume smugly that everything important revolves around you, you'll turn off other people and the world will pass you by. The secret of life is *outward*, not inward.

If you want to make friends and communicate effectively, always remember that the action is out there. The more you pay attention to other people, the more attention they'll give to what you say. Therefore, my advice is: *Keep your nose out of your navel, and keep your attention focused on others.*

Everyone Has a Hot Button

If you focus your total attention on the people you deal with, you'll soon discover they're all different individuals who react to different things. They all have what salespeople sometimes refer to as a "hot button." Only when you find out what their special interests are and press that hot button can you really turn them on.

Columbus learned this during the several years he tried to sell his idea of sailing westward to find a shorter route to the spices and riches of the orient. All the monarchs and titans of trade he approached thought it was a flaky idea with too high an investment and too great a risk.

He discovered that Queen Isabella had an overwhelming interest in securing herself a choice place in heaven by helping to convert many nonbelievers to the true faith. Wisely, Christopher eased up on his previous sales pitch about spices and gold. Instead, he pointed out that he'd be sailing to lands populated solely by infidels all ripe for conversion by the priests he'd take along on his voyage. Isabella told her advisers to forget about the cost and the risks; she'd finance three ships.

The Clues Are All Around You

Most hot buttons are easier to identify than Isabella's. Usually you can spot them readily if you simply keep your eyes and ears open.

The furnishings of many homes and offices spell it out for you. Photos of activities obviously dear to the heart of the occupant. Decorative prints and paintings of sailboats, horses, hunting scenes, fishing, skiing. Trophies and awards.

The style of decor can also tell you much. Is it traditional or modern, flamboyant or cautious, in tone and design? It you enter a business office that displays no nonfunctional touches whatever—just strictly business—you'd better skip the personal chitchat.

When You Share an Interest, You Make a Friend

Once you get behind the mask we all wear (the "persona," Dr. Jung called it) and discover what a person's deepest interests are, you can build friendships that will not only open closed doors but also be educational and enjoyable.

When you learn that Joe in the finance department is an avid gardener, ask him how his tomato plants are coming along. You'll not only make his day, you may learn something, and perhaps receive a bag of vegetables, come harvest season, because he likes you and the two of you get along so well in your work.

If you take the time to learn about people, you may discover that the quiet young woman in marketing is a hotshot skier, the research manager is a Girl Scout leader, the senior vice president is a devoted family man who thinks the sun rises and sets on his grandchildren.

Nothing in the world is as interesting as people. If you're willing to listen to them, you can learn more than from all the textbooks ever written. They'll be glad to give you all sorts of information—not only about their hobbies or special interests, but about business and general topics as well.

Once you begin to share confidences about their personal activities and achievements, you're *someone who understands them.* We all need that, no matter what our social or economic level may be. Those who understand us are those we like to help.

How to Shine Up Your Frame of Mind

If you focus your attention on others, tuning in to their interests and desires, you're headed in the right direction. But there's another factor to consider: your *attitude.* It shows, and it influences the reception you get from others.

To get started on the right track each morning, give some attention to your inner feelings as well as to your countenance. Consider how you feel about yourself and about those you'll be in contact with during the day.

The starting point is to have a good image of yourself.

We all tend to have self-doubts and depressed moods at times; then we sell ourselves short. This isn't good for our mental health or the way we deal with people. In fact, psychiatrists tell us that much of the trouble in the world is caused by people who are unhappy with themselves, and therefore with others. The unruly child and the adult in deep trouble often share the common characteristic of a low self-image. Those are extreme cases. But even a little lack of confidence slows us down. And it shows.

If you have a negative attitude about a person you'll be dealing with, this shows too. When the person senses your dislike or low opinion, it may very well sour your relations and spoil the outcome of your meeting.

A Simple Way to Improve Your View of Self and Others

I call it the card trick, but there's really no trick to it. It's basic psychology you can put to work to build your self-confidence and your liking for the people around you.

Let's start with you. Suppose you have an important appointment today or a big meeting that means a lot to you. And you're worried about it—worried that you may not have the capabilities to carry it off. How can you build up your confidence, reassuring yourself that you're a capable person with an excellent chance for success?

I suggest you get yourself a 3 × 5 card and write the letters of your name on it. You can use your first name, last name, or nickname. Try this exercise all three ways at different times.

After each of those letters you've written on the card, write an adjective that you honestly feel applies to you. Choose adjectives that are most appropriate for the task or situation you face at the moment.

Let's take the letters of my last name, and let's suppose I'm getting ready for a meeting to discuss a possible transfer to an overseas assignment. Here's how I might see myself:

W—Widely traveled

A—Articulate

L—Language-oriented

T—Take-charge guy

O—Objective

N—Nonabrasive

Looking at myself that way, I can see that I have a lot to offer in that job I'm hoping to get in my firm's international office. I can approach the coming meeting with the president of our company with confidence that I'm a good candidate. I have reminded myself of several traits I have that would be valuable in dealing with new people in other countries.

I'm going to keep that card in my pocket and look at it several times to keep myself charged up. In addition, reviewing it will help me remember some of the personal characteristics—my travel experience, language abilities, diplomatic personality—that I should be sure to point up in the interview.

Focus on the Positive

You have a wide range of possibilities when it comes to selecting upbeat adjectives to describe yourself. They're easy to find in the dictionary. For example, here are some of the adjectives you'd find under "A" in Webster's; if this letter's in your name, which of these would describe you?

Able, Accessible, Accomodating, Accomplished, Accurate, Achiever, Action-oriented, Adaptable, Administrator, Adventurous, Aesthetic, Affectionate, Aggressive, Agreeable, Ambitious, Amiable, Analytical, Anecdotist, Animated, Appreciative, Artistic, Assertive, Assiduous, Astute, Athletic, Attuned, Audacious, Available, Aware

Besides improving your view of yourself, it's often important to develop a better view of others. Sometimes it's difficult to think well of certain people you deal with, but you ought to try. Even though it's a struggle, you can find some good points in everyone if you search hard enough.

For example, suppose the bearcat's name is Jones. Resist your first impulses to think of him as Jackal, Obstinate, Nasty, etc. Try hard to think of some redeeming qualities:

J—Jogger (at least he keeps his body in trim)
O—Orderly (doesn't leave things in a mess)
N—Nonsmoker (won't stink up your office)
E—Energetic (will pull his weight, if you can get him to cooperate)
S—Self-made man (probably had a hard time early in life)

So, if you think about it, even that obstinate fellow Jones has a few redeeming features you can put on your card. Keep those good things in mind as you approach your meeting, and maybe the two of you can even get to like each other a little.

Put on a Happy Face Each Morning

It's more fun to be happy than sad. It's also more productive, because nobody likes a grouch.

When you start your day on a happy, positive note, even if you have to force yourself to do it, things are likely to continue in the same vein.

That's because a cheerful outlook is self-fulfilling; people you deal with tend to respond to you in a cheerful, positive way—not always, of course, but mostly. You have to play the percentages, and they're in your favor if you get off to a good start each morning.

> Be pleasant until 10 o'clock in the morning and the rest of the day will take care of itself.   ELBERT HUBBARD

When you're dressing in the morning, take a second to stare deliberately at that person in the mirror and assess what you see. If you're looking at a sourpuss, change that. Immediately. Think of something good that happened the previous day; there must have been one bright spot in the day. Or imagine something good you're expecting. Or concentrate on someone or something you really like. It might be your lover or chocolate ice cream, depending on your proclivities. How about both?

Before you leave the bedroom, be sure your face makes as good an impression as your clothes. *It's even more important.* It's you!

The Proven Value of a Smile

Aside from the fact that it just plain feels better when you go through life with a smile, there's a provable dollar-and-cents advantage to a happy expression.

To verify this, simply recall the face of your favorite waitress. She's a smiler, isn't she? Greets you with a wide one every time. Her service may not always be the best, but even if the kitchen holds up the orders, she gets fewer complaints. And bigger tips than her coworkers.

Even candidates for President of the United States discover that smiling, or not smiling, has measurable results. The political pollsters generally agreed that one of the biggest factors in Richard Nixon's defeat in his first run for the presidency was that he smiled too seldom and too briefly for the television cameras. In his second campaign he was careful to open every speech with a broad smile and to keep smiling frequently to project a warmer image. It worked.

The Magic "Yes" Sign

Behavioral psychologists tell us that it pays to smile when asking for the order. They say the salesperson who uses a smile is flashing a subtle "yes" sign at us. We're inclined to echo the visual yes with a verbal one. In their training programs for salesclerks, some department stores include instructions to smile; they find that smiles improve sales results by at least 10 percent.

> *Don't Work So Hard:*
> *You must activate 43 muscles*
> *to frown, but only 17 to smile.*

Research organizations that conduct personal polls, such as mall intercepts, invariably stress the need for the interviewer to smile when approaching a prospective interviewee. The shoppers intercepted have nothing to gain, yet most of them readily stop to give up their time and personal information to the pollster. Their pay is usually nothing but a smile.

Keep Score on the Results of Your Morning Smiles

Promise yourself right now that you're going to give the smile-in-the-mirror technique a try, starting tomorrow morning, and are going to keep a record of how well it works for you.

Each morning all week, mentally chalk up how many "bounce-backs" you get from your warm, genuine friendliness. Smile at each person you meet and notice if they smile in return, or ignore it.

I'll bet that if you smile at 12 people, and really let it well up from within you, you'll get close to a dozen smile-backs.

That's a good start to a good day.

> *When we sing, everybody hears us.*
> *When we sigh, nobody hears us.*
> RUSSIAN PROVERB

Handle Egos Tenderly

Everyone has an ego, some bigger than others, and all of our egos bruise easily. That's because the ego, in its broader sense, is your self-esteem, your pride.

Dr. Sigmund Freud pointed out that the ego is a powerful force deep inside every human being. He called it *the desire to be great* and listed it as one of the two primary reasons behind all our actions. (He defined the other great motivator as the desire for sex.)

The one unpardonable sin is to trample on someone's ego. If you destroy a person's human dignity, that person is going to get even with you at some time in some way. The orientals refer to it as causing a person to lose face. They never forget or forgive it, and neither do you or I.

A variety of bad habits can hurt feelings and cause trouble. You know what they are, but do you always steer clear of them? Here's what you want to avoid:

- *Don't look for arguments.* You can't win a bitter argument. When you must disagree (as is often necessary), do it tactfully. Never say the other person is "wrong." Besides avoiding bruised feelings, it's more effective to admit that you can see the reasoning of the other side and then quietly to point out those reasons which you believe to be more compelling. Some give-and-take lets the other person save face.

- *Never reprimand in public.* This is the ultimate no-no, yet I've known otherwise intelligent business managers who make a habit of chewing out subordinates in front of an audience. So have you. This sort of boss drives out the best people; only the desperate ones will put up with it.

- *Don't knock others; be positive rather than negative.* It turns people against you when they hear you running others down. They have enough problems without being subjected to negative attitudes that depress and possibly embarrass them. Don't knock your job or your firm either—not in any way. When you do, you set up doubts that destroy any credibility you might have.

When a man points a finger at someone else, he should remember that three of his fingers are pointing at himself.
LOUIS NIZER

In place of these ego-bruising bad habits, there are many pleasant things we can do every day to cement personal relations.

Remember What Your Mama Taught You—Be Polite

In business especially, many of us Americans tend to get carried away in our drive for action and let ourselves act rudely. This reputation for brusqueness can be a handicap in approaching foreign executives; many don't realize that when you seem impatient or outspoken (by their standards), you don't mean to be impolite. The wide discrepancy in language attitudes, for example, is illustrated by the following note from a Chinese magazine editor, rejecting a manuscript:

> We have read your manuscript with boundless delight. If we were to publish your paper, it would be impossible for us to publish any work of a lower standard. And as it is unthinkable that in the next thousand years we shall see its equal, we are, to our regret, compelled to return your divine composition, and to beg you to overlook our short sight.

That's not our style. But how delightful an attempt to soften a blow that is bound to cause some pain.

Nothing Succeeds Like Kindness

This has been a keystone of religious teachers from Buddha to Jesus. It's known as the Golden Rule: "Do unto others as you would have them do unto you." Old stuff; heard it when you were a kid. But do you follow it now that you're an adult?

Maybe you're more impressed by the cynical school of business philosophy that preaches, "Look out for number one" or "Knife thy neighbor." If that's your modus operandi, remember that those who live by the knife die by the knife. As one of my former business colleagues liked to phrase it, "As you climb the ladder of success, don't spit on the people below you; some of them are going to make it to the top someday."

Granted, you do come across people who aren't easy to like, but even if you can't bring yourself to love them, you can still be kind to them. At the minimum, if you can't think of anything good to say about them, don't say anything at all. It might just be that if you proffer the hand of friendship sometime, they'll be so surprised that they'll take it.

Cynics may believe there's no place in business for such niceties, but the evidence indicates otherwise. Ewing Kauffman, the billionaire CEO of Marion Laboratories, told me specifically that he follows the Golden Rule as the basis for operating his company. And he added, "It's not because I'm religious—I don't consider myself a religious person—but I believe it's *just good business practice*. Once in a while you may get taken. But overall, the company that always tries to be fair to others will end up financially better than one that doesn't. It's worked that way for us."

The Art of Mirroring

One of the newest (and best) techniques extolled by sales-training experts is called mirroring. Correction: It's something the finest salespeople have been practicing since the early days of the wheeler-dealers in their camel caravans on the silk and spice routes between the east and the west. But it's been enjoying a well-deserved renewal of interest.

This technique is valuable not only to those who sell a product, but to those who must sell themselves and their ideas—and who does that exclude?

The basis for it is that people tend to react more favorably to others who are similar to themselves. They are more relaxed with and more open to suggestion from those who look, dress, act, and speak in a similar, familiar way. Conversely, the sales rep or other persuader who acts and/or talks differently is a stranger who faces obstacles.

Conclusion: You'll have an easier time of selling yourself or your product or proposals if you *mirror* the actions and speech of whoever is on the buying end. Doubtless you already do some of this, even if subconsciously, as you strive to put your most acceptable self forward in your professional environs.

You know that wild sports jackets and slit skirts don't go over well at IBM or the trust department at a bank; nor do pinstripe suits at a fledgling computer company in Silicon Valley. Now the new twist that sales trainers emphasize is that before calling on a prospective buyer, the salesperson should determine the personal characteristics of the buyer and make a conscious effort to copy them. This includes the buyer's speech characteristics.

How's Your Pacing?

Copying speech patterns is sometimes called pacing, although it involves more than tempo. Of course, the tempo of talking, which tends to vary from north to south in our country, should be considered by the salesperson. But the type of language—educational level, country or city orientation, differences by age or sex, regional vernacular—must be considered too. Reflecting these can increase rapport.

What You Should Know about
Interactional Synchrony

An interesting sidelight from recent studies of the effects of mirroring and pacing is that your body movements follow the speech patterns of someone you're talking to if you're emotionally in synch with that person. Movies reveal that not only does the speaker's body move to the beat of his or her voice, but the listener reacts to the same rhythm with synchronous body movement. They "dance" together in conversation when the vibes are right.

This synchronous movement (called interactional synchrony) varies in intensity, depending on how in tune the views of the two conversers are. The start of a disagreement dampens it. And if lack of interest in the conversation sets in, that's the finish.

Look for this verbal-physical synchrony when you get into a close, harmonious dialogue. If you see it, you're pressing all the right buttons and can easily close the deal, whatever that may be. If your dancing partner stops moving to your tune, you know the magic has gone.

What Everyone Hungers For

Everyone wants it. We can hand it out free. Yet often we are stingy in dispensing this coveted commodity. It is *praise*—the hunger that lurks deep in every human psyche.

If you remember the teachings of Dr. Freud, you know that absolutely everyone wants to amount to something. And what's more important to you as a communicator, everyone desires to be recognized as a person of some worth. Sigmund didn't have to tell you that; you see evidences of it all around you daily.

An Experiment in Psychology

A professor of psychology conducted an interesting experiment among a random group of his neighbors. Those he chose for his test were all casual acquaintances. And all, so far as he knew, were ordinary people with no great accomplishments; he had no idea what these neighbors had been doing recently but assumed it was nothing of great significance. To each of these ordinary men and women he sent the message: *"I understand congratulations are in order. I'm delighted to hear about it. You should be very proud."*

He sent out 12 such cards; he received 12 replies almost instantly, either by phone or mail. All warmly expressed thanks for his recognition of their recent accomplishments or good fortune. Many indicated some surprise that he had heard about their personal triumphs, but none denied they had something noteworthy to be congratulated about.

The achievements they acknowledged ranged all the way from getting a new job, becoming an officer in a local club, rating near the top in a sports tournament, getting a promotion at work, and coaching a successful Little League ball team to becoming a grandparent for the third time. A wide variety of events—but all, to them at least, a source of pride and deserving of recognition.

It behooves us to identify the good things about others and the good things they do. And to *recognize* them. This doesn't require insincere flattery, but merely giving recognition freely where it's merited. Why be stingy, when it's so easy to be generous, and so important in building friendships?

Two Words That Can Move Mountains

They cost you nothing; they have a powerful effect. Yet few people use them nearly as often as they should. What are they? *"Thank you."*

Absolutely everyone likes to be thanked. For helping you. For doing a job well. For performing a routine service in your office, at a store where you shop, at a gas station, in the home, wherever. Often a simple "thank you" means more to people than money.

Are you stingy with those words? Do you tend to take good service or generous cooperation for granted? If you do, you may find that it dries up.

The great lack is not in expressing thanks for the big things, the obvious things. Generally you can't avoid that. But say, "Thank you," when it's not expected and see what a reaction you get. That's when you notice people's faces really light up with pleasure, and with surprise.

- When was the last time you sent someone a thank-you note just on general principles? It could be just to say how much you appreciate their continual cooperation or the support you can count on. Try it.

- When was the last time your firm sent a thank-you note to its steady customers? Not to sell them anything; just to say how much you appreciate their business. Try it.

- You send your spouse or friend a card or gift on anniversaries, birthdays, holidays, but how often do you send a thank-you note or card, with or without a gift, on no special occasion? Try it.

OH, NO!

The Morgan Guarantee Trust of New York instructed its employees, "Avoid saying 'Hello.' This elsewhere pleasant and familiar greeting is out of place in the world of business."

FROM *ESQUIRE*, JANUARY **1984**

19
Remember Whatsizname?

Remember that a person's name is to that person the sweetest and most important sound in any language. DALE CARNEGIE

In advising how to make people like you, Dale Carnegie recommended that you learn to remember people's names. Further, he warned, "If you don't do this, you are headed for trouble."[1]

Sensitivity about names starts in infancy. What's the first thing a child learns to take pride in? Her name. Mistake Millie for her sister Margaret, and you create frustration and irritation. Her name is her identity, her unique possession—and you'd better not forget it.

One of the most demeaning things that can be done to a person is to deliberately take away his name. What's the first thing done to a person when he's put into prison? His name is taken away and replaced by a number. His self-esteem is destroyed by labeling him a nonperson—one without a name.

Names Mean Votes to Politicians

Politicians, who prosper or perish depending on their popularity, know that remembering a name is the sincerest form of flattery; forgetting

---

[1]From Dale Carnegie, *How to Win Friends and Influence People*, Pocket Books, New York, 1981.

it is an insult. It was always so. Back in 500 B.C., the statesman Themistocles was purported to know the names of all 30,000 citizens of Athens. In more recent times, Democratic party chairman James A. Farley and President Lyndon B. Johnson were noted for their phenomenal memory for names. So was the long-time political boss and mayor of Chicago, Richard Daley.

How effective is this faculty in the political field? My son gave me a personal illustration of what it can do. He lives in a suburb of Chicago. Several years ago, when Daley was still mayor, my son attended a large civic party. Daley was at the door, where he greeted each of the several hundred guests as they arrived and asked all of them something about themselves. My son, Scott, was surprised at the personal attention the mayor lavished on each person who came in the door. He had always been critical of the Chicago political organization, and of Daley especially, yet he admits he found this attention not unpleasing.

Personal Playback Pleases

Scott was more surprised a few hours later when Daley again stationed himself at the door to speak to each departing guest. He not only addressed each of the several hundred people by name but also commented on something they'd told him earlier. He repeated their home location, their occupation, or the names of mutual friends, etc. He remembered where my son had grown up and the business he was in.

When Scott recounted this to me, I asked him if this personal attention and the recollection of his name had changed his negative attitude toward the mayor. His answer: "I still don't approve of his political tactics, *but you can't help liking the man*."

If even someone you're prepared to dislike can mellow you by showing personal interest (even though you know it's politically motivated), how much more effectively can you use such a technique with those who are open to friendship?

A Direct-Mail Secret

Direct-mail marketers, who are extremely cost-conscious people, can reach you simply by addressing their mailings to "Resident" at an address, but they rarely do. Instead, they spend millions of dollars every year to buy lists of *names* of people in specific neighborhoods. Why?

Because they know that when you see your own name on the envelope you are much more likely to open it. And if they go one step further, using a computer-typed letter that repeats your name several times, they can increase the pull of their mailing still more. Much more.

Personalization Can Increase Sales
by 50 Percent or More

You realize that the insertion of your name throughout a sales letter is simply a gimmick achieved by a machine. You know it's part of a mailing program that went out to thousands or even millions of people. But you like it.

Just the fact that someone tried to add a personal touch to that impersonal sales letter by recognizing that your name is important inclines you to buy the product. Someone has told you that you're not just a number or an address to them. You're a person, an important one worth a little extra effort and courtesy.

Take a lesson from the computer people; put names and personal information into *your* memory banks too. You can do it without much difficulty. And you'll find, as the direct marketers have, that the personalized approach always pays off whether you're meeting people in business, school, daily chores, or social situations.

Why You Can't Remember
Names

If you're like most people, you probably say, "I can't remember names." If you're like most people, it's no wonder.

Think of a typical situation you're in when being introduced to a group of new people and of what you do to meet that situation.

What Happens When You're
Introduced

Maybe you're at a business meeting or a convention where a friend pulls you into a circle of half a dozen men and women you've never met before. Maybe you've just walked in the door at a cocktail party, and your host and hostess lead you into a chattering throng with the admonition, "Here are some friends we want you to meet."

In either case, the noise level is apt to be high. You're the stranger in the crowd, and all eyes turn on you. The introductions are hurried, and while they're being made, your chief concern is what kind of impression you're making on these people. What's the result?

You may not even *hear* the names, or not hear them clearly. So it's not surprising if you can't repeat them just 60 seconds later. *You never knew the names in the first place.* Isn't that why you hesitate to call new acquaintances by name when you bump into them again a few minutes later? And why you notice they don't use your name either?

You need to take just two simple, obvious steps to cure this initial failing:

- *Listen—really listen.* Concentrate your full attention on hearing each name. If the introducer slurs the name, or if the surrounding noise makes it difficult to hear, ask to have it repeated. And look at each person carefully during the introductions; associate the name with the face. Don't be looking around the room to see who else is present.

- *Get it straight.* Don't let the introducer race on to the next name until you're sure you have the first one straight. If there's any doubt about the pronunciation, ask to have it repeated. In fact, it's a good idea to *repeat each name aloud yourself as you hear it.* This slows down the introductions and clarifies any misunderstandings. You may also ask the person to spell his or her name if it's at all unusual. Don't hesitate to do this; it's taken as a compliment, and it helps impress a name on your memory.

These two easy steps alone can increase your remembrance of names many times over. Your mind is a much better memory device than you may give it credit for. Once you put something into it—a clear, sharp impression—your mind will retrieve it when you wish. At least it will have a chance to do so.

How to Sharpen Your Memory

After you listen to a name and get it straight, there are two other steps, just as simple, that can add strength to the memory impression:

- *Repeat, repeat, repeat the name.* You learned this principle in school: Repetition strengthens memory. So at the time of the introduction say, "I'm so glad to meet you, Miss Brandt."

  Use her name again during the conversation. Maybe you can even make some reference to the name while you talk. For example, you may be able to recall that you once had a friend of that name; this will create a memorable association.

  And by all means, at the end of the initial meeting say, "Miss Brandt, I've enjoyed meeting you and certainly look forward to seeing you again." Each repetition deepens the impression in your memory.

- *Write it down.* If you meet many new people, there's no better way to get their names clearly in your possession than to write them down on a pocket memo pad or 3 × 5 card. Do this right after your meeting, while the names are still fresh in your mind.

Techniques of Name Association

There are other more complex methods for improving your memory of names, lists, data. Experts in the field have written entire books on improving our remembrance of names and faces, and some hold seminars.

The main technique they teach is how to associate a name and face with something else. Sometimes a rhyme. Often a picture image. For example, "Jim Adair has curly hair" is an easy rhyme. An example of a picture image for Franklin Raintree might be a visual of Benjamin Franklin sitting on top of a tree in a downpour of rain. These are relatively simple examples; sometimes they get extremely complicated. In the foregoing example, I'd probably recollect the name as Benjamin Shower.

You may want to avail yourself of some special courses if your goal is to become a whiz at memory, but you can improve a great deal if you merely keep in mind the four easy steps listed above.

The Best Way Out of a Common Embarrassment

It happens to everyone at some time. Despite your efforts to memorize names, you come face-to-face with somebody whose moniker you simply can't recall. What's worse, they remember yours.

What can you do in that situation? If you're alone, you may be able to pretend you remember, but simply not address the person by name. That's not too good, for the person will probably see through your subterfuge. But the tactic won't work at all if you're accompanied by someone; then you must get the name to make introductions, or else you'll appear very rude. There are two possible solutions:

1. *Prove that you recall the face, if not the name.* Do this by stating the situation where you last met. For example, you might say, "Gee, it's been a long time since we saw each other at that party at the Smith's house, hasn't it? I enjoyed that, and enjoyed meeting you and your husband. But I must confess I can't at the moment put the name with the face. You are...?" By this technique, you'll at least get credit for partial recollection.

2. *Admit your memory lapse, but indicate strongly that it won't happen a second time.* After you apologize and are told the name, you might say, "I must remember that...Jennie Jones, Jennie Jones...I want to be sure it stays in my memory this time." If you have a pen and paper in your pocket, you can make still more of a production of your determination to imprint the important name on your mind. Say, "I'm going to write that down, because you're a person I mustn't forget." The fact that this is done so seldom will impress the other person with your sincere interest.

And, of course, either technique—repeating the name several times or writing it down—will help you not to repeat your mistake and face the same embarrassment the next time you meet.

The Relationship Determines How Much Is Too Much

Although everyone likes the importance of being recognized by name, you can overdo it. How often you should call someone by name depends on your relationship. Three professors of psychology proved that repeated "name calling" can build a favorable image for you—or do just the opposite if you're suspected of ulterior motives.[2]

For example, the professors used videotapes and audiotapes of supposed job interviews in which name-using varied markedly. When people reviewed these tapes, they thought the interviewer was friendly if she used the applicant's name frequently. But when a job applicant repeatedly addressed a prospective employer by name, he was suspected of being insincere and phony.

Similar results were obtained in other tests, where groups of male and female college students were introduced and then left to talk together for 15 minutes. Unknown to the women, half of the men were instructed to address the women by name at least six times during the conversation; the others were not to repeat names. Later, the frequent name-users were rated by the women as phony and trying too hard to make an impression. Again, ulterior motives were suspected.

In tests where this element of suspicion was not present, the results were different. A female student interviewed two men at a time about topics of current interest. In each case, she treated the men identically except that she called one by name a single time and the other by name several times. When asked for their reactions to the interviews, both men would say she liked better the one she called by name. And in each case, that man liked her significantly better than the other did.

[2]C. L. Kleinke, R. A. Staneski, and P. Weaver, as reported in C. L. Kleinke, *First Impressions: The Psychology of Encountering Others*, Prentice-Hall, Englewood Cliffs, N.J., 1975.

20
Your Telephone Personality

If the phone rings when you're in the shower, it's a wrong number.
COOPER'S LAW

Which of the following statements about the telephone do you think are true?

- The telephone is an irritating interruption throughout my workday.
- It's a major time waster.
- It's one of my best and most cost-efficient means of communication.
- It's the tool I use more often than writing letters or even face-to-face contact.
- To many of the people I deal with, it's *me!*

If you answered, "All of the above," you're 100 percent correct. In many surveys, businesspeople place the telephone either near or right at the top as a source of irritation and a time waster. But you couldn't possibly do your job without it. And many of your business contacts meet you face-to-face rarely or never; *they know you only as a personality who comes to them over a wire.*

Before considering ways to minimize your irritation and save your time in telephoning (and it can be done), let's evaluate what sort of impression you make on those people on the other end of the line. In general, of course, this will parallel the chemistry you generate in the flesh—how well you establish rapport by the way you listen, talk, act courteously, etc. All the things you've previously read about. But there are peculiarities in the ways people tend to use Alexander Bell's marvelous invention—ones that can be annoying.

Pet Peeves

You may not ever make the mistakes listed below. Your telephone techniques are just about perfect, aren't they? But just in case you might slip once in a while, or in case some of your subordinates need guidance, here are four common practices to avoid.

1. Don't Play "Guess Who." How many times have you answered the phone when the caller fails to identify herself or himself, but rolls right into the conversation as if you'd just parted company 10 minutes ago? Even if it's someone you talk to frequently (and often it isn't), your mind has been occupied with other matters, and all voices are not distinctive. So as the caller jabbers along, you wonder, "Who in hell is this?" Eventually the subject matter may give you the necessary clue, but in the meantime *you're not concentrating on the message*. Sometimes you may even face the embarrassment of having to ask who's calling.

Whenever you make a call, even to a close friend or associate, always give at least your first name. If the association isn't very close, give your full name.

The same holds true when you answer the phone. Identify yourself, along with your company or department if that's appropriate. Whether calling or receiving, playing guessing games is neither polite nor businesslike.

2. Allow at Least a Minute for Your Call to Be Answered. How many times have you dashed to reach a phone, when you've been a distance away, only to have the ringing stop just as you grab the receiver? If you don't appreciate that, don't do it to others.

The thing to remember is that *it takes about 10 rings to equal a minute*. Count 'em. If you're an impatient, type A personality (like me), it may seem you're waiting an interminable time for an answer, when in reality it has only been a fraction of a minute. You'll be more generous if you count to 10 rings, allowing a full 60 seconds.

3. Don't Run Out on the Person You're Calling. Does anything steam you more than this? You pick up the telephone (which has just interrupted your important activities) and you hear: "Mr. Bighead is calling. If you'll hold, please, he'll be right with you." Only he doesn't get right with you. You can hear him finishing a conversation with someone in his office.

Even if the wait is brief, it's arrogant to assume that the receiver of your call should hold the line until you get good and ready to talk.

Make your own calls. Or, if your secretary gets the number, stay on the line. If you happen to be a big wheel, that kind of considerate conduct may surprise some people. But pleasantly.

4. Don't Play Hard to Get.   There are various reasons why you may not be reachable at times, or why you may not want to talk to someone (that's discussed later in this chapter). However, each situation can be handled without raising the suspicion that you're avoiding calls. It's a matter of providing information so callers don't jump to wrong conclusions.

- *When you leave your office,* either turn on an answering machine, have your calls forwarded to someone else, or arrange to have a nearby colleague answer your phone. Then people won't have to dial you over and over to no avail.

- *When you get your messages,* return them promptly. If you delay too long, callers may assume you're just not interested in them.

- *When a call is interrupted by another,* don't put the first party on hold for a lengthy time. Apologize when the interruption occurs; say you'll return to them immediately; then do it. After all, the first party has priority; you need talk to the second phoner only long enough to get a number and promise a call back.

How to Save Time

Let Your Fingers Do the Walking

That's more than a slogan for the yellow pages. Your phone can save you miles of walking right in your office building. Although you never want to eliminate at least one daily stroll to see what's happening (management by walking around), your telephone can save you unnecessary trips and multiply the contacts you make each day.

That's the good part. The hazard is that it's easy to let that wonderful machine take control. If you allow it to interrupt at any time, for any length of time, you're no longer the manager—it is.

Don't Let Your Phone Bully You

You know people who'll drop anything or anybody whenever the telephone rings. They may be working on a crucial project with a tight deadline. Or they may have someone in their office who's come a thou-

Control your telephone.
Don't let it control you.

sand miles to see them. Yet when that bell sounds, they give instant priority to whoever's on the line, no matter how trivial the call's purpose may be. Their days are a disjointed series of interruptions, and they accomplish little.

There are several solutions.

Screening. If you have a secretary, let that person run interference for you. An immediate statement that you're not available at the moment can be followed with a polite inquiry as to the reason for the call. In many cases, a secretary or someone else can handle the matter. At other times, you can call back later. If the big boss or an important client happens to be on the line, your secretary can always make the quick switch to "Oh, I see him [or her] coming down the hall now. Just one moment, please."

The Answering Machine. Without the luxury of a secretary, you can still block out some free time to work and think on an important assignment, protected from a barrage of calls. Obviously, you can't shut off the phone too much of the time, and for some people it may not be possible any of the time.

You must weigh the priorities: How important is a period of open time in your particular job on a particular day? If your switching off of the telephone is questioned by associates or a superior, can you justify it? At one firm I worked for, it was corporate policy for *everyone* to enjoy one call-free morning each week, and it was amazing how much more each of us accomplished in those few precious hours. It's not a bad policy.

Bunching Calls. When you have several calls to return, try to make them all at once. It's tempting to procrastinate and delay some of them, but that breaks up your day. Get the chore over with! It'll save you time in the long run.

Choice of Language

Since you're intelligent and friendly, you're always careful to be diplomatic and polite in everything you say over the phone. Right? However, your telephone personality as it's perceived by many callers is often shaped by what they hear *before* you get on the line. The switchboard operator who first takes the call and the secretary or assistant who may answer your phone represent you. They determine the first impression outsiders get of you and your company, and it's very important. Do you know for sure what sort of impression it is?

During the past few weeks, I've jotted down things I've heard when I've made calls. They've included:

- "I don't know where he is. I can't keep track of him."
- "She's not here yet; she's late this morning."
- "I don't know anything about that."
- "That's not my department. Sorry."
- "What's 'at? Speak up, will yuh?"
- "She's around here somewheres."
- "Why don't you call back later. Maybe somebody can help you then."

All these responses have been from substantial companies from which you'd expect better. In several instances, I was phoning as a customer thinking about making a sizable purchase. In one case, I had to make three calls before reaching anyone able or willing to locate a basic bit of information for me.

Let's hope no one gets responses of this quality at your office. *But do you know for sure?* If there's any doubt, it would pay to check. Have someone at home call your office while you listen in. Determine exactly what they're told and how they're told it when they ask several questions.

Expert Help Is Available—Free!

Most people get at least some cursory training before they're allowed to take over a switchboard, but few lower-level office personnel receive any guidance as to what to say before they're allowed to answer telephones. There's no excuse for this. The local telephone company in any area is loaded with excellent, easy-to-understand training booklets they're aching to impart free of charge to their customers.

I have several from Southwestern Bell in front of me at the moment.

I could quote you some of their dos and don'ts and suggestions for the best wording to use in various situations. But you'll do much better to call your local representative for a supply of booklets to pass around. If you're the department head, instruct everyone to read them. If you lack such authority, quietly drop a booklet on those desks where they're needed.

Telemarketing—An Economical Way to Build Business

The telephone is taken for granted as the obvious tool for saving time and money in just about every business function. However, many companies still have barely scratched the surface in marketing by telephone. This is surprising since an industrial sales call made in person now costs nearly $200. *A call by phone costs about one-tenth as much.* In light of these facts, perhaps your company could benefit by developing a telemarketing personality.

That's not something to be undertaken haphazardly. High-pressure telemarketing run out of boiler shops is not beneficial to a company image. But skilled, concerned sales people who know how to make lasting friends over the phone are precious gems.

Hallmark Cards, where I worked for several years, supplements its field sales force with a large staff of telemarketers who keep in close touch with smaller dealers who might otherwise be called on infrequently. In developing a new, direct-marketing operation of specialized products at that firm, the first people I hired were telephoning experts who made personal contacts from our customer mailing list.

The special techniques of telemarketing are adaptable to many problems. And not to others. Experts such as Murray Roman and Skip Weitzen have perfected many aspects of the art. Each has written a comprehensive handbook (filled with case studies) that could help you find your way in the telemarketing field:

- Murray Roman, *Telemarketing Campaigns That Work*, McGraw-Hill, New York, 1983. Describes 18 successful telemarketing campaigns, with complete details on strategies and techniques used and results obtained.

- Skip Weitzen, *Telephone Magic*, McGraw-Hill, New York, 1987. Gives ideas on how to use the telephone effectively in many facets of marketing.

21
Never Stop Questioning

*My greatest strength as a consultant is to
be ignorant and ask a few questions.*
PETER DRUCKER

Skillful use of questions is a priceless ingredient of communication. Without it, you can be in deep trouble. Here's a story about that.

A stranger from up north was fishing from a rickety pier at the edge of a small lake in the Florida Everglades. The sun was jabbing hot needles through his shirt; the air was so soggy he could almost squish it between his fingers; only a few fish had shown even a nudging interest in his bait. After a few hours of parboiling, he began speculating about reeling in his line and enjoying a quick swim before heading back to his lodgings. But he'd been warned to beware of poisonous snakes in this area.

A boy came walking down the road and paused to eye the fisherman. The man nodded to him and asked, "Sonny, are there any snakes in this lake?"

"No, sir," the boy answered. "Nary a one."

With this reassurance, the man stripped off his outer clothes and dipped into the cooling water. As he splashed around a bit, he noticed movement in the thick reeds nearby. "Hey, kid," he said, "are you positive there aren't any snakes in here? I heard this was moccasin country...ever seen any in this lake?"

"Nope," the boy replied.

Uneasy as the reeds stirred again, more vigorously this time, the man persisted. "How come there aren't any snakes here?"

"Alligators ate 'em all," the boy explained.

The fisherman made a common mistake. He asked the wrong questions, received misleading answers. Fortunately he persisted and eventually learned what he needed to know. That's one of the main reasons we ask questions—to learn, to get information—but there are others.

Reasons for Asking Questions

1. To Learn.   This is the commonest goal. And the kind of questions most often used to achieve it are direct *closed-end* ones, such as the fisherman tried. They're called "closed end" because they generally inspire answers of only one or two words, and that's the end of it. For instance:

"Are there any snakes?" Answer: "No."
"How long have you lived here?" Answer: "Five years."

As the fisherman example indicates, closed-end questions eliciting brief answers can lead to misunderstandings. I've often been at odds with research people who employ closed-end questions to find out what consumers like, dislike, or may do. My premise is: "Let me write the questionnaire and I can prove anything you wish."

If you're really fishing for information, you can often learn more with an indirect approach—*open-end* questions that invite lengthier replies. Just one of them may start a conversation that'll last for several minutes and open up vistas you never knew existed. For example:

"What bothers you when you do your laundry?" The answer to this will tell a soap company more than a page full of "yes or no" answers.

"How do you like to spend your leisure time?" Be prepared for a lengthy chat when you ask this, and expect to learn a great deal about the speaker if you listen perceptively.

2. To Show Your Interest in Others.   Questioning people about their hobbies, interests, families, jobs, etc., is a wonderful way to let them know you're interested in them. So is asking, "What do you think about this?" or "What's your opinion?" or "What's your experience been in these matters?" You show you care.

3. To Arouse Interest.

Q: Isn't it surprising that...?

Q: Do you know that...?

A question enables you to present a thought in a more provocative way than making a flat statement. The question draws the reader in because it requires the reader to think and possibly to answer.

4. To Clarify.

Q: Do you mean...? (Rephrase the question.)

Q: Exactly how much will we have to pay? (Get a specific answer, instead of settling for a generality.)

A frequent cause of misunderstandings is the failure to ask the questions necessary to clarify an ambiguous statement. We sometimes hesitate to question a speaker because we're afraid of offending. Instead, we guess at what the person means, and perhaps guess wrong.

5. To Get Feedback.

Q: What advantages do you see in this new program? (Find out if the other person has really been listening and is really interested.)

Q: What will you tell your people about it?

Just as we must be sure we understand others, we want to be certain they're getting our message. The best way to verify this is through questions that elicit feedback of our thoughts, so we can determine if the message received is in sync with the message we sent out.

6. To Get Agreement.

Q: Don't you agree that...?

Q: That's what you want, isn't it?

Q: Would you rather have the blue car or the red one?

A series of questions can be a means of bringing someone step-by-step to agreement with your ultimate goal. Smart salespeople use the question technique constantly. We're all selling something all the time.

7. To Disagree without Confrontation.

Disagreeing is a part of social and business interaction that can be unpleasant and disastrous to future relations if we do it bluntly with a "You're wrong!" approach. A question can soften the blow and be much more effective than a confrontational statement, because it forces the other person to do the proving and the arguing. When opinions clash, avoid a verbal clash by asking quietly and pleasantly:

Q: Why do you doubt that?

Q: If you don't like this solution, how do you propose to solve the problem?

Q: Your plan has some very good points. But what assurances do you have that there won't be a large cost overrun, as we've had before?

8. To Keep the Talker Talking.

Q: Will you tell me more about that?

Q: What did you do next?

Sometimes it takes quite a while to draw people out and get all the information you want. They may need encouragement to keep going until they get to the point.

9. To Avoid a Question You Don't Want to Answer.   When an insensitive person hits you with an embarrassing question, you have three choices: (a) Allow yourself to be bullied into answering; (b) refuse to answer, either with a blunt refusal or by ignoring the query; or (c) *answer with a question of your own.* The first two routes are hazardous, but the "U-turn" question puts the discomfiture back where it started:

Q: What tax bracket are *you* in?

Q: Why don't *you* do it?

Who's Afraid to Question?

Many of us become fearful of asking too many questions and end up asking too few. It's better to be curious than ignorant.

Sometimes we're hesitant about showing our lack of knowledge. We pretend to understand when we don't, and we're likely to end up in a mess as a result.

Sometimes we're too shy or compliant to clarify a vague point or to question something we don't agree with. We're afraid we may seem to doubt the veracity or the ability of the speaker. But if we don't question doubtful statements, we're giving tacit agreement. Later that can lead to an unpleasant question being put to us: "If you didn't agree, why didn't you say so?"

Children and Geniuses Aren't Afraid to Question

Children question constantly; that's how they learn. It's also how they show the enthusiasm we admire. Even though they may wear us down at times with their continuous questions, we're captivated by their need to know, and we want to help them.

And it's interesting to note that those adults who know the most seem to retain their childlike curiosity.

> *The important thing is never to stop questioning.* ALBERT EINSTEIN

Ben Franklin's Secret

Who can help but admire the Philadelphia printer, publisher, philosopher, scientist, inventor, politician, postmaster general, ambassador, diplomat, bon vivant, etc., who maintained a wide-ranging curiosity till the end of his long life?

Franklin was a questioner extraordinary. With no formal engineering training, he questioned views on electricity that savants had believed for centuries and he replaced them with new concepts that shook the scientific world. He questioned why books should not be available to everyone and founded the first public library. He questioned everything in his hometown, from fire prevention to hospital care to education, and founded such organizations as a fire company, a city hospital, and a college, which became the University of Pennsylvania.

Old Ben, the philosopher, also had a rare insight into the psychology of questions. He knew they changed conversation from a one-way harangue to a lively back-and-forth exchange of ideas. He knew that questions demanded two-way participation, brought people closer together, warmed up a meeting.

Making a Friend of an Enemy

Even in situations where animosity existed, Franklin realized that certain questions could smooth it out. He tells of doing this to thaw a relationship with a former friend who was becoming an enemy.

He had become embroiled in a political contest with the man and had defeated him; communication between the two instantly became sparse and cold. Franklin might have tried to apologize for any bruises the battle had caused his associate, but it was a fair fight, and an apology could have been taken as patronizing. Instead, he decided to avoid any mention of past unpleasantness and *ask a favor* that recognized his adversary's preeminence in another field.

Franklin knew that the other man was proud of his fine collection of books and especially of one very rare volume. He sent a note stating that he had heard much of this marvelous book, knew he couldn't find it anywhere else, and would really like to read it. "Would you be so kind as to lend it to me?" Franklin asked his disgruntled former friend.

The man promptly sent his precious book to Franklin. The next time the two met, they chatted amiably. Their differences had been healed.

The principle of asking for a favor—whether it be requesting information or some other form of assistance—warms many relationships. The young businessperson who asks advice of a senior executive may discover a friendly sponsor who'll volunteer other guidance from time to time.

> It's better to know some of the
> questions than all of the answers.
> JAMES THURBER

My Favorite Questions

Many of our questions are ones we must ask to get specific information or clarify it. The questions I enjoy most are *optional*. I add them not because a conversation couldn't proceed without them, but because it bubbles along so much more productively with them.

If your day-to-day relationships seem to have no more fizz than stale beer, try popping some of this fresh effervescence into them. Remember that all sorts of people, no matter how important they may be, get a pleasant lift when their opinions are valued or their aid is requested. Be kind enough to ask:

- "Will you help me?"
- "What would you do in these circumstances?"
- "What do you think about this?"
- "Do you have any suggestions?"
- "What's your opinion of this approach?"
- "What has your experience been in these matters?"
- "Will you tell me what you know about this situation?"
- "Have you ever had this kind of problem?"

Remember also that not only important people need their egos massaged occasionally. Don't be too proud to ask advice or help from those on your rung of the ladder or below. You may be surprised at how much help they can give, and how much some of them know.

Summary

The Story of
the Wise Man

Once upon a time there was a young man who was despondent about his progress, careerwise. He had done everything right: matriculated from a prestigious grad school, dazzled a recruiter from a Fortune 500 firm, switched jobs three times with the aid of the very best headhunters, and accepted nothing but fast-track assignments. Yet after four long tiresome years, he was still far from a vice presidency.

Having read this book and determined that maybe communication was his problem, he came to me for advice. Or maybe to get his money back. Anyhow, I asked if he'd tried any of the suggestions in the book.

"Not yet," he answered. "I was looking for some totally new discovery, you know. Maybe a new formula or something. Those things in your book, like paying attention to people and asking questions, checking facts, remembering names and all that...they're OK. But they're mostly just commonsense ideas discovered a long time ago. Right?"

"What did you expect?" I asked. "A wise man named Dale Carnegie wrote several books on this problem, very good ones. They've helped millions of people. And they're based on commonsense ideas that have been around a long time too. In fact, here's what Mr. Carnegie said about them:

> The ideas I stand for are not mine
> alone. I borrowed them from Socrates; I
> swiped them from Chesterfield; I stole
> them from Jesus. And I put them in a
> book. If you don't like their rules, whose
> would you use?   DALE CARNEGIE

"Well," said the young man, "I don't rightly know whose I'd use. But I sort of had something different in mind. This stuff sounds like work; it's not high-level staff operation like I'm trained for. Don't you have something shorter, more compact, you know? Maybe one short statement or a graph that puts it all into coordinates that lead to the bottom line?"

I thought for a moment and then suggested, "I'm not too good at graphs, but a wise man named Elbert Hubbard had a brief statement I've always liked. Maybe it would suit your purpose."

> *Every man is a damned fool for at least*
> *five minutes every day. Wisdom consists*
> *of not exceeding the time limit.*
>   ELBERT HUBBARD

"That's good, very good," the young man agreed, "but not very specific. I'd like it to sum up everything—the secret of communication and the secret of life—*in 10 words or less*. Yes, that's what I need!"

Sadly I shook my head and told him I knew no such magic maxim. The only person who might, I advised, was a holy man, reputed to be the Wisest of the Wise, who lived on a mountaintop in the Himalayas. I gave the young man directions as best I could, and he vowed to seek out the ultimate wise man.

For weeks he traveled by plane, bus, and jeep to the village in the Hindu Kush near the mountain just a yodel across the valley from Everest. He hired two Sherpa guides, who hoisted him aboard a pony that plodded halfway up the peak, beyond where the clouds bumped its sides. From there, the Sherpas pushed and pulled him on foot up a trail that was merely a zigzag scratched into the rock.

Long after he was sure his lungs had burst and his legs would never move again, they reached a ledge notched into the mountainside. His guides settled him to a sitting position, bowed to a figure he could see dimly, muttered a few reverent words, and then skittered back down the trail.

From the cold, exertion, and lack of oxygen, the young man's skull felt empty and his eyeballs felt like frozen oysters. Mouth agape, he gulped icy air until his pulse gradually calmed and he could focus his squinting eyes. As he'd hoped, the silent figure sharing his mountainous perch was undoubtedly the one he sought: a round-faced cherub with a long white beard, high swelling forehead, and Mongolian eyelids. Clad in a saffron cotton robe and seated in the lotus position. The whole bit. The Wise Man stared unblinkingly and smiled, but did not speak.

Eventually the young man managed to get his teeth together so he could smile back and introduce himself. The Wise Man rose, entered the mouth of a cave, and returned with a cup of steaming yak butter, which he proffered to his guest. The rich liquid curled the young man's tongue but made a pleasantly warm puddle in his stomach. Relaxed a bit, he told the guru his problems and begged for a solution.

The Wise Man spoke in the unhurried pace of one ruled by no watch, appointment book, or calendar. His words puffed out in separate little whiffs that instantly solidified into ice crystals that sparkled briefly in the clear cold before fluttering to the ground.

"In all the world out there," he waved his hand, "everyone wants to be listened to." Pause. "Few are." Pause. "No one all the time." He stopped for a long while as if worn out by the unaccustomed verbosity.

"There are many ways to reach the hearts of others through their eyes and ears. But whatever ways you choose, they will work only if you keep this in mind, always."

The young man leaned forward eagerly for the next words. And waited. And waited. Finally they came—four slow, frosty puffs:

"Life   is   a   boomerang."

The young man listened for the rest of the maxim, but the pundit spoke no more. His gaze was fixed out on the abyss, where there was nothing but miles of emptiness.

"Maybe I'd better sleep on it," the young man said, mostly to himself. There was no reaction from the monk. "It's short alright, sort of catchy too. Maybe there's some meaning there I don't see right now."

That night, in the guest room of the cave, the young man slept fitfully. It was not the chill or the whistling of the wind that made him toss and turn, but the enigma of the four curious words.

In the morning, after another beaker of yak butter and a handful of rice, the young man sought to clarify the great truth he'd received. "Do you mean, O Wise One," he asked, "that we get back what we give? Like if we're considerate of others, and listen as well as talk, and be polite and get interested in them and such…then maybe they'll give more consideration to us and our ideas? Is that it, huh?"

The wise man took all this in without moving or speaking, but there was a sparkle in his eyes and definitely a smile on his lips.

Despite this seeming approval of his analysis, the young man still felt confused as to how the four enigmatic words answered his problems. He persisted, "I can see that applies to me personally. I know you have to give as well as take, and I try to do that...sometimes. But does this boomerang stuff work in business too?"

"Hmm," the young man mused, half to himself. "I always thought it was the opposite: Do unto others before they do unto you. Isn't that the American way?" He "hmmed" again. "But I guess those companies that go all out to please their customers with good service and products and a big smile every time...they seem to do OK. Better than OK."

The Wise Man beamed approvingly now, the ends of his lips curving upward like the points of a torii gate. He repeated:

"Life is a boomerang."

As he did so, as if to dramatize his aphorism, he took from the folds of his robe a gleaming crescent of polished ebony. Drawing back his arm, he flipped the airfoil deftly so it soared out a great distance, banked as gracefully as a gyrfalcon, and returned precisely to his waiting fingers. Smiling encouragingly, he handed it to the young man.

"Oh, no, I couldn't." The young man tried to give back the strange device, but his host smiled persistently, so he felt obligated to take a shot at tossing it. He feared he'd do it wrong, and hated to look like a fool in front of such an erudite and skilled master.

His fear was soon confirmed. After an awkward slash, the boomerang bounced off a jagged rock at the brink of the precipice. The wood shattered into brittle shards that fluttered away into the void.

Sheepishly the young man looked to the other for comment. The Wise Man had not stopped smiling, nor did he blink an eye during the mishap. But he moved his shoulders ever so slightly in what might have been a shrug as he now said, *"You didn't put your heart into it."*

So now you know it all.

There are many routes to better use of language, greater success in getting people to listen to you and respond to your ideas. Study them all. Use them. But remember this:

In everything you do in life, and especially in communicating, success comes not from arrogantly charging ahead and knocking everyone out of your way. It comes from drawing others into the circle of your endeavors.

It's a matter of give and take. Listening is more important than eloquence. A quiet question that elicits the ideas of others is far better than a loud declaration. Good conversation is a Ping-Pong game in which all participate. Good writing takes into consideration not just your own convictions but also the interests of your readers. Good rapport is the result of understanding that comes from feedback and sensitivity to the messages of others. Yes,

> *Life is a boomerang. It brings you back*
> *what you send out.*

And that includes the *sincerity* of your signals. You won't gain true acceptance or cooperation from messages contrived with skill alone. To ensure a warm response, you must communicate with honest feeling as well as intelligence.

You have to put your heart into it.

Index

About the Author

Donald Walton was vice president-creative and an account supervisor at a top-twenty advertising agency. He became the first new-product developer at the Franklin Mint and managing director of one of its divisions. He was a marketing executive at Hallmark Cards, Inc. He is a popular speaker and a consultant on communications. This is his third book. His last, a biography of his friend Norman Rockwell, was a national best-seller and book-club selection.